Susan Mortimer's
Create-a-Notebook Bible and History Series:

Remembering God's Awesome Acts

Teacher's Manual

Illustrated and Written

by

Susan Mortimer

For individual teacher use only!

Permission is given to copy only the Discussion, Speech and Drama Pages for use in individual classes. Please respect this limited copy permission. No other portion of this book may be used for any other purpose in any form without the written permission of the author.

Copyright © 1997 Susan Mortimer
731 W. Camp Wisdom Road
Duncanville, TX 75116

ACKNOWLEDGMENTS

This book would not yet be ready to print were it not for the help of two very important people—Esther Nordman, who helped me as a secretary (we took turns teaching each others' children while the other one worked), and my sister, Betty Smith, who said, "It has to get done—there are kids who need it!" (She put her words into action and drove four hours one way to work nonstop for three to five days at a time while her husband took care of their four young children.) Thank you both!

I would also like to thank my children, Sheri, Wendy, and Christopher. I wrote this with you in mind. May you fall ever more in love with God.

A special thanks to my best friend and most important supporter, my husband, Greg. You are the best thing that ever happened to me. Thank you for letting me buy the books I needed and for being there for me during the long hard process!

The Biblical Family Tree of Man

Genesis 4 - 11   Copyright © 1991, 1996 Susan Mortimer

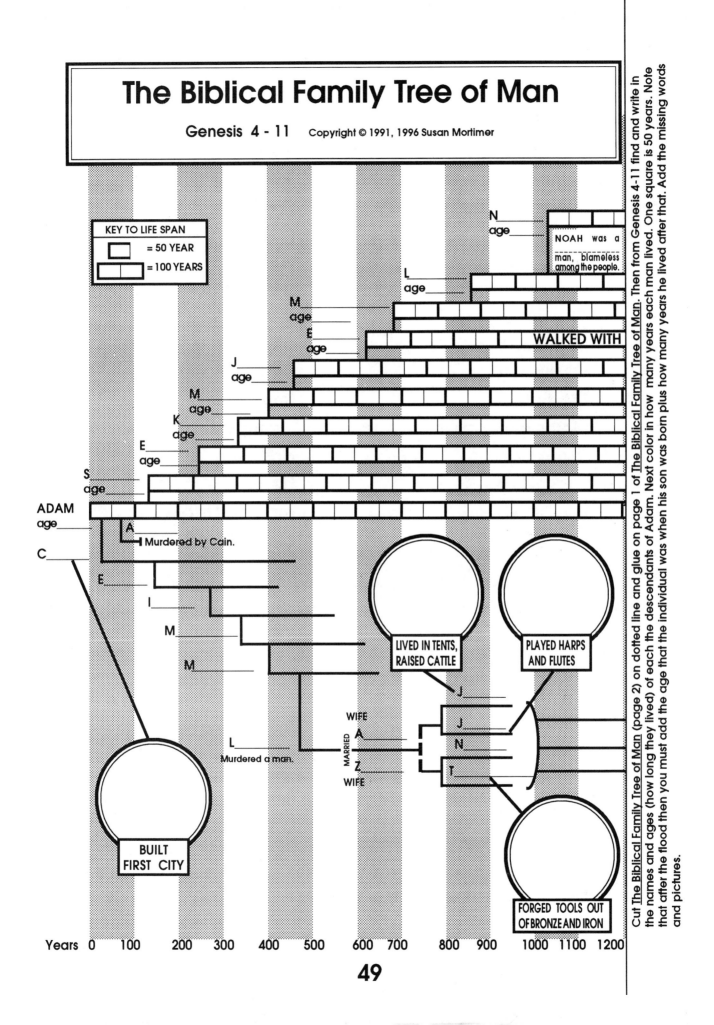

KEY TO LIFE SPAN

☐ = 50 YEAR

☐☐ = 100 YEARS

N
age

NOAH was a _____ man, blameless among the people.

L
age

M
age

E
age

WALKED WITH

J
age

M
age

K
age

E
age

S
age

ADAM
age

A
Murdered by Cain.

C

E

I

M

M

L
Murdered a man.

LIVED IN TENTS, RAISED CATTLE

PLAYED HARPS AND FLUTES

WIFE
MARRIED A
Z
WIFE

J

J
N
T

BUILT FIRST CITY

FORGED TOOLS OUT OF BRONZE AND IRON

Years 0   100   200   300   400   500   600   700   800   900   1000 1100 1200

Cut The Biblical Family Tree of Man (page 2) on dotted line and glue on page 1 of The Biblical Family Tree of Man. Then from Genesis 4-11 find and write in the names and ages (how long they lived) of each the descendants of Adam. Next color in how many years each man lived. One square is 50 years. Note that after the flood then you must add the age that the individual was when his son was born plus how many years he lived after that. Add the missing words and pictures.

Read Genesis 4 to figure out the clues below. Then match each name with their meaning.   Copyright © 1996 Susan Mortimer

Abel	wandering
Adah	to lead (flocks)
Adam	ground
Cain	breeze, breath
Eden	pleasure
Eve	metal forger
Enoch	shadow
Irad	dedicated
Jabal	living
Jubal	pleasant
Lamech	he who flees
Mehujael	trumpet
Methshael	strong youth
Naamah	acquired
Nod	beauty
Tubal-Cain	man that is of God
Zillah	blotted out by God

1. 'El' in a name means 'god'. Of two names that end in 'el', the father's name means 'blotted out by God,' and his son's name means 'man that is of God.'

2. All those who are living came from her. Her name means 'living'.

3. A descendant of Cain used his strength to kill a youth. His name means 'strong youth'.

4. His name tells what he came from. The Hebrew for ground is 'adamah'.

5. Troubled by having to flee his home, Cain names his grandson 'he who flees'.

6. "I will be a restless wanderer on the earth," said Cain. The land he went to means 'wandering'.

7. The name of the only daughter mentioned means 'pleasant'.

8. Lamech's three son's names each have meanings that go with their professions.

9. The wonderful garden with the 'Tree of Life' was named 'Pleasure'.

10. Cain dedicated the first city to his first born. This son's name means 'dedicated'.

11. Like a gentle breeze or a breath, he was here--then he was gone. The name of the first man murdered means 'breeze' or 'breath'.

12. Lamech's first wife was named 'beauty'. His second wife's name means 'shadow'.

13. When he was born, his mother Eve said, "With the help of the Lord I have acquired a man."

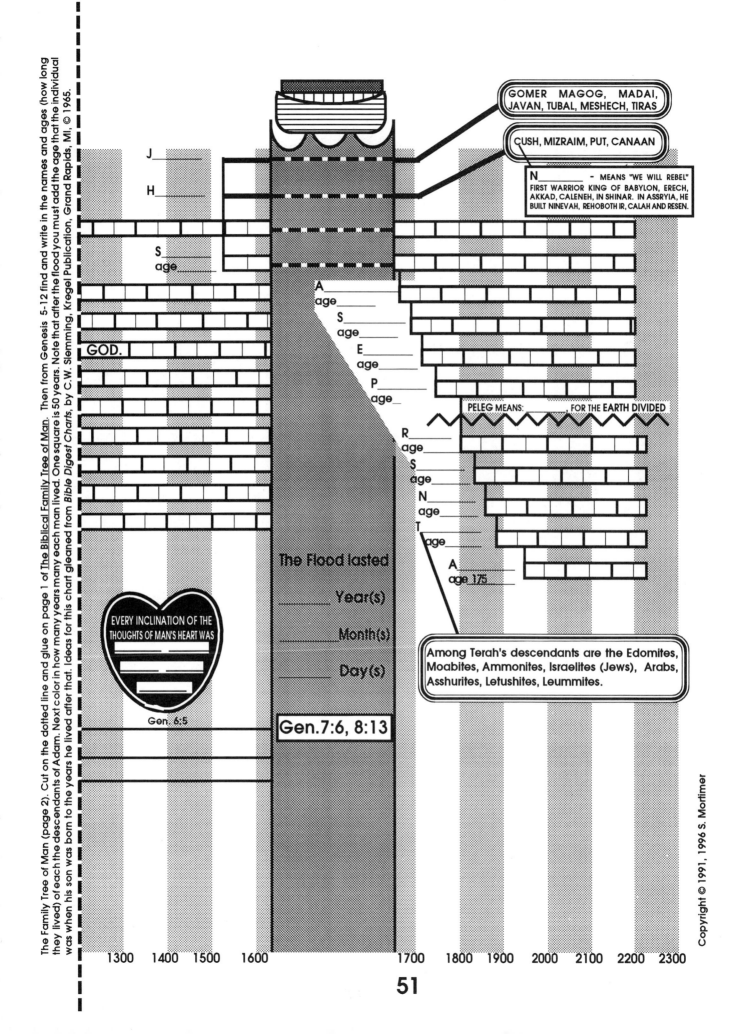

The Family Tree of Man (page 2). Cut on the dotted line and glue on page 1 of The Biblical Family Tree of Man. Then from Genesis 5-12 find and write in the names and ages (how long they lived) of each the descendants of Adam. Next color in how many years many each man lived. One square is 50 years. Note that after the flood you must add the age that the individual was when his son was born to the years he lived after that. Ideas for this chart gleaned from *Bible Digest Charts*, by C.W. Slemming, Kregel Publication, Grand Rapids, MI, © 1965.

J _____

H _____

GOMER MAGOG, MADAI, JAVAN, TUBAL, MESHECH, TIRAS

CUSH, MIZRAIM, PUT, CANAAN

N_____ - MEANS "WE WILL REBEL"
FIRST WARRIOR KING OF BABYLON, ERECH, AKKAD, CALENEH, IN SHINAR. IN ASSRYIA, HE BUILT NINEVAH, REHOBOTH IR, CALAH AND RESEN.

S _____
age _____

A _____
age _____

S _____
age _____

E _____
age _____

P _____
age _____

PELEG MEANS: _____ FOR THE EARTH DIVIDED

R _____
age _____

S _____
age _____

N _____
age _____

T _____
age _____

A _____
age 175 _____

GOD.

EVERY INCLINATION OF THE THOUGHTS OF MAN'S HEART WAS

Gen. 6:5

The Flood lasted

_____ Year(s)

_____ Month(s)

_____ Day(s)

Gen. 7:6, 8:13

Among Terah's descendants are the Edomites, Moabites, Ammonites, Israelites (Jews), Arabs, Asshurites, Letushites, Leummites.

1300   1400   1500   1600   1700   1800   1900   2000   2100   2200   2300

BUILDING MY OWN CHIASMUS

A chiasmus is an inversion of parallel phrases, clauses, sentences or paragraphs. The whole story of the flood is one large chiasmus. Try your hand at writing in this style and put your final copy on this page. Write it in story form on the next page. You may use one of the ideas below. The corresponding letters should have corresponding ideas.

The Chiastic Structure of _____

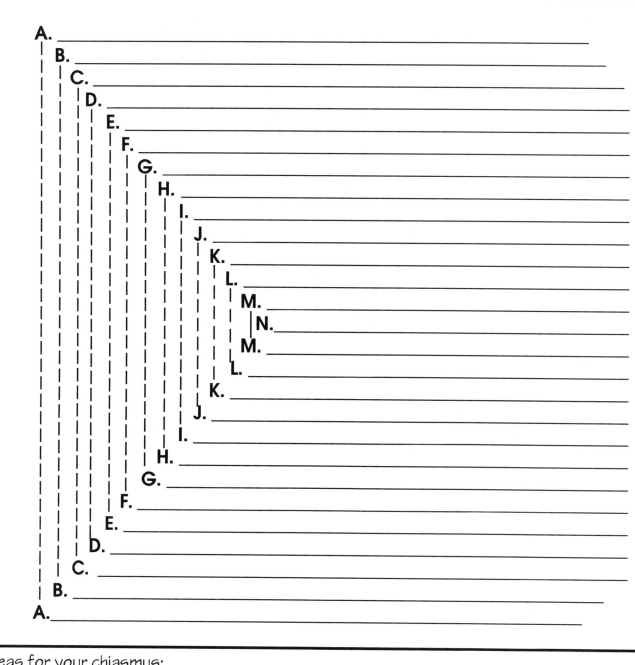

A. _____

B. _____

C. _____

D. _____

E. _____

F. _____

G. _____

H. _____

I. _____

J. _____

K. _____

L. _____

M. _____

N. _____

M. _____

L. _____

K. _____

J. _____

I. _____

H. _____

G. _____

F. _____

E. _____

D. _____

C. _____

B. _____

A. _____

Ideas for your chiasmus:

Climbing a mountain and coming back down

Being born, growing up, getting old

Doing bad deeds and reaping the consequences

Going on a vacation trip and coming back home

Getting sick and getting well

Helping someone and reaping the consequences

or any storyline with a series of events that can be matched, point by point.

CHIASTIC STRUCTURE OF THE FLOOD

A chiasmus is an inversion of parallel phrases, clauses, sentences or paragraphs. The whole story of the flood is one large chiasmus. Fill in the missing lines by selecting the best answer from the bottom of the page. The corresponding letters should have corresponding ideas.

The Chiastic Structure of the Flood

Genesis 6 - 9 (Verse numbers in parentheses.)

A. (6:1) Men increased in number on the earth

B. (6:10) Noah and his three sons, Shem, Ham, and Japheth

C. (6:12-13) Since man's heart is only evil, earth will be destroyed (by flood)

D. (6:18-20) God makes a covenant with Noah

E. (6:22) Noah builds ark

F. (7:1-3) God commands to enter ark

G. (7:4) 7 days wait until God sends rain

H. (7:10) 7 days wait before flood came

I. (7:14) Last animal enters the ark

J. (7:16) The Lord shuts the door

K. (7:17) 40 days and 40 nights the floods come

L. (7:19) Highest mountains covered

M. (7:24) 150 days waters prevail

N. (8:1) BUT GOD REMEMBERED NOAH

M. (8:3) _____

L. (8:5) _____

K. (8:6a) _____

J. (8:6b) _____

I. (8:7) _____

H. (8:10) _____

G. (8:12) _____

F. (8:15-16) _____

E. (8:20) _____

D. (8:21) _____

C. (8:21) _____

B. (9:19) _____

A. (9:19) _____

Sentence Bank

- ○ 7 days wait to send out dove
- ○ Noah opens window of the ark
- ○ 150 days waters recede
- ○ Noah builds altar
- ○ 7 days wait to send out dove again
- ○ Though man's heart only evil, earth will NOT be destroyed (by flood)
- ○ God makes a covenant with Noah and all life on earth
- ○ People increase and scatter over the earth
- ○ God commands to leave ark
- ○ Mountain tops become visible
- ○ 40 days water abates
- ○ First creature (a raven) leaves the ark
- ○ Noah and Shem, Ham and Japheth

BEFORE ABRAHAM WAS BY ISAAC KIKAWADA AND ARTHUR QUINN, ABINGDON PRESS NASHVILLE © 1985, PG. 104

GENESIS—BEGINNINGS

Fill in this crossword puzzle as a review after you have studied the sections on the family tree of man. Use the word bank at the bottom of the page. If you are not familiar with the meaning of a word, look it up!   © 1996 Susan Mortimer

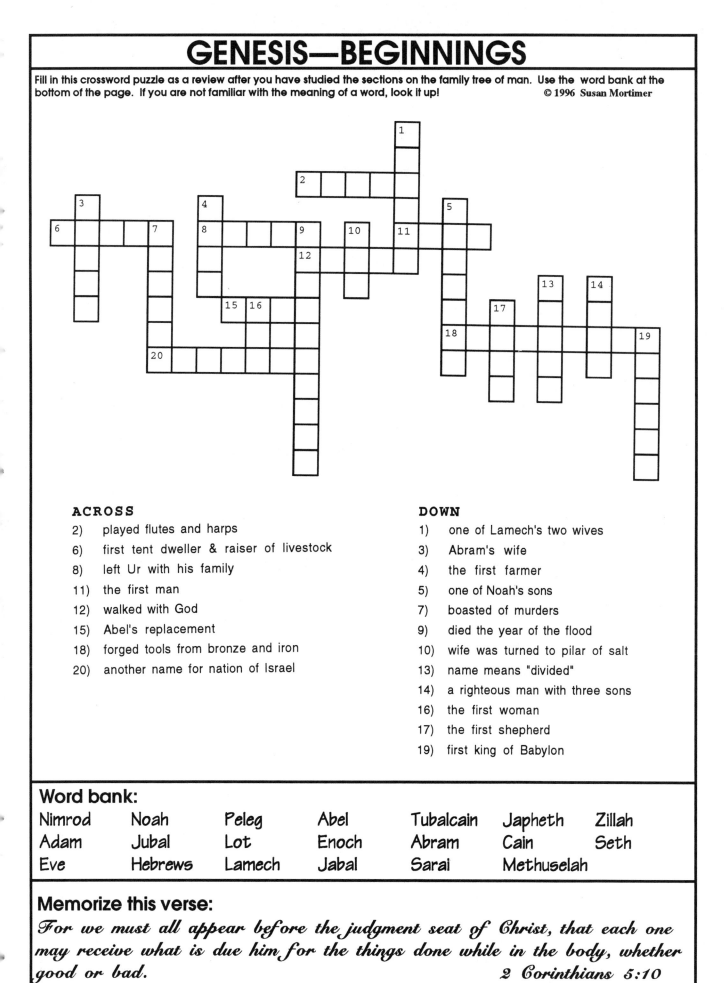

ACROSS

2) played flutes and harps
6) first tent dweller & raiser of livestock
8) left Ur with his family
11) the first man
12) walked with God
15) Abel's replacement
18) forged tools from bronze and iron
20) another name for nation of Israel

DOWN

1) one of Lamech's two wives
3) Abram's wife
4) the first farmer
5) one of Noah's sons
7) boasted of murders
9) died the year of the flood
10) wife was turned to pilar of salt
13) name means "divided"
14) a righteous man with three sons
16) the first woman
17) the first shepherd
19) first king of Babylon

Word bank:

Nimrod	Noah	Peleg	Abel	Tubalcain	Japheth	Zillah
Adam	Jubal	Lot	Enoch	Abram	Cain	Seth
Eve	Hebrews	Lamech	Jabal	Sarai	Methuselah	

Memorize this verse:

For we must all appear before the judgment seat of Christ, that each one may receive what is due him for the things done while in the body, whether good or bad.   *2 Corinthians 5:10*

CHIASMUS IN GENESIS

Copyright © 1996 Susan Mortimer

A chiasmus is an inversion of parallel phrases, clauses, sentences or paragraphs. The writer builds to an apex or focal point (which is the turning point of his story), and then recedes to an ending, matching each point. Here are two examples.

In the Hebrew word order, this is how Genesis 6: 8-9 would read.

A. Noah
 B. found favor in the eyes of the LORD
  C. these are the generations of Noah
   D. Noah was a righteous man
   D. perfect he was
  C. in his generation
 B. with God walked
A. Noah

Genesis 7:21- 23

A. Every living thing that moved on earth perished
 B. birds,
  C. livestock, wild animals, all the creatures that swarmed over the earth
   D. and all mankind
    E. everything on dry land that had the breath of life in its nostiles died
    E. everything on the face of the earth was wiped out
   D. men
  C. and animals and the creatures that moved along the ground
 B. and the birds of the air
A. were wiped from the earth

In the first selection, the focal point is "Noah was a righteous man, perfect he was." Then each beginning and ending point are matched. What phrase matches "these are the generations of Noah"?

_____

What phrase matches "with God walked"?

_____

What is the focal point of the second selection?

_____

_____

What phrase matches "and the birds of the air"?

_____

What phrase matches "Every living thing that moved on earth perished"?

_____

Now draw lines connecting each matching point in the second selection.

BEFORE ABRAHAM WAS BY ISAAC KIKAWADA AND ARTHUR QUINN, ABINGDON PRESS NASHVILLE © 1985, PG. 86-95

TABLE OF CONTENTS

OPEN LETTER TO STUDENTS

(PLEASE READ BEFORE BEGINNING THIS COURSE)

Welcome to the beginning of a new course. We will be going over what you will be studying in the coming months.

Remembering God's Awesome Acts is different from traditional textbooks which treat only one subject. This program is more of a classical approach, and blends many subjects together into one cohesive unit. It is primarily Bible and History. However, it also includes a complete drawing course, a structured creative writing class, speech, and drama. In addition, geography, anthropology, archeology, and linguistics are studied.

The point of each element is to give a better understanding of the Bible. Therefore, not every subject will be taught every day or even every week. The focus is on studying issues, playing with concepts, mastering skills, and learning discernment and logic.

Your student notebook is not a "workbook." It is a creative effort to be shared with others. Therefore, corrections need to be done discretely. Writing assignments should be fully corrected before transcribing them into your "notebook."

Keep in mind that the end result should not be just the rote memorization of facts, but to gain a higher level of understanding. Your goal should be to gain wisdom, understanding and a deeper love for God.

BIBLE

If you has never studied the Bible before, this is a great place to start. This will give you a strong foundation in understanding who God is and His awesome power.

If you feel that you have studied Genesis and the beginning of Exodus before, take heart—this is a fresh approach that brings the whole Bible into play. There is so much to cover in these chapters: the creation of the universe, the forming and fall of man, the start of civilization and languages, and the humble beginnings of the Jewish people. Even more than this, you will be getting the background for understanding passages throughout the Bible.

Jesus is emphasized from beginning to end. Every story points to Him! God knew the plan for salvation and set it in motion from the beginning of time. It is as if God is saying, "I don't want you to miss Jesus when he comes. I will point towards him this way, and if you miss that, I will point to him in another way." The sad reality is that although God pointed to Jesus from every possible angle, there are many who still miss him. May you not be one of them.

The Bible text chosen for the student notebook is the New International Version (NIV). If you elect to use another version, you may do so, however, there will need to be a few minor adjustments to some of the student pages.

DISCERNMENT

Discernment goes far beyond just retaining the facts. It involves knowing the *issues* behind the facts and making sound judgments and decisions based on that information. You, as God's children, should not be raised in a sterile environment, unexposed to the outside world. You need to be developing antibodies against wrong philosophies and twisted truths. What better way to expose these falsehoods than in the bright light of the Bible. We need to grow up not naive and gullible, but wise with eyes that see right to the heart of the issue, being able to discern right from wrong.

HISTORY

This book intertwines Bible and history. It presents the study of history in order to understand the Bible (Ur, Sumer, and Egypt), and the study of the Bible in order to understand history (Adam, Abraham, Isaac, Jacob, Joseph, and Moses.) Viewing the Bible not just as a historical document, but as a handbook for daily living, makes the journey not only fascinating but life-changing.

SOCIAL STUDIES

Genesis tells us how languages began, so you will be studying how languages have expanded to over 6400 languages in the world today. You will study a language from every continent as well as countries from around the world. These country studies focus on more than just information about a country—that is, major products, climate, and so forth. They were created to help you see the country from God's perspective by including the nation's prayer needs, major religions, and how many portions of scriptures have been translated into the various languages. This will help you expand your horizons and begin to pray more effectively for the lost of the world.

ART

The art lessons are progressive and designed to be self-taught. Drawing forces you to slow down and spend time looking at and appreciating the details of God's creation. Every skill that is developed makes our lives richer as individuals and opens more windows of opportunity. Work to uncover your talents and to use them for the glory of God. If this is the first art class you have taken, see Teacher's Manual pages 57-64 for more suggestions and examples of what other students have done. Seeing what others have done will encourage you to try harder and spend the time and effort to do your best.

CREATIVE WRITING

Many students agonize over writing assignments. Parents and teachers grow weary trying to teach them. The creative writing in this book is set out to be structured enough to help the reluctant student and yet open-ended enough to give wings to the eager writer. The writing assignments are very diverse and are often illustrated with surprising examples from the Bible. There is a section on Teacher's Manual pages 39-56 that show writing examples done by other students. This section will show you the quality of work that is expected. It is even more important for you if you are working on your own. These samples will inspire and direct you.

DISCUSSION

This course lends itself well to being used as a group course. It does not take a lot of preparation time and can be used by students with a broad age-and-ability range. If you are doing it by yourself, try to find times to get together with others who are using the course. This will give you a forum to share and get feedback on your writing assignments and art projects. It is a time to explore ideas and insights that you have been learning. It is also a time when you will get reading assignments from supplemental books.

SPEECH/DRAMA

Giving speeches and performing in a drama can serve several purposes. The most universal fear is speaking in front of a group. This needs to be understood and worked on in a setting that is comfortable and secure. Confidence increases each time you present a speech or perform in a drama. Having visual aids and a script to begin with will make it easier. These lessons give you the tools and opportunity to witness to others in an open and nonthreatening way. Planning and setting up times to teach will also help you develop organization skills and responsibility.

LOGIC

Logic problems are set up and taught so that with only a few clues and deductive reasoning, you can extract a wealth of information. This is done by using logic problems to teach biblical and historical information.

You will also use logic in following the steps taken by the individuals who figured out how to read hieroglyphics and cuneiform.

Logic and deductive reasoning help to create individuals who will be making the important contributions in the future.

GEOGRAPHY

Drawing maps of the areas discussed will give you a feel for the location and placement of the historical events and background for biblical characters. In this book there is a unique twist to geography which combines time, events, and location. This enables you to simultaneously follow the events of an individual's life and his location at the time of the event.

ANTHROPOLOGY/ARCHEOLOGY

In-depth study permits you to vicariously participate in the uncovering of ancient cultures. Places and events talked about in the Bible are sometimes taught as mere myths. However, Jesus said that even the rocks would cry out, and with each uncovering of an ancient city or a stone tablet, the rocks cry out that the Bible is true.

This book gives real problems from the real world. Hieroglyphics are not used merely as a game, but are accurately taught so that you can translate some actual stories written by the ancient Egyptians.

The gods and pharaohs are studied, not just on a factual level, but in order to have a clear understanding of who they were in relation to God's chosen people. The Egyptian gods are studied extensively for the express purpose of understanding what the issues were when

God challenged and defeated them through the plagues. You will discover that the issues God was confronting the people in Egypt so long ago are the very issues that need to be addressed by every individual, regardless of his culture, religion, or time period in history. This will help you trust God more as you begin to understand how powerful and awesome He really is.

This book contains some information that would be hard or nearly impossible to find elsewhere. However, research will be required of you in order to get a thorough historical background of the time periods covered. You will be required to write reports on basic historical facts that are readily available in encyclopedias and libraries. *Do not skip these research assignments* or you will have an incomplete understanding of history and you will not be getting all the benefits of this course.

LINGUISTICS

Finally, there will be language studies from every continent. They, like the art lessons, will build on skills so that at the end of the unit, the student will be able to do actual in-depth language studies. Studying languages can be exciting. Although languages vary greatly, these techniques used to teach college students, enable languages to be within anyone's grasp. This study will also develop an appreciation for the work of translators and missionaries and may even challenge you to become one.

FURTHER READING AND RESEARCH

You will need access to some type of reference books (such as encyclopedias or other resource books) for many of the writing assignments. Some recommendations are included at the end of this manual. However, feel free to use what you have available.

In closing I would like to encourage you to take charge of your own education. Try to use this time in your life wisely. Study hard and do your best so that you will be ready when the opportunities arise, to step in, fully equipped, for the task set before you.

Sincerely,

Susan Mortimer

LESSON PLANS

UNIT 1: WHO IS GOD?

INTRODUCTION
Much of this Teacher's Manual is meant to be read aloud to the student. Directions specifically for the teacher will be in italics parentheses.

DISCUSSION
Teacher's Manual Page 66—The History of History

Points to bring out: *(Read through the lesson and do the activity from previous Teacher's Manual page 66 before assigning the following notebook page.)*

HISTORY
Bible Reading: 2 Timothy 3:10–17
Notebook Page 5: The History of History

Points to bring out: What does the word "history" mean to you? Have you ever wondered why you were born at this particular place and time in history? Keep these thoughts in mind as you work through your notebook page on history.

BIBLE
Bible Reading: Genesis 1:1–2:3
Notebook Pages 6–7: Genesis 1

Points to bring out: We will be looking at the story of creation in a new way. Our focus will be to visualize the poetry by looking for repetition of words and phrases. This will help us "see" the beauty and poetry in God's word. This is not to be a word-for-word translation, but more of a note-taking activity. Listen or read the Bible reading and fill in the missing words, then illustrate it.

ART
Bible Reading: Psalm 148:1–14
Notebook Pages 8–9: Shapes and Shadows 1 and 2

Points to bring out: God created all that we see. He gave us light so that we can see the shapes and shadows of everything around us. By learning to draw the basic shapes, we will be able to draw God's world. Drawing forces us to slow down and spend time observing the details in the world around us.

DISCERNMENT
Bible Reading: John 1:1–14
Who was present at creation?
Notebook Page 10: The God of Creation

Points to bring out: There is a lot to be learned from the account of creation about who and what God is and is not. By analyzing the God of the Bible, we will be able to see the sharp contrast with false religions.

CREATIVE WRITING
Bible Reading: Psalm 8:1–9
Notebook Pages 11–12: Writing with Acrostics

Points to bring out: Psalm 119 is an acrostic poem, with each section beginning with a letter of the Hebrew alphabet. In this writing assignment, show how we do not worship all creation but enjoy and respect it since it points us to the Creator. Look on Teacher's Manual pages 42-43 for examples done by other students.

ART
Bible Reading: Proverbs 8:1–36
Notebook Page 13: Shapes and Shadows 3

Points to bring out: Today you will practice all the things you have learned so far about shapes and shadows. Make sure you fill the page with your drawing. In order to draw well, you must forget you know what the object is. Drawing should be like a math problem. You need to look at each items as a shape with shadows all in specific relationships to each other. Ask yourself as you are drawing: How far is this line from the other? What angle do I draw next? How dark is this shaded area compared with another? See Teacher's Manual pages 57-64 for more help in drawing.

UNIT 2: WHO IS MAN?

SPEECH/DRAMA

Teacher's Manual Pages 67-68— Adam and Eve (2 pages)

Points to bring out: *(Prepare a copy of the Teacher's Manual pages 67-68 for each student to give them at the end of the class.)* This will be the first lesson of its kind. These speech and drama classes will take some time to gather the materials and to practice. However, the spiritual truths they portray are well worth the effort. I will be presenting a lesson for you, not for your entertainment, but for you to learn how to teach the lesson yourself. So listen carefully, and try to visualize how you will teach the lesson to younger students in a Sunday School class, a Bible club with neighborhood children, family members or relatives, or even senior citizens. This will give you an opportunity to share your faith with others.

HISTORY

Bible Reading: Genesis 2:1–25

Notebook Pages 14–20: Confessions of Paleontologists, Neanderthal Man—Science or Fiction, Neanderthal Update

Points to bring out: These pages show the perspective of man from the humanist/evolutionist viewpoint. In their own words, these scientists show how unscientific their methods are.

DISCERNMENT

Bible Reading: Proverbs 1:1–33

Notebook Page 21: Paleontology Quiz

Points to bring out: Discernment is an important skill to develop. This is done by learning to analyze everything we see or read and not just accept it. We also need to learn to make judgment calls and conclusions based on our foundation, the Word of God.

ART

Bible Reading: Psalm 119:105–112

Notebook Page 22: Drawing with Light

Points to bring out: Visual light allows us see all of God's physical creation. Spiritual light, in and through us, enables others to see God, the source of all light. Memorize Matthew 5:16.

CREATIVE WRITING

Bible Reading: Genesis 2:1–25

Notebook Page 23: Practicing Hebrew Poetry

Points to bring out: English poetry is hard to translate, for it is based on rhyming words. Words with the same meaning in other languages do not translate with the same rhymes. However, Hebrew poetry is based on restating thoughts, and therefore can be translated easily. Because of the way poetry is written in the Bible, we can enjoy it in English, but only if we learn to recognize it as such. These pages will help us identify the elements of Hebrew poetry and increase our awareness of it as we read the Bible in the future. See some samples of Hebrew poetry done by other students on Teacher's Manual pages 44-45.

Notebook Page 24: The Poetry of Man and Woman

Points to bring out: God demonstrates a loving and respectful relationship with man. In addition, there are so many things that we can know about early man just from the account of creation and looking at what the Bible has to say about Adam. Adam was created as a totally capable and functioning human being. He had a language, the ability to think abstractly and to create new words. God delighted in his abilities and brought the animals to him to see what he would name them.

ART

Bible Reading: Isaiah 64
We are the work of God's hand.

Notebook Pages 25–26: Drawing the Hand 1 and 2

Points to bring out: The hand is one of the aspects that emphasizes the uniqueness of man. No other animal was created with the dexterity of the human hand. Memorize Psalm 119:48a. See Teacher's Manual page 59 for samples drawn by other students.

BIBLE

Notebook Page 27: Versatile Hands

Points to bring out: Many aspects of man that are unique from the animal world can be expressed through the hand. The Bible uses the hand to show our humanity. This page will help you build skills in looking up and finding verses in the Bible.

CREATIVE WRITING

Bible Reading: Proverbs 31:1–31

Notebook Pages 28–29: Hands Show Humanness

Points to bring out: Learning to take abstract ideas and write a cohesive paper is a very necessary skill. The form and suggestions are to help you learn to get your thoughts and ideas into a polished paper. The writing assignments should be done over a period of several days. It will take that much time for you to think about what you want to say. You are to begin with a rough draft, polish it, and copy the final corrected version in your book. With any writing assignment in this book, if you need additional pages, attach them to your notebook page. See Teacher's Manual page 46 for an example.

ART

Notebook Page 30: Drawing Your Hand 3

Points to bring out: The amazing design of the way the thumb and fingers come together enables man to do many things that are uniquely human. Memorize Ecclesiastes 9:10a. If drawing your hand seems too hard, first try tracing it on a separate piece of paper. Then follow the instructions on how to draw your hand. You will be able to see what needs to be changed or what to do next by referring back to your traced hand on the first piece of paper. When you have finished drawing, your hand should match perfectly with both the traced page and the drawing. There are samples of other student's drawings in the Teacher's Manual page 59.

UNIT 3: THE FALL OF MAN

DISCERNMENT

Bible Reading: Psalm 119:89–104

Notebook Page 31: Twisting the Truth is Wrong

Points to bring out: The words that begin with "wr" have a unique common denominator that you will discover as you do this page.

BIBLE

Bible Reading: Genesis 2:16; 3:1–7

Notebook Page 32: Twisted Truth

Points to bring out: This page gives us a picture of how Satan twisted what God said into a lie. God is constantly reaching out to man, and Satan is constantly trying to twist what God says. It is critical to learn to discern what is the element of truth and what Satan has twisted.

DISCERNMENT

Bible Reading: John 8:42–47

Notebook Page 33: The Author of Lies

Points to bring out: The same thing that happened in the Garden of Eden is still going on today. Satan's tactics haven't changed.

HISTORY/SOCIAL STUDIES

Bible Reading: Romans 1:1–32

Notebook Pages 34–35: Religions of the World Write-up; Religions of the World

Points to bring out: Mankind was created with a "hole" in his soul that only God can fill. If people have rejected or do not know or understand God, they will try to fill the void with other religions. *(The home is a good place to be "vaccinated" against the attraction to other religions.)*

CREATIVE WRITING

Bible Reading: Genesis 3:8–19

Notebook Page 36: Poetic Justice

Points to bring out: This page helps us take a closer look at the curse that affects us all.

BIBLE

Notebook Page 37: Questions on the Fall

Points to bring out: By bringing in the New Testament insights and comparing Adam to Jesus, we can get a broader picture of the fall of man *and* God's solution.

DISCUSSION

Teacher's Manual 69—Sin, Separation and New Life

Points to bring out: Listen closely to this lesson. You will be using the information for today's writing assignment.

CREATIVE WRITING

Bible Reading: 1 Corinthians 15:35–59

Notebook Pages 38–40: The Garden of Eden Revisited

Points to bring out: Thinking through the tactics or weaknesses of people that result in sin will help you to be on the guard against it. In order for your play to be effective, you must present a sin so twisted that doing it would appear to be the good and noble thing to do. Then you must conclude by showing that sin never pays. Your writing assignments should be done over a period of several days. You are to begin with a rough draft, polish it, and copy the final corrected version in your book. There is a sample of such a play on Teacher's Manual page 47-48.

REVIEW

Bible Reading: Psalm 90:1–17

Notebook Page 41: Review of Words

Points to bring out: This page is a review of what you have studied. It will help "cement" the concepts in your mind. Fill in the crossword without looking back at previous work. Memorize Romans 1:25.

DISCUSSION

Teacher's Manual Page 70—Anger

Points to bring out: *(Anger is a hard subject to talk about. In the Teacher's Manual is a discussion on several issues to do with anger. Read it aloud with the student before he does his page.)*

BIBLE

Bible Reading: Genesis 3:20–4:7

Notebook Page 42: A Study on Anger

Points to bring out: See the discussion above.

BIBLE

Bible Reading: Genesis 4:8–16

Notebook Page 43: An Attitude of the Heart

Points to bring out: God is always reaching out to us. The whole Old and New Testaments cry out for us to love God with all our heart, soul, and mind. King David and Cain both committed sin. However, when Cain sinned, he did not show a change of heart, whereas King David did. It is important to think through the issues of sin and forgiveness.

ART

Bible Reading: Ecclesiastes 3:1–22

Notebook Pages 44–45: Symmetry

Points to bring out: Balance and symmetry are important in both life and art. Memorize 1 Corinthians 14:40. See Teacher's Manual page 60-61 for samples drawn by other students.

CREATIVE WRITING

Bible Reading: Matthew 23:1–39 Jesus gave His life to make a change in a bad situation. Look for His righteous anger.

Notebook Pages 46–48: Making a Difference

Points to bring out: In order to dedicate oneself to a cause, it takes a lot of passion and compassion. Most people who have made a difference in our world have done so by recognizing that something was wrong and then dedicating their lives and energies to change it. Let's discuss what kinds of causes would be good to be involved in and why. Then we will discuss what kinds of causes would not be good to be associated with and why. What should our underlying motivation be?

HISTORY/SOCIAL STUDIES

Bible Reading: Genesis 4:17–26

Notebook Pages 49, 51–52: The Biblical Family Tree of Man

Points to bring out: Before the flood, man had built cities, raised livestock, forged bronze and iron, and made musical instruments. In the pre-flood world, men lived to be almost a thousand years old. After the flood, men were once again evil. Their lifespan dropped in half after the flood and dropped dramatically again after the days of Peleg. Begin working on these pages today, filling in the information you find in today's Bible reading.

BIBLE

Bible Reading: Genesis 4:1–26

Notebook Page 50: Names Have Meaning

Points to bring out: Much is lost in the biblical accounts if we do not understand that the names of people and places have significant meanings. Studying the names will bring new insights into God's Word. Pay particular attention to the similarities of the names, and at the same time, distinct differences in their meanings for the descendants of Cain and the descendants of Seth. On the Family Tree of Man page, fill in the information you found in today's Bible reading.

REVIEW

Bible Reading: Genesis 5; Genesis 9:2; Genesis 11:10–32

Notebook Page 53: Genesis—Beginnings

Points to bring out: This crossword puzzle will help you review what you have studied. Fill it in without looking back. Then memorize 2 Corinthians 5:10. When you have finished, fill in the information on the Family Tree of Man page that you found in today's Bible reading.

UNIT 4: GOD SAVES NOAH

SPEECH/DRAMA

Teacher's Manual Page 71-73—Noah and the Flood (3 pages)

Points to bring out: *(Prepare a copy of the Teacher's Manual pages for each student to give them at the end of the class.)* These speech and drama classes will take some time to gather the materials and to practice. However, the spiritual truths they portray are well worth the effort. I will be presenting a lesson for you, not for your entertainment, but for you to learn how to teach the lesson yourself. So listen carefully, and try to visualize how you will teach the lesson to younger students in a Sunday School class, a Bible club with neighborhood children, family members or relatives, or even senior citizens. This will give you an opportunity to share your faith with others.

BIBLE

Bible Reading: Genesis 6:1–9:19

Notebook Pages 54–55: Chiasmus in Genesis; Chiastic Structure of the Flood

Points to bring out: The chiastic (ki-as-tic) structure may be a new writing form for you. Because of having to pass down information by oral tradition, the chiastic approach helped the listeners to remember the story. God built a chiasmus (ki-as-mus) into the story of the flood. The intricacies and details stand out in a new light when we look at it from this perspective. If you first locate the focal point or turning point of the story, it all becomes much clearer.

CREATIVE WRITING
Bible Reading: Genesis 9:20–10:21
Notebook Pages 56–57: Building My Own Chiasmus

Points to bring out: Some ideas for your chiasmus might be: going up a mountain and back down again; starting and ending a day; doing a series of wrong things, getting caught, and reaping the consequences. Be sure to build up to a decisive turning point and have matching ideas for each event in your series. See Teacher's Manual pages 49-51 for some examples.

ANTHROPOLOGY
Bible Reading: Matthew 24:36–51
Notebook Page 58: The Flood—The One Universal Story

Points to bring out: Stories of a universal flood are found on every continent and in many countries.

ZOOLOGY
Bible Reading: Luke 17:20–35
Notebook Page 59: Noah's Zoo

Points to bring out: Out of all the animals that would have needed to be on the ark, only a small percentage of them are larger than a sheep and most of them are smaller than rats.

HISTORY
Bible Reading: Psalm 107:23–32
Notebook Pages 60–61, 63–64: The Ships; The History of Wooden Ships (2 pages)

Points to bring out: The Ark is the largest wooden ship ever built. It was not a cute little boat with elephants and giraffes hanging off the sides, but a mammoth structure.

BIBLE
Bible Reading: 1 Peter 3:8–22
Notebook Pages 62, 65: How big was the ark?; Animals All Aboard

Points to bring out: The size of the ark was more than adequate to hold all the animals.

ANTHROPOLOGY
Bible Reading: Hebrews 11:7
Notebook Pages 66–68: The Epic of Gilgamish (3 pages)

Points to bring out: Why are we studying The Gilgamish Epic? The reason is that many scholars use it to discredit the Bible. A blatant example from Princeton University declares that its course, **The Bible and Western Culture** "extends back before the *Book of Genesis* 'in the beginning . . .' by including discussion of the ancient epic tradition and the influences of the oldest epic, *Gilgamish*, on the Hebrew Bible." It goes on to say, "The influence of *Gilgamish*, the oldest known epic, on Semitic mythology is seen in the initial part of the Hebrew Bible. Many elements of epic literature . . . are elaborated in a more complex way in the Pentateuch. *Gilgamish* offers a useful historical context for all inquires into biblical literature." (from Greatest Lectures by American's SuperStar Teachers, Spring Catalog, 1997, page 22). What they are saying is that they believe the Bible to be "mythology" and the beginning of it is nothing more than an elaborate rewrite of the Gilgamish epic. They, in effect, are cutting down the Bible at its very roots in order to discredit the whole of it.

We, as believers in the Bible, use the Gilgamish epic to show that the Bible is true since, although it is myth form, it contains the flood story. We say that we should find such stories around the world, and we do. The selections from the Epic of Gilgamish that are included here, were taken from a literal word-for-word translation of an original text. Careful attention was given to maintain the integrity and flavor of the original. Most translations of Gilgamish for the English-speaking world give only a summary or overview of the text. They bring out only the points that match up with the Bible, but they do not give enough information to give a firm grasp of the issues. By working from the original, we are able to deal with specific issues and be discerning in our conclusions.

DISCERNMENT

Bible Reading: Revelation 18:1–18 What is in store for these gods and their followers?

Notebook Page 69: Evaluating the Sumerian and Babylonian Gods and Goddesses

Points to bring out: The gods and goddesses of Sumer and Babylon are exact opposites of the true God. When most religions speak of "god" they are not speaking of the God of the Bible. Their "gods" are not good, not all-knowing, not always there, not all-powerful, but are reflections of human beings, with all their shortcomings.

DISCERNMENT

Bible Reading: Proverbs 5:1–23

Notebook Page 70: Truth and Twisted Truth in the Epic of Gilgamish

Points to bring out: The Epic of Gilgamish agrees with the biblical account of the flood story on some points, but where it differs, it is not believable. In addition, in a society where promiscuity was rampant, the people recognized that their main goddess, the female goddess of promiscuity was not worthy of respect, and that sex outside of marriage is destructive and not admirable.

Later in this book, you will be studying about Judah, one of the sons of Jacob, who mistook his daughter-in-law for a temple prostitute (of the Canaanite version of Ishtar). The Bible deals frankly and openly with sin of all kinds, including sexual sin. Therefore, when someone makes an accusation about someone in the Bible behaving a certain way *(as many have done, even attacking the chastity of our Lord Jesus),* we can look in the Bible to find out for ourselves whether or not it is true.

DISCERNMENT

Bible Reading: Psalm 119:33–48

Notebook Page 71: Comparing the Bible with the Gilgamish Myth

Points to bring out: *(If this page is used as a test, make sure the student knows what will be covered on it before test time.)*

GEOGRAPHY

Bible Reading: Genesis 10:21–32

Notebook Pages 72–75, 77–78: Continental Drift; The World Today (2 pages)

Points to bring out: The continents fit together so well (especially Africa, South America, Australia, and Antarctica) that it seems to confirm that not that long ago it was one land mass. It could have divided in the days of Noah and Peleg. Peleg's name means "division" or "earthquake." *(Note: The circles on the World Today pages will be used in later lessons.)*

ART

Bible Reading: Luke 6:20–42 Jesus had a way of showing us that our perspective of things is not the same as His.

Notebook Pages 79–80: Perspective (2 pages)

Points to bring out: Perspective is important to make objects appear three-dimensional. It is achieved by making things that are closer look bigger than things far away.

BIBLE

Bible Reading: Revelation 20:11–21:8 Where is the most important place to have your name written down?

Notebook Pages 80–81: Names Have Meaning 2 & 3

Points to bring out: Studying the names will bring new insights into God's Word. See what you can learn from these names.

UNIT 5: DISPERSION OF MAN

ARCHEOLOGY
Bible Reading: Psalm 127:1–2
Unless God is included in a project, all work is in vain.

Notebook Page 82: Building a Ziggurat

Points to bring out: Using logic skills, you will uncover that one of the most ancient buildings, the ziggurat, was probably similar to the Tower of Babel.

ART
Bible Reading: Matthew 19:16–29
Notebook Page 83: Perspective 3

Points to bring out: By putting into practice what you have learned, you should be able to draw these structures in perspective. Memorize Ephesians 3:17b–19. See Teacher's Manual page 62 for samples drawn by other students.

BIBLE
Bible Reading: Genesis 11:1–32
Notebook Page 84: Building the Tower of Babel

Points to bring out: Built into the biblical account of the Tower of Babel is another chiasmus. Notice that from man's perspective, the tower reached up to the heavens. However, from God's perspective, He had to come *down* to see the tower. You start at the bottom of the left-hand side of the page and work your way up and over to the right-hand side.

CREATIVE WRITING
Bible Reading: Isaiah 46:1–13
Notebook Pages 85–86: Babbling Blocks the Building of Babel

Points to bring out: Lost in the translation of the story telling how languages began are the alliterations (that is, the same sound being used over and over again) and puns (jokes based on words that sound the same). This writing assignment will help give you a feel for how it was originally written. See Teacher's Manual page 52 for an example.

ARCHEOLOGY
Bible Reading: Psalm 121
Our help is from heaven, not from high places on earth.

Notebook Pages 87, 273: Ziggurats; Pyramids and Temples (2 pages)

Points to bring out: All around the world there are pyramid structures used as temples and tombs which suggest a common beginning—perhaps the tower of Babel. Study them. Then carefully cut out the bottom half of page 273 from the yellow pages at the back of your notebook. Leave the top half there for a later assignment. Finally, cut and glue the pictures onto the World Today map in their correct locations.

GEOGRAPHY
Bible Reading: Psalms 100:1–5
Notebook Pages 88–89: Nations from the Sons of Noah

Points to bring out: After the flood, all people descended from the three sons of Noah and spread out from a central point to eventually cover the entire world. This page shows where the descendants of the sons of Noah migrated. It does not include all of them, but the ones that can be traced in history.

SOCIAL STUDIES
Bible Reading: 2 Corinthians 5:1–21
Notebook Pages 90–91: A World of Languages

Points to bring out: European languages are most commonly the official languages. However, there are now over 6,500 languages in the world that came from the handful of languages which began at the Tower of Babel.

REVIEW
Bible Reading: Romans 8:1–39
Our physical heritage is not important, our spiritual position is!

Notebook Page 92: Deluge and Dispersion Review

Points to bring out: Use this page as a review. Understanding the meaning of words is important in studying any subject. Memorize Genesis 9:16.

INTRODUCTION

The dispersion of the nations has resulted in thousands of languages and cultures. The goal of this unit is to help you gain an appreciate for other cultures and to acquire a vision for the people and their needs. In addition, it will open windows of understanding and a concern for the spiritual needs of these people.

In this unit study of languages and people from around the world, you will be doing several things. The first will be learning how to do portraits and to appreciate different facial features from around the world. The lessons are done sequentially to slowly build up portraiture skills so that in the end, you will be able to draw portraits. Using a pencil, you will lightly draw in the "guidelines" on the large face and follow each step shown on the left-hand side of the page. When the drawing has been completed in pencil, only the features should be traced with ink and the pencil marks should be erased. (Make sure to get a good drawing pen.) By doing the "guidelines," you will learn to draw with the correct placement and proportions.

We recommend using a current *Operation World* by Patrick Johnstone, for the hard-to-find information on the Getting to Know a Country page. If this book is not available, a chart is included in the Teacher's Manual with the basic information needed, but only for the specific countries studied in this unit. The focus of this second part of each section will be learning to understand about countries from a Christian point of view—that is, not only learning about major products and climate, but also the nation's prayer needs and how many portions of scriptures are translated into the various languages. This will help you see the country's needs from God's perspective.

You will then write a report on the country including information not covered on the previous country study page. This could include the history of the country, current events from magazines and newspapers, missionaries or friends that you may know from the country, and so forth.

Finally, there will be language studies from every continent. They, like the portrait drawing, will build on skills so that at the end of the unit, you will be able to do actual in-depth language studies. Studying languages can be exciting and although languages vary greatly, these techniques, used to teach college students, enable languages to be within anyone's grasp. This study will also develop an appreciation for the work of translators and missionaries and may open your eyes to becoming one. You may want to do clothing and foods from the countries, too. If there are several students, each may be assigned different countries to research and report on.

ART

Bible Reading: Acts 10:1–48

Notebook Page 93: Faces from Around the World: Asia

Points to bring out: The first portrait drawing focuses on how to draw the eyes, nose and mouth. Using a pencil, lightly draw in the "guidelines" on the large face and follow each step shown on the left-hand side of the page. When the drawing has been completed in pencil, only the features should be traced with ink and the pencil marks should be erased. By using the "guidelines," you will learn to draw with the correct placement and proportions.

SOCIAL STUDIES

Bible Reading: Psalm 46:1–11

Notebook Pages 94–95: Getting to Know a Country (Choose any Asian country.); My Report on (country)

Points to bring out: These country study pages are designed to give more than just the factual information. They also present the people from God's perspective with spiritual and prayer needs. Many people in Asian countries practice Eastern religions, such as Buddhism. Earthquakes and monsoons affect the lives of Asians who live near the ocean. Memorize Revelation 5:9b.

LINGUISTICS
Bible Reading: Psalm 98:1–9

Notebook Page 96: Vietnamese Language Study (Vietnam)

Points to bring out: You will see that languages are logical by using logic to match words in this Vietnamese translation exercise.

ART
Bible Reading: Psalm 2:1–12

Notebook Page 97: Faces from Around the World: Latin America

Points to bring out: This portrait drawing lesson will help you expand on what you have already learned, by doing both the features and the face shape. Remember to first lightly draw in your "guidelines" with a pencil.

SOCIAL STUDIES
Bible Reading: Psalm 65:1–13

Notebook Pages 98–99: Getting to Know a Country (Choose any Central American country.); My Report on (country)

Points to bring out: Central American countries have experienced great turmoil in the past decade. Civil wars, unstable governments, and poor economies make life difficult. These countries are nominally Roman Catholic; however, most of the people do not have an understanding of the gospel.

LINGUISTICS
Bible Reading: Psalm 113:1–9

Notebook Page 100: Mezquital Otomi Language Problem (Mexico)

Points to bring out: You will learn that by knowing only a few words of Mezquital (mes-key-tahl) Otomi (oh-toe-me), a whole array of sentences can be created.

SOCIAL STUDIES
Bible Reading: 1 Corinthians 13:1–13 Begin memorizing this chapter today. Love is more important than many things, including knowing many languages.

Notebook Page 101: Getting to Know a Country (Choose any South American country.)

Points to bring out: Bible translators are working in South American countries to translate scriptures into the languages of the many language groups in these countries. One group, previously known as the Aucas, murdered five young missionary men in the 1950's. Today many in that group have become Christians. The group is now known by the name they call themselves, Waorani (wah-oh-rah-nee). You will be doing a translation from that language.

LINGUISTICS
Bible Reading: 1 Corinthians 13:1–13 Continue memorizing the chapter.

Notebook Pages 102–105: Waorani Language Study (Ecuador)

Points to bring out: With only sixteen words, a whole story can be told. However, this language is not spoken with the same grammatical structure as English, so you must rewrite it to sound more natural in English.

ART
Bible Reading: 1 Corinthians 13:1–13 Continue memorizing the chapter.

Notebook Page 106: Faces from Around the World: Africa

Points to bring out: You have now advanced to drawing the whole face with only a few "guidelines." Make sure that you do all the steps shown on the left-hand side so that you learn correct placement and proportion.

SPEECH/DRAMA
Teacher's Manual Page 76— Missions; Getting to Know a Country

Points to bring out: *(Prepare a copy of the Teacher's Manual page for each student to give them at the end of the class.)*

This lesson will be a little different. You will have to do some research on missions and missionaries to present to a group.

SOCIAL STUDIES

Bible Reading: 1 Corinthians 13:1–13 Finish memorizing the chapter and say it for someone outside of your family.

Notebook Pages 107–108: Getting to Know a Country (Choose any African country.); My Report on (country)

Points to bring out: War, famine, drought and disease have hit many African countries hard. There are many people there who follow animistic religions, however, many more are Muslims.

LINGUISTICS

Bible Reading: Psalm 22:22–31

Notebook Pages 109, 275–278: Igala Language Study (Nigeria) (Two of the pages are in the yellow section of the student notebook.)

Points to bring out: The Igala (ee-gah-la) language is quite complex. The nouns all begin with vowels and the verbs with consonants. But it gets a little tricky, so you must go slow and figure it out step-by-step.

ART

Bible Reading: Psalm 24:1–10

Notebook Page 110: Faces from Around the World: Middle East

Points to bring out: You should be getting quite good at drawing faces by now! Don't forget to keep your proportions accurate.

SOCIAL STUDIES

Bible Reading: Psalm 146:1–10 Mohammed was a man who began the Islam, the religion of Muslims. What does the Bible say about such a man?

Notebook Pages 111–112: Getting to Know a Country (Choose any Middle East-ern country.); My Report on (country)

Points to bring out: It is a crime to convert a Muslim to a different religion. Consequently, many of the Arab nations are primarily Muslim, the fastest growing religion in the world. Christians in these countries are often persecuted. Practice seeing these people from God's perspective, with spiritual and prayer needs.

LINGUISTICS

Bible Reading: Psalm 96:1–13

Notebook Pages 113–114: Turkish Language Study (Turkey)

Points to bring out: You will be doing the Turkish language problem a little differently, in that numbers and simple drawings will be used for part of the translation instead of words. Notice what the word for man is, *Adam.* By now you should be able to do a lot of the translation without much help from the clues.

ART

Bible Reading: Isaiah 9:1–7

Notebook Page 115: Faces from Around the World: Australia

Points to bring out: You are on your own in drawing this portrait. Make it as large as possible to fit in the space allowed.

SOCIAL STUDIES

Bible Reading: Isaiah 49:1–7

Notebook Pages 116–117: Getting to Know a Country (Study Australia.); My Report on (country)

Points to bring out: Many Australian aborigines still speak their own languages and live in the bush away from the modern city life. They are primarily animistic, while the city folk are primarily humanists and atheists.

LINGUISTICS

Bible Reading: Romans 10:1–21

Notebook Pages 118–121: Ooldea Dialect (Western Desert, Australia)

Points to bring out: You will be doing one final story and translating the Ooldea (ool-dee-ah) language into good English. What have you learned about languages? Do you think you would be able to learn a language that has never previously been written? Research mission groups that do

Bible translation, such as Wycliffe Bible Translators and New Tribes Mission.

ART
Bible Reading: Romans 11:1–36

Notebook Page 122: Faces from Around the World: Whatever country you are in.

Points to bring out: You will be learning to draw a live portrait in this lesson. Have someone sit in a chair facing you. The subject needs to pick a focal point behind you to look at in order to stay still long enough for you to draw the portrait. Tell the subject to feel free to blink as needed, but not to move his head or body. You should go through all the steps you have studied, drawing the rough draft and "guidelines" in pencil and then finishing the picture with ink. Make sure the placement is correct before starting to work on the details. See Teacher's Manual pages 63-64 for samples drawn by other students.

SOCIAL STUDIES
Bible Reading: Psalm 33:1–22

Notebook Pages 123–124: Getting to Know a Country (Choose any country on your continent.); My Report on (country)

Points to bring out: Find out what the spiritual needs of your country are. What can you do to help?

LINGUISTICS
Bible Reading: Acts 2:1–47

Notebook Page 125: Indo-European Languages—Roundabout and back again.

Points to bring out: In the days after the flood, there were only a few languages. Today there are thousands. How did all the languages develop? This page will show how a multitude of languages developed out of one. From a single language, many languages were derived that are not mutually understandable.

Notebook Pages 126–127: IndoEuropean Language Wheel

Points to bring out: This chart show how many different languages developed from one original language. You will have to use logic to figure out where each language goes on the wheel.

HISTORY/SOCIAL STUDIES
Bible Reading: 1 Corinthians 9:19–27; Galatians 3:26–29

Notebook Pages 128–129: The Human Race

Points to bring out: There is more variety between individuals within a group than between the races. And within a particular race, there is a broad range of skin color. For example, Caucasians have skin color from white to yellow, to tan to dark brown, and so forth. God cares about one race—the human race. The Bible never refers to "race" but instead to "tribes" and "nations."

UNIT 6: THE GOD OF ABRAHAM, ISAAC, AND JACOB

SPEECH/DRAMA
Teacher's Manual Pages 77-78—Three Lives and Three Choices (2 pages)

Points to bring out: *(Prepare a copy of the Teacher's Manual page for each student to give them at the end of the class.)* These speech and drama classes will take some time to gather the materials and to practice. However, the spiritual truths they portray are well worth the effort. I will be presenting (or assign someone to present) a lesson for you, not for your entertainment, but for you to learn how to teach the lesson yourself. So listen carefully, and try to visualize how you would teach the lesson to younger students in a Sunday School class, a Bible club with neighborhood children, family members or relatives, or even senior citizens. This will give you an opportunity to share your faith with others. The lesson today will show how choices we make in life have far-reaching consequences.

BIBLE

Bible Reading: Genesis 12:1–20

Notebook Pages 130–131, 133–134: Practice for Abraham's Journey (2 pages; Abraham's Journey (2 pages)

Points to bring out: In our journey to heaven, we must leave the land of sin and follow where God leads. An interesting point here is that both Ur and Haran, where Abraham began his journeys, were dedicated to the moon god. The Sumerian name for the moon god was "Sin." So Abraham, too, had to leave the land of "sin" and follow God's leading.

Abraham spent his life moving from place to place. It is hard to understand his life unless we see where he was at different times. This new way of charting keeps track of both time and location. The information will be filled in over several days, as you read through the daily reading assignments in Genesis.

BIBLE

Bible Reading: Genesis 13:1–18

Notebook Page 132: Follow Along Family Tree of Abraham

Points to bring out: You will fill in the information on this page as you are reading through Genesis. It is not to be completed in one sitting, but to be kept up as you work through the unit.

ARCHEOLOGY

Bible Reading: Genesis 14:1–24

Notebook Pages 135, 137, 138: Ur of the Chaldeans (Sumerian Society)

Points to bring out: Abraham grew up in the city of Ur, one of the most wealthy, educated, and advanced cities in the Middle East at that time. By studying the culture of Ur, you will have a better understanding of what life was like in Abraham's day.

BIBLE

Bible Reading: Genesis 15:1–21

Notebook Page 136: Covenant with Abraham

Points to bring out: God spoke many times to Abraham, restating and adding to His covenant with him. This page will help you get a clear and complete picture of the covenant that was made. Again, it is to be filled in over a period of time, as you find the information in your reading of Genesis. It is important to emphasize that God's promise to Abraham was not limited to Abraham and his descendants, but that God wanted to bless all nations in every period of time through him.

ANTHROPOLOGY

Bible Reading: Genesis 16:1–16

Notebook Pages 139–141: Where Animals Were First Domesticated; Israel and the Arab Nations

Points to bring out: There are very few domesticated animals in the world today. Out of those that are domesticated, the majority of them were first domesticated in the Middle East. This is as we would expect to find, because this is near the area where the ark landed and where civilization began again.

ARCHEOLOGY

Bible Reading: Genesis 17:1–27

Notebook Pages 142–143: The Development of Cuneiform

Points to bring out: Writing has been around for millenniums. Cuneiform was the method used at the dawn of recorded history.

ANTHROPOLOGY

Bible Reading: Genesis 18:1–33

Notebook Pages 144–145: Life in the Fertile Crescent; A Tour of the Fertile Crescent

Points to bring out: The first page will help you review and sort the information you have been studying about the Fertile Crescent. On the second page, picture yourself as a young person in Abraham's times and take a visitor from this century on a tour of your town. You won't be able to include all the information you have gathered, but choose some major points and make your report informative but interesting.

BIBLE

Bible Reading: Hebrews 7:1–28

Notebook Page 146: Melchizedek and Jesus Compared

Points to bring out: We don't know a lot about Melchizedek, but we do know that he was a righteous person. Abraham recognized him as such, and brought him tithes and offerings. This story, as do others in the Old Testament, points us to Jesus who became our eternal high priest.

BIBLE

Bible Reading: Genesis 19:1–29

Notebook Page 147: God Rescues the Righteous

Points to bring out: From the beginning of time, God has been warning, protecting and saving the righteous. He will continue to do so until the end of time.

(After the student finishes the notebook page, have a discussion about the following. Suggested answers are included, but there are probably many more.) There are several connections between the story of Noah, Lot and the End Times. Can you think what some of them would be?*

*(*1. There was great wickedness in the land. 2. There was to be destruction of the wicked. 3. God revealed his plan of salvation to the righteous. 4. People were living life as usual up until the moment of destruction. 5. God rescued/will rescue the righteous.)*

ARCHEOLOGY

Bible Reading: Esther 8:1–13
This edict was probably written in cuneiform. The Xerxes (zerk-sees) you will study about today was most likely the king who married Esther.

Notebook Pages 148–150: Cracking the Code of Cuneiform

Points to bring out: At first the cuneiform markings will look like chicken scratchings to you, but as you follow the process discovered by George Grotenfend, you will begin to recognize actual words.

ANTHROPOLOGY

Bible Reading: Genesis 19:30– 21:21

Notebook Page 151: Firsts from Ur: the First Known Spoiled and Lazy Son

Points to bring out: Until recent times, scholars believed that early people were limited in their language and intelligence. They questioned the Bible for being too advanced for the time period it was said to be written in. However, since some of these ancient languages are being decoded, we are finding out that they reveal highly intelligent people. The writings of these early people reveal that they experienced the same dilemmas we do today. Cuneiform writing, because it was preserved in clay, is some of the earliest writing found. After its code had been cracked, a whole world of clay writings from the area and time period of the beginning books of the Bible, were made accessible. Most of the tablets of clay were record keeping. Records of how many sheep or cattle, how much grain was harvested, fill tablet after tablet. But there were also stories, myths, religious songs, and letters. Some we find amusing even today.

One of the most common scripts found from that time period was a writing assignment for young students. They had to copy down a story of a poor student who was whipped constantly in school for his poor academic skills. Then his father invited his teacher over for a meal and gave him fine clothes. After that the student excelled in school. This shows that bribery was not just going on even back then, but was promoted!

There were also comical materials that could have been used by the first stand-up comedian. The script tell how a clever servant has to constantly change his position to agree with his fickle master:

"Servant, agree with me."

"Yes, my Lord, yes."

"I will love a woman."

"Yes, love, my Lord, love. The man who loves a woman forgets all his pains and troubles."

"No, servant, I will not love a woman."

"No, do not love, my Lord, do not love. A woman is a pitfall, she is a sharp iron dagger, which cuts a man's throat."

(*The Legendary Past Mesopotamian Myths*, Henrietta McCall British Museum Publications, 1990)

What you will be reading in your notebook is a letter from a father to a rebellious son. It could be written by many fathers today. People have not changed since time began.

BIBLE

Bible Reading: Genesis 21:22– 22:24

Notebook Page 152: Abraham Steps out in Faith

Points to bring out: The agony in what God asked Abraham to do is shown graphically in how he performed each step, painstakingly, and deliberately. We can see the change in the pace of the story once God provided the ram to take Isaac's place. Instead of describing each step—such as he took the ram, he bound the ram, he placed it on the wood, he reached out his hand, he took the knife—it just says, he took the ram and sacrificed it. There was no agony for Abraham in the sacrifice that God provided, only joy and thanksgiving!

CREATIVE WRITING

Bible Reading: Genesis 23:1–20

Notebook Pages 153–154: Stepping Out in Faith

Points to bring out: Your assignment is to develop a paper featuring a character who has a difficult task to carry out. Show the tension and anguish of each step taken to do what is right. Then have a distinct turning point, where the story comes quickly to a joyful ending. See Teacher's Manual page 53-54 for some examples.

ART/SOCIAL STUDIES

Bible Reading: Genesis 24:1–32

Notebook Pages 155–157: Beast of Burden (3 pages) *(Note: Do not allow students to look ahead until the first page has been completed.)*

Points to bring out: The requirements for an ideal beast of burden for the desert seem to be virtually impossible to fulfill. However, God has provided such a creature.

SPEECH/DRAMA

Teacher's Manual Page 79— Rebekah, the Needle in the Haystack

Points to bring out: *(Prepare a copy of the Teacher's Manual page for each student to give them at the end of the class.)* There are times in our lives that God performs the impossible for us. These events help us to know that He is in charge and enables us to trust Him with our day-to-day lives. Keep in mind that you will be teaching this lesson to a group.

BIBLE

Bible Reading: Genesis 24:33–67

Notebook Page 158: Mission Possible

Points to bring out: The servant of Abraham was the one who would have inherited all of Abraham's wealth if Abraham had not had a son. However, we see a gentle spirit in this servant, who is faithful and trusting both Abraham and his God.

BIBLE

Bible Reading: Genesis 25:1–26:35

Notebook Page 159: Isaac and Jesus Compared

Points to bring out: Isaac is a picture of Jesus, up to a point. But Isaac, although loved and cherished by his father, was still like us, human with a sinful nature. His sacrifice, although painful to Abraham and those he loved, would have done nothing to help a lost and dying world. Jesus was the only sacrifice that would fulfill the requirements of our holy God.

LOGIC

Bible Reading: Genesis 27–28; Galatians 4:21–31

Notebook Page 160: Abraham's Sons

Points to bring out: Often it is overlooked that Abraham had two wives besides Sarah, and a total of eight sons. It is informative to study the names of Keturah's sons. Their names reveal much about the relationship between Abraham and these sons. Ishmael and the sons of Keturah joined with the tribes of Joktan (Peleg's brother) and became the ancestors of the Arab nations. Isaac, the son of the free woman, was to continue the lineage to Jesus.

SPEECH/DRAMA

Teacher's Manual Pages 80-81—The Struggle (2 pages) (Do not discard the cut-out cards on page 2.)

Points to bring out: *(Prepare a copy of the Teacher's Manual pages for each student to give them at the end of the class.)* Cut apart The Struggle cards and fold as directed. These will be used to do a play. You will be doing it today and will perform this for another group later.

BIBLE

Bible Reading: Genesis 29:1–32:23

Notebook Page 161: Leah and Rachel's Struggle

Points to bring out: Strife and contention hurts not only those who are fighting, but all of those around them. The struggle between Rachel and Leah affected their children and grandchildren as well. Stories in the Bible allow us to see the entire picture of a person's life, not only his actions, but the consequences of them as well. If we could see our lives from this long-term perspective, we would be more determined to settle problems and to work through things before they get out of hand.

BIBLE

Bible Reading: Genesis 32:24–35:29

Notebook Page 162: Jacob's Ladder

Points to bring out: Rung by rung, Jacob worked his way down the ladder of life until he reached the bottom. At that point, he had to flee for his life and leave his home. Rung by rung, God dealt with each issue that had brought Jacob down, until finally he was a changed man. God wants us to be wholly devoted to Him. So

He often brings events in our lives that point out our weaknesses and show us that we cannot manage our lives without Him. Jesus is the answer to all our struggles!

UNIT 7: JOSEPH IN EGYPT

INTRODUCTION

As you study the Egyptian gods and goddesses in this unit, look for the story behind the story. See what these gods were really like and compare them with the God of the Bible. Note how misconceptions of nature and science played into the Egyptians' concepts of the spiritual world. Read the stories carefully, for when we study the plagues, many of the issues presented will be the ones challenged by God and demonstrated to be false. After 430 long, hard years in Egypt, the Israelites had a deep understanding of the gods of Egypt. Consequently, they knew exactly what the issues were that God was challenging. By studying these ancient myths in the light of the Bible, a new dawning of spiritual understanding will flood our souls. So bright will be the light, and so great the contrast, that we will stand in awe as we remember God's awesome acts.

SPEECH/DRAMA

Teacher's Manual Pages 83-84—The Story of Joseph (2 pages)

Points to bring out: *(Prepare a copy of the Teacher's Manual pages for each student to give them at the end of the class.)* You'll have fun with the class today. Remember that you'll be doing it for your own class later. We'll be studying Joseph. Joseph's life was full of difficulties, but God worked good out of it all.

SOCIAL STUDIES

Bible Reading: Psalm 105:1–22

Notebook Page 164: Getting to Know a Country (Egypt)

Points to bring out: This page will help us get our bearings on the country of Egypt today.

LOGIC

Bible Reading: Genesis 36:1–37:36

Notebook Page 165: Rulers of Egypt

Points to bring out: Egypt has had the longest running governmental system in the world. This logic problem will help us to get a feel for its lengthy history and unique rulers.

CREATIVE WRITING

Bible Reading: Genesis 38:1–30

Notebook Pages 166–167: Egyptian History

Points to bring out: Learning to do research is an important skill. By researching the history of Egypt and writing a report, you will be learning about Egypt and at the same time learning to find and process information on your own. Try to include the time when the pyramids were built and when the pharaohs began to be buried in the Valley of the Kings. *(Your library may have a copy of the excellent article, "Secrets of the Princes' Tomb" in Time magazine, May 29, 1995, Vol. 145, No. 22.)*

HISTORY

Bible Reading: Genesis 39:1–23

Notebook Pages 168–169, 273: Key to Egyptian Sites on the Nile River; Egyptian Sites on the Nile River (2 pages) *(Note: The cut-out page is in the yellow pages at the back of the student notebook.)*

Points to bring out: There are clues in each sentence to help you figure out the locations of these Egyptian sites.

GEOGRAPHY

Bible Reading: Genesis 40:1–23

Notebook Page 170: The Rise and Fall of the Nile River

Points to bring out: The Nile River was and is the life-line of Egypt. Most of the country gets only 1–8 inches of rain per year, so all of life depends on water from the Nile. Look back at your map on domesticated animals to see the Nile River in its entirety.

BIBLE

Bible Reading: Psalm 37:1–40

Notebook Page 171: Family Feud

Points to bring out: From this account we can see how the consequences of a parent's sin are passed on to the children and grandchildren. But God gives us an amazing promise in Exodus 20:5b. Although the children reap the results of the sins of their fathers to the third and fourth generations, He shows love to a thousand generations to those who love Him and keep His commandments.

CREATIVE WRITING

Bible Reading: Ephesians 1:1–2:10

Our thankfulness to God overflows into our thankfulness for others.

Notebook Pages 172–173: Good Families

Points to bring out: We need to be aware that God has placed people in our lives to help us on the journey. We need to take time to reflect on and thank those who have been a faithful witness and helped us along the way.

ART

Bible Reading: Romans 9:1–24

Notebook Pages 174–176: Egyptian Art; Formula for Egyptian Figures (2 pages)

Points to bring out: You will become a master Egyptian artist in no time by studying these pages and following their prescribed formulas. The Egyptians were more concerned about following the required pattern of drawing than in depicting people as they really look. Try to stand like the people in the Egyptian art. Get up and stand sideways, twist from your waist up so that your shoulders are pointing forward while your feet and head are still sideways.

ARCHEOLOGY

Bible Reading: Colossians 2:1–23

The "mysteries" we discover from reading hieroglyphics do not even compare with what we receive from the Holy Scriptures.

Notebook Pages 177, 179–180: Solving the Hieroglyphic Mystery

Points to bring out: The deciphering of the Rosetta Stone gave archeologists the key to hieroglyphics and opened up the written world of ancient Egypt for study. Remember that these archeologists were individuals who, with logic and patience, were the first to break the codes of ancient written languages. Often we feel that discoveries can only be made by the most educated in a particular field of learning. However, more often than not, it is the newcomers to a field who, with their fresh insight and enthusiasm, make some of the most important contributions.

Teacher's Manual Pages—Hieroglyphic flash cards (8 yellow pages in back of teacher's manual)

Points to bring out: Hieroglyphics are relatively easy to learn and by doing flash cards every day, you will be able to read actual manuscripts in hieroglyphics. You will review the flash cards you have studied and add one new sheet daily. You will need this information for future notebook pages. Begin with the first sheet today.

CREATIVE WRITING

Bible Reading: 1 John 3:8; Ephesians 6:10–13; and James 4:7

Sometimes we think that our enemy is our brother, parents, or someone who really bothers us. But our real enemy is a spiritual enemy.

Notebook Pages 178–181: The Deceit of the Devil

Points to bring out: The devil can deceive us into thinking wrong ideas. He distracts us from what is important and discourages us from continuing the good fight of faith. This page should inspire a whole array of different types of papers. There is no right or wrong way to go about creating your own. Use the words as a stepping stone to write a profound essay.

Teacher's Manual Page—Hieroglyphic Flash Cards

Points to bring out: Review the flash cards you have studied and add the second

sheet today. You will need this information for future notebook pages.

DISCERNMENT

Bible Reading: Proverbs 4:1–27

Notebook Pages 182–183: Theories About the Pyramids

Points to bring out: Pyramids have always fascinated men. How were they made, and what, if any, magical powers do they have? You will be reading a few of the many theories that have arisen over the years. Use discernment to decide which of these theories are reasonable.

Teacher's Manual Page—Hieroglyphic Flash Cards

Points to bring out: Review the flash cards you have studied and add the third sheet today. You will need this information for future notebook pages.

ARCHEOLOGY

Bible Reading: Colossians 3:1–25

Notebook Page 184: Hieroglyphic Determiners in English

Points to bring out: You do not have to know the ancient Egyptian language to be able to read Hieroglyphics since the determiners give much of the meaning. See how easy it is to figure out these words even with all the vowels missing.

HISTORY

Bible Reading: Genesis 41:1–37

Notebook Pages 185–186: Pyramid Structure of Egyptian Government; Second-in-Command to Pharaoh

Points to bring out: This information on the Egyptian government came from secular and not biblical sources. You will see a little later on how the biblical account of Joseph and his rise to power follows this design. The pyramid structure gives a good illustration of the government of ancient Egypt and shows the important position of the vizier.

Teacher's Manual Page—Hieroglyphic Flash Cards

Points to bring out: Review the flash cards you have studied and add the fourth sheet today. You will need this information for future notebook pages.

BIBLE

Bible Reading: Genesis 41:38–43:15

Notebook Page 187: Joseph as Vizier of All of Egypt

Points to bring out: Joseph, as we have studied, experienced many years filled with many problems. But Joseph was faithful to God and accepted whatever task or hardship he was given. Because of this, when the opportunity was set before him to become the vizier of all Egypt, he had the skills, the experience, the patience, and the wisdom to take on the task. If you learn to take every experience that comes into your life as an opportunity to grow, you will be prepared for whatever destiny God has in mind for you.

Teacher's Manual Page—Hieroglyphic flash cards

Points to bring out: Review the flash cards you have studied and add the fifth sheet today. You will need this information for future notebook pages.

ARCHEOLOGY

Bible Reading: 1 Timothy 6:1–21

Notebook Pages 188–190: Hieroglyphic Dictionary (2 pages), Spell and Figure

Points to bring out: On this page, you will be seeing the different components of a word. You will be writing out both the determiners and the spelling for a word. At the bottom of the page, you will see how it would be said in English. Notice as you translate that the grammatical structure is different than in English. For example, they would have said, "born he" while we would say, "he is born." Use the hieroglyphic dictionary as a quick reference when doing hieroglyphic translations today and in future lessons. (Again, as with all translations, there are acceptable variations for correct answers.)

Teacher's Manual Page—Hieroglyphic Flash Cards

Points to bring out: Review the flash cards you have studied and add the sixth sheet today. You will need this information for future notebook pages.

ANTHROPOLOGY

Bible Reading: Genesis 43:16–44:34

Notebook Page 191: The History of Egyptian Mythology

Points to bring out: This is the introduction to a study of the Egyptian gods to prepare you for understanding who and what the issues were when God challenged each "god" and defeated them with the plagues. This author studied extensively to provide you with enough information to be totally overwhelmed by the contrast and the mighty power of our God over the principalities of this world.

ANTHROPOLOGY

Bible Reading: Psalm 104:1–35

Notebook Pages 192–194: The Gods of Egypt (2 pages); The Egyptian Story of Creation

Points to bring out: Use the information from The Gods of Egypt pages to figure out which name to write in the blanks. As you read through the story, contrast it with the biblical story of creation.

Teacher's Manual Page—Hieroglyphic Flash Cards

Points to bring out: Review the flash cards you have studied and add the seventh sheet today. You will need this information for future notebook pages.

ANTHROPOLOGY

Bible Reading: Psalm 19:1–14

Notebook Page 195: Myth of Ra, the Sun God

Points to bring out: This myth was an effort to explain how the sun would get from the west back to the east every morning from the ancient Egyptian perspective of a flat world. Now is your chance to see if you can put together what you have learned about Egyptian hieroglyphics in translating some actual script.

The determiners have been darkened so that you can focus on them and not worry about the spelling of those words. Your translations might vary slightly because some words can have different ways to be expressed. For example, two earths could be written as "earths," "two lands," "two earths," and so forth. There is room for some variation and still be correct. The names for "Nut" and "Ra" are next to their pictures.

Teacher's Manual Page—Hieroglyphic Flash Cards

Points to bring out: Review the flash cards you have studied and add the last sheet today. You will need this information for future notebook pages.

CREATIVE WRITING

Bible Reading: John 7:37–41
The water of the Nile was the source of life for Egypt. Jesus, flowing through us, produces living water.

Notebook Pages 196–197: The Mighty Nile, The Mighty Nile Report

Points to bring out: You have been given a lot of information about the Nile River. Here is your chance to put it all together and add more to it. Do the clustering first, write a rough draft, and then write your finished report in your book.

BIBLE

Bible Reading: Genesis 45:1–24

Notebook Pages 198–202: Joseph—The Original "That's Good, No, That's Bad" Story

Points to bring out: Sometimes, when hard or bad times come into our lives, we get discouraged, angry and give up. Joseph's life shows a person who is constantly pulling himself up, just to be knocked down again. His trust in God and positive attitude in all of this is something we need to internalize as we learn to trust God with our own ups and downs. You will be using your completed pages later.

SPEECH/DRAMA

Teacher's Manual Pages 83-84— Joseph—The Original "That's Good, No, That's Bad" Story (3 pages)

Points to bring out: One of the most encouraging lessons from the life of Joseph is that God works every circumstance out for his good. What are some difficult times that you have had in the past? How did God use that experience for something positive in your life? The next time you have something that seems "bad" happen to you, focus on what good will come out of it and learn be thankful ahead of time. We will be using your completed Joseph Story to do a play. We will practice it together and then plan who to perform it for later. *(Schedule a performance for a group of senior citizens, a Sunday School class, a family get-together or some similar group.)*

CREATIVE WRITING

Bible Reading: 2 Corinthians 1:3–11

Notebook Page 203: My Original "That's Good, No, That's Bad" Story

Points to bring out: Have fun with this assignment. Think carefully about a time when a lot of bad things happen that could be turned around into something good. Write a rough draft first and put your final copy in your book. You may attach more pages if necessary. See Teacher's Manual page 55 for some examples.

ANTHROPOLOGY

Bible Reading: Psalm 145:1–21

Notebook Page 204: Determiners Determine Meaning

Points to bring out: Determiners were used as Egyptian shorthand. Instead of having to write out each letter, they represented words. That is what makes it possible for us to read hieroglyphics today without even knowing the ancient Egyptian language. Some of the determiners will be ones you have not studied, but if you think about it carefully, you will be able to figure them out. If you just try to make the phrases make sense, you will be able to figure out some of the things you might not know.

ANTHROPOLOGY

Bible Reading: Psalm 106:35–48
What happens when we mingle with the customs and practices of the people around us and forget to worship God?

Notebook Pages 205–206: The Story of Osiris and Isis

Points to bring out: The following story is one of the most important myths of ancient Egypt. It deals with a common theme found in most cultures around the world. On a physical plane, the story deals with the cycle of vegetation where plants die in the fall and come back to life in the spring. On a spiritual level, it is about man's death and his hope for eternal life. In the ancient world, this drama was re-enacted yearly, often with sinful and evil ceremonies. Most of the practice of human sacrifices around the world was in relation to this issue. Satan again is twisting one of God's eternal truths into something very wrong and evil. The truth is that there *did* have to be a sacrifice and death to pay for sin and that with this death there is hope for eternal life. But this death does not happen yearly; it was *once for all*. It was Jesus' death on the cross that enables us to have eternal life.

ART

Bible Reading: Proverbs 3:1–35
God's wisdom should permeate every area of our lives.

Notebook Page 207: Mythology and Math

Points to bring out: The ancient Egyptian mythology permeated all aspects of life including mathematics.

BIBLE

Bible Reading: Genesis 45:25–47:31

Notebook Page 208: The Father Rejoices

Points to bring out: Have you ever been separated from someone you dearly love? It is pure joy when you can be together again. Imagine what it would be like if you thought that person had died and then found out that he was still alive!

BIBLE

Bible Reading: Genesis 48:1–49:22

Notebook Page 209: Jesus Fulfills Prophesy to Judah

Points to bring out: Judah was a man of questionable character. However, he was the one that God chose to be the ancestor of Jesus. What is encouraging to see is that God used him in spite of himself. Twice in his life Judah humbled himself—once when he was willing to take Benjamin's place as a slave and again when he realized that he was more to blame than his daughter-in-law, Tamar, for what had happened. God uses weak and sinful creatures who are willing to humble themselves and admit their wrongdoing.

CREATIVE WRITING

Bible Reading: Jude
The Israelites started out doing well in Egypt, however, they became enslaved. We, too, can become ensnared and enslaved by things that seem to be O.K. but are not.

Notebook Pages 210–211: Life in Ancient Egypt; A Tour of Ancient Egypt

Points to bring out: Use all the information you have learned about ancient Egypt for these pages. Write your tour in Egypt from the perspective of a young person living during that time.

Because the Israelites were so careful not to make any graven images, there are very few representations of them. The drawing at the top of your tour page is of an early Semitic tribe, perhaps similar in appearance to the early Hebrews. Use additional pages as needed.

BIBLE

Bible Reading: Genesis 50:1–26

Notebook Page 212: Joseph and Jesus Compared

Points to bring out: Joseph was a person of greatness, both in character and honor. But he is only a shadow of the true

Savior of mankind. Joseph saved men from physical death by giving them bread to eat. Jesus saves mankind from eternal death by being the "bread of life."

HISTORY

Bible Reading: Philippians 2:1–18 God did become man and lived among us.

Notebook Pages 213, 215–216: Write–up of Egyptian Dynasties; The Eighteenth Dynasty Family Tree

Points to bring out: Many pharaohs took on names and titles that linked them with Egyptian gods. Names such as Thuthmosis, Rameses and Seti show that they believed they were the gods, Thoth, Ra, or Set on earth. The pharaohs of Egypt had many names and titles, including their "Horus" name, for they believed that they were "Horus" incarnate (god in human flesh). When they died, they believed they would become Osiris (god of the afterlife).

The pharaoh, as a god on earth, was expected to protect Egypt and all its people. He was responsible for ensuring the annual flooding of the Nile, an abundant harvest, freedom from pestilence and disease, as well as protection from invasion by neighboring nations.

Because the ancient Egyptian royal families considered themselves to be gods, they often married each other instead of marrying a "mere mortal." Consequently, their hereditary gene pool became very inbred, causing many deformities.

The truth in this matter is that God did become man—Jesus became Immanuel, or "God with us." And the truth is that is He is God now.

ANTHROPOLOGY

Bible Reading: 1 Thessalonians 4:13–18 What is the Christian's view of death?

Notebook Pages 214, 217–218: The Egyptian View of Death, The Egyptian Gods Judging the Dead

Points to bring out: The ancient Egyptians believed that a man's deeds were weighed at his death to determine his eternal fate.

SPEECH/DRAMA

Teacher's Manual Page 85-87—The Way of the Cross (3 pages)

Points to bring out: *(Prepare a copy of the Teacher's Manual pages for each student to give them at the end of the class.)* Mankind today still has many ideas of what it takes to get into heaven. This play demonstrates some of those thoughts. You will be doing it today and for a group later.

ANTHROPOLOGY

Bible Reading: Exodus 1:1–2:25

Notebook Page 219: Names in Hieroglyphics

Points to bring out: Today you will see that, in hieroglyphics, names have meaning. Expect some surprises.

ARCHEOLOGY

Bible Reading: Colossians 1:1–29 Pharaoh was a man and his death accomplished nothing for his people. What did Christ's death accomplish?

Notebook Pages 220–221, 223–224, 279–288: Mummification, The Crypt of King Tutankhamen, King Tut's Crypt (6 pages) *(The last five pages of King Tut's Crypt are found in the yellow pages at the back of the student notebook.)*

Points to bring out: These pages give a clearer understanding of how Egyptian kings were buried. The relatively recent discovery of the crypt of King Tut by an Englishman, Howard Carter, in 1922, brought with it a proliferation of rumors about "The Curse of King Tut." Newspapers eagerly reported the deaths of anyone who was remotely associated with the opening of the tomb; however, most of those deaths could be traced to pre-existing conditions or to unrelated events. In a study done of the 26 people who had actually been at the opening of the tomb, six died within the decade while most of the others lived many more years to be 60 to

80 years old. Howard Carter himself lived until 1939, a full seventeen years after the discovery.

CREATIVE WRITING

Bible Reading: John 15:1–17
What does Jesus say about friends?
Notebook Page 226: Letter to a Friend
Points to bring out: God has a specific purpose for bringing each person into your life. Sometimes these people are there to help you, sometimes you are there to help them. Write a letter to a friend who does not know where he will spend eternity. Speak with love, concern and authority to show him the way to the cross of Jesus Christ.

ART/ARCHEOLOGY

Bible Reading: Deuteronomy 4:1–36; 5:1–21; and 7:1–26
Read these passages as you work through these translations and illustrations.
Notebook Pages 227–234: Sorrows of Isis

Points to bring out: This lesson will be the culmination of the study of hieroglyphics and Egyptian Art. You will be doing it over several days. You should be able to translate easily and draw illustrations in true Egyptian style.

Egyptians did their artwork on paper as well as stone. Their paper was made out of the papyrus plant that grew in the Nile. Strips of the stem were cut and laid down in layers. They were then hammered so that the natural starches in the plant would glue the layers together to form the paper. You can make something that looks very similar to this by following these instructions.

(Needed materials: brown paper bags, liquid starch, waxed paper, scissors, cookie sheet, acrylic or poster paints, gold paint pen.)

Step 1: Cut the bags into 1 inch wide strips and 8–10 inches long.

Step 2: Pour a small amount of liquid starch onto the cookie sheet. Dip a strip into the starch, running your thumb and finger down the length of the strip to remove excess starch and ensure even coverage.

Step 3: Place the strips in straight horizontal rows on the waxed paper.

Step 4: Make a second layer of vertical rows on top of the horizontal rows. Be sure to place any writing that is on the bag in the center so that it is not visible from the top or bottom.

Step 5: Allow to dry. Then draw and paint an Egyptian picture on your "papyrus paper." Use the gold paint pen to highlight your picture.

Make at least one of these pictures the appropriate size and topic to glue on one of the illustration pages in the Sorrows of Isis story.

DISCERNMENT

Bible Reading: Colossians 2:1–23
Notebook Page 235: Are Isis and Horus Like God or Like Humans?
Points to bring out: The Egyptian cult that worshipped Isis and Osiris belong to what is collectively called, the "Mystery Religions." These religions were practiced with secret ceremonies and only the initiates were allowed to participate. What a contrast Christ offered—openness and freedom, not secrecy and slavery. The truth is that there is a mystery to man's relationship with God, but it has been revealed through Jesus Christ. Let's read today's Bible reading together. And then in your notebook, you will be able to visually see that the goddess is mostly "clay" with few truly god-like characteristics.

UNIT 8: MOSES LEADS THE ISRAELITES OUT OF EGYPT

ANTHROPOLOGY

Bible Reading: Ephesians 2:5–9
Notebook Page 236: Plight of the Farmers
Points to bring out: This report, written in 1400 B.C., shows how hard life was for the people on the bottom layer of the social pyramid of Egypt. The Israelites would have had many of the same struggles

and dilemmas, trying to keep their families fed while being forced to work on the pharaohs' projects.

SPEECH/DRAMA

Bible: Psalm 105:23–38

Teacher's Manual Pages 88-92— Moses Learns the Power of God (5 pages)

Points to bring out: *(Prepare a copy of the Teacher's Manual pages for each student to give them at the end of the class.)* This lesson will be a challenge for you to prepare and give, but the benefits and enjoyment of your students will be worth it!

BIBLE

Bible Reading: Exodus 3:1–4:31

Notebook Page 237: Terribly Tongue-tied

Points to bring out: Even though Moses realized that God promised to be with him, he still felt inadequate to the task. Do you let your feelings of inadequacy keep you from doing the things God asks you to do?

BIBLE

Bible Reading: Exodus 5:1–23

Notebook Page 238: God's Promise to His People in Bondage

Points to bring out: God is a God of power and action. He is also faithful to His promises. The Israelites had gone from being the welcomed family of the Vizier, Joseph, to being slaves. The small clan of seventy had multiplied to hundreds of thousands. The Egyptians became fearful that they might revolt, so they tried to kill every Hebrew baby boy. It was to this oppressed people that God spoke, through Moses, reminding them of His promise to their ancestors. Though release from their desperate situation appeared to be humanly impossible, with God, anything is possible. God was going to show His mighty power— not just to free the Israelites, but to encourage us today.

ANTHROPOLOGY

Bible Reading: Psalm 102:1–28

Notebook Page 239: Two Stories About the Sun

Points to bring out: This story was included to show that the gods of Egypt not only were born, but also grew old and senile.

Many people today generally believe that man consists of body, soul, and spirit. The Egyptians believed there were more components than this. One of those was their secret name. By discovering what this name was, a person received the special power from the owner of that name. This is what Isis did to Ra. Isis showed no compassion and love, but only a callous striving to gain power at the expense of others, a theme that recurs throughout history.

ANTHROPOLOGY

Bible Reading: Psalm 95:1–11

Notebook Pages 240–242: Comparison of the Gods and Goddesses; Tracing the Days of the Week Back in Time

Points to bring out: Upon closer study, the gods and goddesses in many different ancient cultures basically boil down to the same ones, only with different names given them in the different languages.

The gods and religions from around the world tend to have many elements in common. There are three simple reasons why this would be.

1. All people live in the same world, governed by the same natural laws. Their religions try to explain the same basic issues of nature, life, and death.

2. All people came from one original group. Though you will find much discrepancy on dates, having come from one group, they would have had a common heritage.

3. We believe that God has been reaching out to mankind with love and compassion from before the beginning of time, while Satan has been trying to imitate, deceive, and twist God's perfect plan.

In this simple exercise of tracing the names of the days of the week all the way back to the dawn of civilization, we can easily see the common thread between the seemingly diverse religions of the ancient world.

Soon we will be seeing God's mighty hand come down on the gods of Egypt. What I want you to realize is that God was confronting not only the gods of Egypt, but all the gods and anything that would seek to take His place from every nation, in any time period, including the present. God will win an overwhelming victory over all the powers and principalities of this world.

When you are finished, above the names of the days of the week, write in the Spanish names: Lunes, Martes, Miercoles, Jueves, Viernes, Sabado, Domingo. Note: Lunes comes from the same Latin root as our word lunar. Domingo come from the Latin root in Anno Domini or A.D. that we use after a date to mean after the "year of our Lord." "Domini" means "Lord."

REVIEW

Bible Reading: Psalm 136:1–26
Read this Psalm responsively.

Notebook Page 243: Ancient Egypt Review

Points to bring out: This crossword puzzle will be a review of what you have studied about ancient Egypt. Fill it in without looking back at previous assignments. Memorize Psalm 78:5b–8.

BIBLE

Bible Reading: Exodus 6:1–30
Notebook Page 244: Moses and Jesus Compared

Points to bring out: The people of Israel were in bondage, but we, too, can be in bondage today. Being enslaved to sin is the worst kind of oppression there is. Sin is a relentless master causing those it controls to become hopeless and beaten down. How wonderful it is to realize that Christ has paid the price to free us from the bondage of sin. The shackles are taken off, and not only are we free, but we become adopted children of God.

DISCERNMENT

Bible Reading: Psalm 115:1–18
Notebook Page 245: Evaluating the Egyptian gods and goddesses

Points to bring out: By now you have a good understanding of the ancient Egyptian culture and its religion. This will give you a firm foundation to have insight into the challenges that God will be presenting to the gods and goddesses.

INTRODUCTION

The confrontations of the gods of Egypt through the plagues marked a real turning point for the formation of the nation of Israel. These deities and the demonic forces behind them could not stand against the power of the Almighty God. And the fact that God was stronger than these "gods" united the Israelites in allegiance to Him. This event was referred to forever after in the annals of Jewish history as a highlight of their national identity. Since He is our God too, we can rest assured that we have nothing to fear from all the powers in heaven and on earth. We are in the protective hand of the Almighty God.

BIBLE

Bible reading: Exodus 7:1–13
Notebook Pages 246–247: The God of Israel Challenges the "gods" of Egypt; The Serpent

Points to bring out: We find the serpent, or dragon, has been worshipped in many cultures throughout history. The Aztecs of Mexico covered pyramids with Quetzalcoatl (ket-sahl-koh-ahtl), a feathered serpent. In India, cobras are worshipped. The dragon, with its serpent-like body is the emblem of China. And fire-breathing dragons abound in mythologies around the world. Behind all these mythologies is Satan—the "father of lies."

BIBLE

Bible reading: Exodus 7:14–24

Notebook Pages 248–249: The God of Israel Challenges the "Gods" of Egypt; The Nile—Lifeblood of Egypt.

Points to bring out: Whether we realize it or not, without readily available water, our farms, communities, cities and country could not exist. This has been true of all mankind. In order to have civilizations, there must be water, and a lot of it. Almost all of the ancient civilizations grew up around mighty rivers: the Tigris and Euphrates of the Fertile Crescent, the Indus River of India, the Nile of Egypt, and the Yellow and Yangtze of China. These rivers symbolized life to their people. The Nile name actually means "life." As we read about the Nile turning to blood, remember that water is the lifeblood of all mankind.

BIBLE

Bible reading: Exodus 7:25–8:15

Notebook Pages 250–251: The God of Israel Challenges the "gods" of Egypt; Frogs

Points to bring out: Universally, man has wondered what will happen to him when he dies. In Sumer, China, Egypt, the United States, Mexico, and Peru, tombs were found that demonstrated these people all had a belief in life after death. Their tombs contained food, clothing, jewelry, cooking utensils, furniture. Sometimes even animals and servants were killed in the belief that they would accompany their master in the afterlife. The truth is that there is life after death. But Satan has deceived many people about what will happen to them when they die. It is Jesus' resurrection from the dead on which we base our hope for Eternal Life with God when we die.

BIBLE

Bible reading: Exodus 8:16–32

Notebook Pages 252–253: The God of Israel Challenges the "Gods" of Egypt; Insects

Points to bring out: The theory of evolution states that inert matter, floating in a primordial sea, was struck by lightning which brought it to life. From this one-celled organism came more and more advanced life-forms which filled the waters and sprang out onto the land. After millenniums, a primitive man evolved from an ape, developed language, writing, music, math, and science. In time, man developed agriculture and civilization.

If you look closely, you can see that all the elements of evolution are found in Egyptian mythology. It is Khepera, the scarab, who gives the spark that brings life to inert matter. It is from the waters of Nu that all life sprang. It is Thoth, in the form of an ape, who brought all knowledge and language to man. And it is Osiris who brought man civilization and agriculture.

None of these accounts are true! They are a twisting of what really did happen. The truth is that someone did give language to man—it was God, when He created Adam as a fully capable human being in His own image. It is true that man developed agriculture and civilization—they had been created by God with these capabilities. And the truth is, that there was a spark that created life—it was the Word of God, saying "Let there be. . ."

BIBLE

Bible reading: Exodus 9:1–7

Notebook Pages 254–255: The God of Israel Challenges the "Gods" of Egypt; Livestock

Points to bring out: Even in this mechanized age, livestock is still vitally important. From livestock we get wool, milk products, meat, fertilizers, and leather. Livestock do work for us, such as plowing fields and pulling wagons. They turn water wheels and grind grain. They carry heavy loads and can take us places that cannot be reached by modern transportation.

The cattle of Egypt, India, and some nomadic tribes in Africa, the water buffalo of Asia, and the bison of the Plains Indians of the Americas have been considered sacred and without equal in importance to those people. It was to a golden calf that the Israelites first turned after leaving Egypt. Baal, a bull god of the Canaanites, kept drawing the people of Israel away from God.

What God provides to enrich and improve man's existence often ends up being the object of their worship. Although most people in our culture do not worship animals, they do tend to put their trust in the source of their livelihood, not in the Source of Life Himself.

CREATIVE WRITING
   Bible Reading: Psalm 103:1–22
   Notebook Pages 256–257: If There Were a Plague Today
   Point to bring out: We may think that the plagues are over and done with and have little to do with us today. However, many of the same issues that were confronted then, continue to be issues today. Although our culture is not tied into nature to the extent that the Egyptian culture was, we can write about a plague that might hit closer to home. Electricity has been chosen as the focus of our plague because it is such an intrinsic part of our culture. There isn't much that touches our lives that in some way does not use electricity. Think through all the things that would be affected. The significance of the plagues show us the issues behind each one. See Teacher's Manual page 56 for an example.

BIBLE
   Bible reading: Exodus 9:8–12
   Notebook Pages 258–259: The God of Israel Challenges the "Gods" of Egypt; Boils
   Points to bring out: Human beings can endure a lot of difficult situations without too much complaining as long as their physical health and comfort are not disturbed. Many societies have developed entire health-care systems based on their religious beliefs. Ancient Egyptian priests were the physicians of their day, combining magical practices with their medical treatments. In many animistic religions, witch-doctors prescribe sacrifices for healing. Other societies demand exorbitant payments and torturous procedures for medical care.

In our modern society, physical beauty and health are a top priority. The Olympic athletes show us the furthest limits that the human body can achieve. Movie stars and models dictate what society deems as perfection and beauty. Most people do not fit in these categories and tend to have low self-esteem because they do not meet these physical standards. If they gain weight or have a pimple, their self-esteem plummets.

The truth is that our bodies are a temple of God, and that God is the great physician. God is more concerned with our spiritual well-being than our physical state or appearance. Apart from God, man is a sinner. Health foods, exercise and beauty products do not change this fact, but only enable one who is lost to be a healthier and better-looking sinner.

BIBLE
   Bible reading: Exodus 9:13–35
   Notebook Pages 260–261: The God of Israel Challenges the "Gods" of Egypt; Hail
   Points to bring out: Since early times, man has tried to harness nature and gain control over the elements. There have been many gods and goddesses for each aspect of weather and nature. Native Americans performed rain dances to entreat the gods for rain. A resurgence of interest in the ancient gods and goddesses of nature are reflected in the modern day terms of "Mother Nature," "Mother Earth,", the goddesses "Gaia" and "Sophia." We see again how man tries to worship the creation rather than the Creator.

BIBLE
   Bible reading: Exodus 10:1–20
   Notebook Pages 262–263: The God of Israel Challenges the "Gods" of Egypt; Locust

Points to bring out: A common theme, found in most religions the world over, is the issue of life and death. On a physical plane, these stories deal with the cycle of vegetation where plants die in the fall and come back to life in the spring. Many of the Middle Eastern and European mythologies have a story where a husband dies and goes to the underworld. He is brought back to the earth by the efforts of his wife for a yearly visit. The rest of the year she mourns his absence and all vegetation dies to reflect her mourning. In Egypt, the couple was Isis and Osiris; in Babylon, it was Ishtar and Tammuz; and in Greece, the characters were a mother and daughter, Demeter and Persephone.

On a spiritual level, these stories are about man's death and his hope for eternal life. In the ancient world, this drama was re-enacted yearly, often with sinful and evil ceremonies. Most of the practice of human sacrifices around the world was in relation to this issue. Satan again is twisting one of God's eternal truths into something very wrong and evil. The truth is that there did have to be a sacrifice and that with this death there is hope for eternal life. But this death does not happen yearly; it was once for all. It was Jesus' death on the cross that enables us to have eternal life.

BIBLE

Bible reading: Exodus 10:21–29

Notebook Pages 264–265: The God of Israel Challenges the "Gods" of Egypt; Darkness

Points to bring out: God created the sun as our source of light. It is the sun's power that gives the earth light and warmth. Its energy enables plants to make chlorophyll which, in turn, provides food for all living creatures. It heats the air and water, which cause the wind and water currents. It evaporates the oceans to form clouds and rain. Without the sun, there would be no life on earth. The twisting of the truth about the importance of the sun has developed into the worship of it around the world. The Aztecs and Incas built

pyramids for their sun gods. The Romans, Greeks, Babylonians, Egyptians, and Hindus were also among those cultures who worshipped the sun. Once again people worshipped the creation rather than the Creator.

BIBLE

Bible reading: Exodus 11:1–12:36

Notebook Pages 266–267: The God of Israel Challenges the "Gods" of Egypt; Firstborn

Points to bring out: If anyone had any doubt at this point about who was the most powerful, or had any question about who to place their trust in, this last confrontation settled the matter. If the people had faith in the security of their family or trust in some god that they felt God had not yet challenged, this last plague would shake their very foundations.

God graciously warned the people ahead of time what to do to avoid the disaster. At the stroke of midnight, the Lord moved throughout Egypt, striking down every firstborn male, both man and animal in the households of those who had not obeyed. Of those, there was not a household in Egypt, from the palace to the lowest servant, that did not lose a son, husband, father or brother. Their homes had lost a sense of security because of the invasion of death.

At this point, even the Egyptians' wealth held no attraction for them. They eagerly gave it to those Hebrew trouble-makers and urged them on their way. And with the departure of their Hebrew labor force, they lost their hope for an easy life in the future.

God proved that family, wealth or anything that we put in the place of Him, cannot stand up to His power. God used this awesome power to free the Israelites physically from their slavery to the Egyptians. But the God of the Bible is our God, too, and He uses this same awesome power to free us from an even more powerful and deadly slavery. This is the slavery to sin and death. No power in heaven or on earth can stand up to our God. And when God is for us, who can be against us?

BIBLE

Bible reading: Hebrews 11:1–40

Notebook Page 268: By Faith

Points to bring out: Faith is trusting in something not seen. The people we have studied in Genesis and Exodus acted in faith. We have gone through their lives and seen how they acted on what they were told to do. They did not know what the results would be, but they trusted in the God who was leading them. We do not know what our future holds, but we do know the God who holds our future. We know He is faithful and true and has had us in mind from the beginning of creation. He is worthy of our trust and faith. May your faith grow as you review the patriarchs.

BIBLE

Bible reading: Deuteronomy 6:1–25; Matthew 5:17; Romans 16:25–27

Notebook Page 269: Jesus, the First and the Last

Points to bring out: Jesus, the first and the last. He was at creation. At the end of time as we know it, He will be the only one worthy to open the seal mentioned in Revelation. And He will rule in eternity. God knew what His plan for our salvation was from the beginning of time. In order that we would not miss seeing that Jesus was the Promised One, He gave us illustration after illustration, all pointing to Jesus. Each one gives us one more glimpse into the true nature and purpose of Jesus Christ. By putting together all the little pieces we have studied from the beginning, we will see the amazing scope and foresight of our Heavenly Father.

CREATIVE WRITING

Bible reading: John 3

Notebook Pages 270–272: Christ our Savior

Points to bring out: Now is a time to reflect on your relationship to Jesus Christ. If you have not asked Him into your life, or have not made Him Lord of your life, now is the time to do so.

Your relationship with Jesus Christ should become richer and deeper as the years go by. Prayerfully write a paper on who Jesus Christ is to you.

RESOURCES AND SUGGESTED READING

Creation to the Flood

Beechick, Ruth. *Adam and His Kin.* Pollock Pines, Calif.: Arrow Press, 1990.

Morris, Henry. *The Genesis Record.* Grand Rapids, Mich.: Baker Book House, 1976.

Noebel, David A. *Understanding the Times* . Summit Press, PO Box 207, Manitou Springs, CO 80829. 1991. Read the section about History.

Petersen, Dennis R. *Unlocking the Mysteries of Creation.*

Sellier, Charles E. and David W. Balsiger, *The Incredible Discovery of Noah's Ark.* New York: Bantam Doubleday Dell Publishing Group, Inc., 1995.

Ancient World History

Casson, Lionel. *Ancient Egypt.* New York: Time–Life Books, 1965

The Usborne Book of the Ancient World. Tulsa, Okla.: EDC Publishing Co., 1991.

The Usborne Book of World History. Tulsa, Okla.: EDC Publishing Co., 1985.

Also ask for catalogs from:
Farm Country General Store, Rt. 1, Box 63, Metamora, IL 61548
Greenleaf Press, 1570 Old Laguardo Rd., Lebanon, TN 37087
Lifetime Books and Gifts, 3900 Chalet Suzanne Dr., Lake Wales, FL 33841

Missions

Johnstone, Jill. *You Can Change the World.* Grand Rapids, Mich.: Zondervan Publishing House, 1992.

Johnstone, Patrick. *Operation World.* Grand Rapids, Mich.: Zondervan Publishing House, 1993.

Look for biographies of missionaries such as Hudson Taylor, Amy Carmichael, Cameron Townsend, David Livingstone. Also, books by Don Richardson, (such as Eternity in Their Hearts), Hugh Steven (many children and adult missionary stories). Sources include:

William Carey Library, PO Box 40129, Pasadena, CA 91114 (Ask for free Mission Resource Catalog)

Wycliffe Bible Translators, PO Box 2727 , Huntington Beach, CA 92647 (Ask for free Wycliffe catalog of books/films/videos)

Library & Educational Services, PO Box 146, Berrien Springs, MI 49103 (Ask for free homeschool catalog)

O M Literature, PO Box 1047, Waynesboro, GA 30830 (Ask for free catalog)

Remembering God's Awesome Acts

Samples of Writing and Drawing Assignments

Help! How do I get started writing?

Both parents and students tend to worry about writing assignments. Students balk at doing them, and parents do not know what to expect from their students or how to help them reach their goal.

I know it inspired my students to see what each other had written. Examples are worth their weight in gold. Seeing what can be done with an assignment will get a reluctant student moving in the right direction. So I have included examples of many of their stories, poems, and essays.

Another great way to get students to write is by getting group together with the same writing assignments. Having a deadline to complete a polished paper motives students to put out the needed effort.

Often students and teachers know there is a problem with how a paper is written but do not know how to fix it. Here are two simple writing assignments to weed out the most common types of errors faced by the beginning writer.

Repetitive words: One of the major problems individuals have with writing is the repetitive use of words. Here is an exaggerated example of that problem. It is easy to see the overuse of simple words. Every other line is the same. The assignment is to make two vastly different but excellent stories from these repetitive and static lines.

> **I walked to a flower.**
> **I walked to a flower.**
> **I picked a flower.**
> **I picked a flower.**
> **I looked at the flower.**
> **I looked at the flower.**

First, do not be too tied to the wording of the original lines. Use it as a jumping off point.

Discuss creative words or phrases to replace the repetitive words. For instance "walked" can be replaced with "strolled," "sauntered," "hiked," "tramped," or "stumbled."

Since the word 'flower' is used so often, you may want to replace it on occasion with a type of flower, such as rose, violet, sunflower, and so forth. It may be appropriate to replace some of them with flower parts: petals, stem, leaves, or roots. Phrases would also help. This can be done by adding descriptive words dealing with size, color, texture, smell, and location.

You may want to make some lines general. Instead of saying, "I walked to a flower," use something like "I strolled down the garden path." "I hiked over Bluebonnet Hill." or "I stomped through the brier patch." Then for variety make the next line more specific.

It is important to get rid of most of the "I's" by rephrasing and connecting the various lines. For instance instead of saying, "I strolled past the vivid red rose. I was captivated by its wondrous smell." It would read better to start with "Strolling past the vivid red rose, I was captivated by its wondrous smell."

Now remember you are to rewrite this story twice, giving each writing a distinct feel and texture that will cause totally different emotional responses from your readers.

After the assignment is done discuss what works and what can be improved. Now that you have been made aware of ways to improve your writing by replacing or rewording repetitive words, make sure you do it in all your further writing assignments.

Weak endings: Often stories, poems, and other writing assignments began strong but have weak endings. In my writing classes, it seems that the last few lines in an assignment are the ones that need the most work. Many times this is because the writers haven't thought through how they wanted their papers to end. Weak endings can also be because the writers got tired and wanted to finish quickly.

More often than not students are happy to fix the problem if it is pointed out in a constructive way. This can be done by rereading the parts that work, and talking about the feeling and emotion, the style and direction the writing is heading. Then show how the ending does not follow through with what is happening. Finally, discuss various options that would work.

Below are two acrostics with the last two lines missing. Copy both and give them strong endings.

Here are a few questions to ask to see if you finished with a strong ending: Do the thoughts hold together? Does it work as a whole? Does the ending bind the writing together as a unit? If you answer yes to these questions, you did what you set out to do.

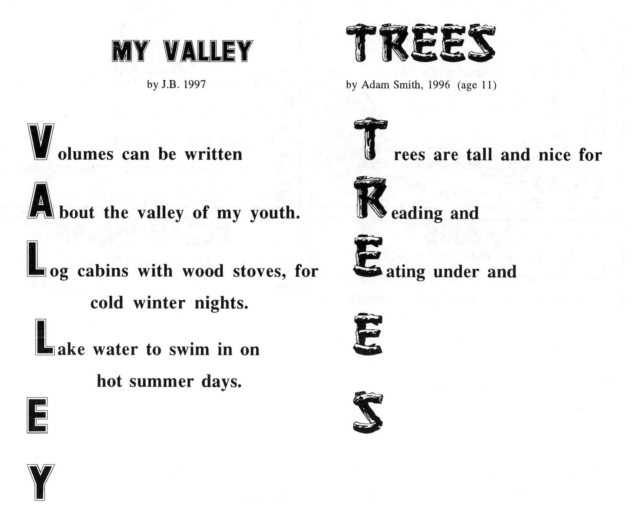

MY VALLEY

by J.B. 1997

Volumes can be written

About the valley of my youth.

Log cabins with wood stoves, for
cold winter nights.

Lake water to swim in on
hot summer days.

E

Y

TREES

by Adam Smith, 1996 (age 11)

Trees are tall and nice for

Reading and

Eating under and

E

S

Now look on page 43 and see how these authors finished their acrostics. Whose do you like better? Why?

Writing is exciting and fun to do. Have the students rewrite and rework their writing assignments until they are polished and professional.

Sample Writing with Acrostics

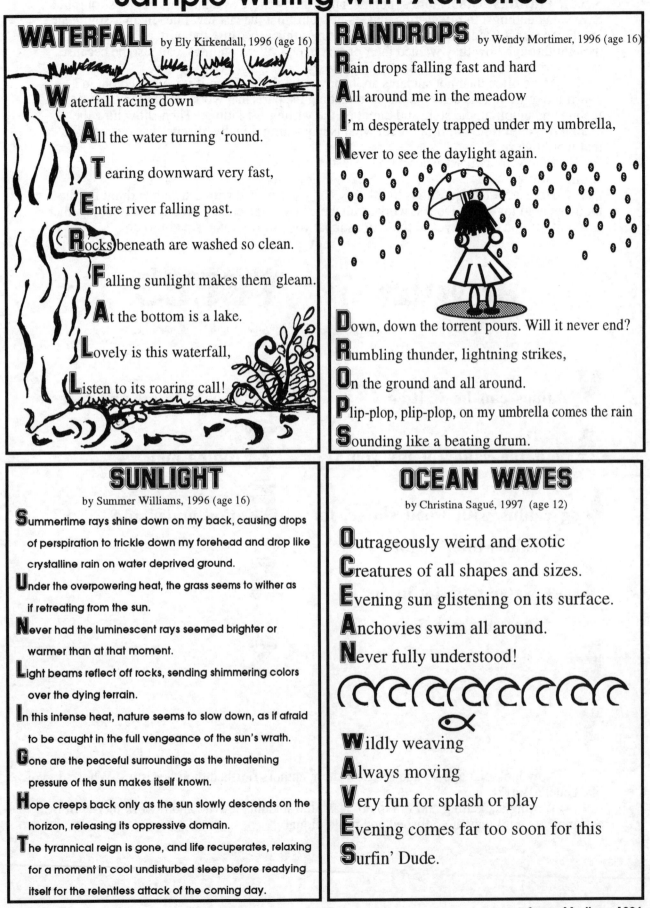

WATERFALL
by Ely Kirkendall, 1996 (age 16)

Waterfall racing down

All the water turning 'round.

Tearing downward very fast,

Entire river falling past.

Rocks beneath are washed so clean.

Falling sunlight makes them gleam.

At the bottom is a lake.

Lovely is this waterfall,

Listen to its roaring call!

RAINDROPS
by Wendy Mortimer, 1996 (age 16)

Rain drops falling fast and hard

All around me in the meadow

I'm desperately trapped under my umbrella,

Never to see the daylight again.

Down, down the torrent pours. Will it never end?

Rumbling thunder, lightning strikes,

On the ground and all around.

Plip-plop, plip-plop, on my umbrella comes the rain

Sounding like a beating drum.

SUNLIGHT
by Summer Williams, 1996 (age 16)

Summertime rays shine down on my back, causing drops of perspiration to trickle down my forehead and drop like crystalline rain on water deprived ground.

Under the overpowering heat, the grass seems to wither as if retreating from the sun.

Never had the luminescent rays seemed brighter or warmer than at that moment.

Light beams reflect off rocks, sending shimmering colors over the dying terrain.

In this intense heat, nature seems to slow down, as if afraid to be caught in the full vengeance of the sun's wrath.

Gone are the peaceful surroundings as the threatening pressure of the sun makes itself known.

Hope creeps back only as the sun slowly descends on the horizon, releasing its oppressive domain.

The tyrannical reign is gone, and life recuperates, relaxing for a moment in cool undisturbed sleep before readying itself for the relentless attack of the coming day.

OCEAN WAVES
by Christina Sagué, 1997 (age 12)

Outrageously weird and exotic

Creatures of all shapes and sizes.

Evening sun glistening on its surface.

Anchovies swim all around.

Never fully understood!

Wildly weaving

Always moving

Very fun for splash or play

Evening comes far too soon for this

Surfin' Dude.

42

Sample Writing with Acrostics

THUNDER

by Eric Sagué, 1997 (age 9)

TERROR IN MY TENT.

HUG MY PILLOW.

UMBRELLA! WHERE IS MY UMBRELLA?

NEVER HAVE I FELT SO UNSAFE.

DURING THE STORM, IT'S LOUD WITH

LIGHTNING FLASHING ACROSS THE SKY.

EXCITED, I JUST CAN'T HIDE IT.

REMEMBERING THAT GOD IS

ALWAYS WITH ME, I SETTLE

DOWN FOR A NICE LONG SLEEP.

TREES

by Adam Smith, 1996 (age 11)

Trees are tall and nice for

Reading and

Eating under and

Enjoying their

Shade.

CACTUS

by J.B. 1997

Cactus thrives on the

Arid, desert sands.

Collecting every bit of available moisture.

Two feet of growth in twenty years.

Under the sun's intensive rays,

Succulent cactus grow slowly on.

MY VALLEY

by J.B. 1997

Volumes can be written,

About the valley of my youth

Log cabins with wood stoves, for
cold winter nights.

Lake water to swim in on
hot summer days.

Evergreens and aspens on
the mountains all around.

Youthful memories to fill a book.

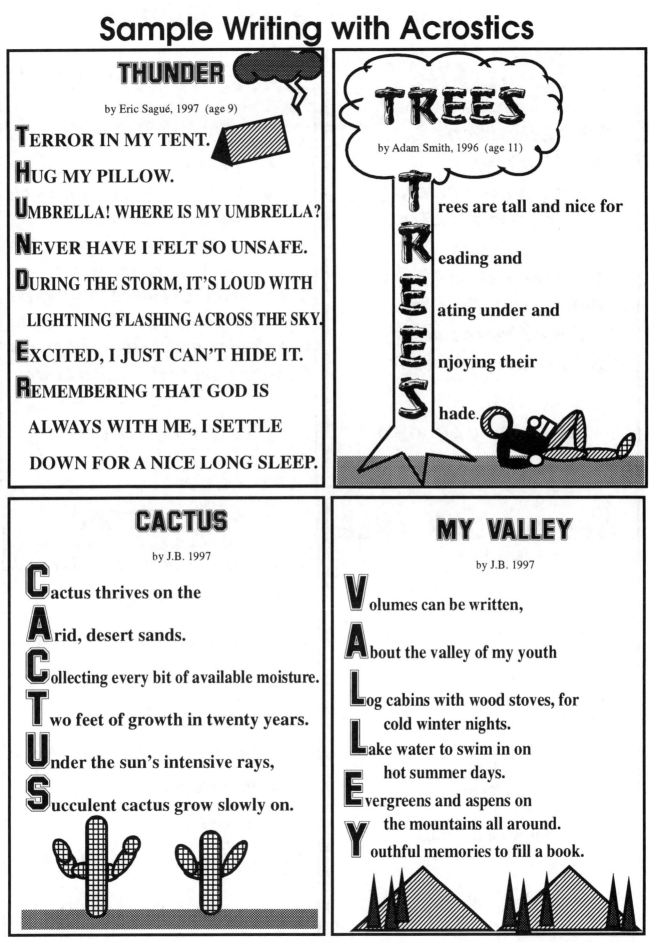

43

Sample Writing of Hebrew Poetry

RESILIANCY

by Wendy Mortimer, 1996 (age 16)

A Grass looks delicate,
A But it is strong.
B People trample it every day,
B But the grass is resilient.
C People cut it down
C But it grows back, just to show them.
D Winter comes, the grass
     dies a slow, cold death,
D But it revives every spring.

A ≠ A   B ≠ B   C ≠ C   D ≠ D

SAFE IN THE LORD

by J.B., 1997

A I will rest in peace in the arms of
     the Lord,
B For the Lord is mightier than all
     the terrors of the night.
A I am hidden within the protection
     of His covering wings.
B For nothing cloaked in darkness
     can stand up to His strength.
C Safe am I under His watchful eye.
C Secure under His vigilant care.

A = A   B ≠ B   C = C

THE OLD OAK TREE

by Ely Kirkendall, 1996 (age 16)

A The old oak tree is blowing
     in the wind.
A Its branches swaying
     in the breeze.
B A chipmunk scampers
     up the tree.
B While a squirrel runs
     down its trunk.
C A blue jay hides
     within its branches.
C And a robin flies
     out from its limbs.

A > A   B ≠ B   C ≠ C

EXHILARATING

by Adam Smith, 1996 (age 11)

A The river twisted around and around,

A Then it straightened out.

B The water tumbled over huge boulders,

B Then grew very smooth and calm.

C All of the sudden, I plunged.

C Diving into a deep pool at the end

     of the waterfall.

D It was chilling.

D But exhilarating, just the same.

A ≠ A   B ≠ B   C > C   D > D

44

DOLPHINS FREEDOM

by Christina Sagué, 1997 (age 12)

A Dolphins swim in the ocean deep.
A Always whirling and jumping up above,
A Breaking the surface so we can see.
B But no fisherman may catch them.
B For their freedom they value
B As much as we value ours.

$$A \neq A = A \ B \neq B > B$$

JOY

by Eric Sagué, 1996 (age 9)

A Joy is sometimes laughter.
B Joy is sometimes tears.
A You can have joy when you are happy.
B You can have joy even when you are sad.
C Joy does not come from what happens to you.
C Joy comes only from God.

$$A = A \ \ B = B \ \ C \neq C$$

TTHE RIVER FLOWS

by Summer Williams, 1996 (age 15)

A The river flows freely.
A Over the rocks it glides.
B Swiftly moving from one place to another.
B Never standing still.
C Sediment washed up with its current.
C Scraping rocks as it rushes by.
D Splash! Goes the crashing waves.
D Showering the banks with water and mud.

$$A > A \ \ B \neq B \ \ C > C \ \ D > D$$

Brother-In-Christ

by J.B.,1996

A Little Brother, my bad example has broken your heart.
A My thoughtless actions have wounded your soul.
B You must not follow my tarnished ways.
B But travel the straight and narrow path towards God.
C You need to see me not just as your Big Brother,
D But as a weary traveller and offer a helping hand when I fall.
C And Little Brother, I need to see you as God does,
D As my journeying Companion, and respect you as my equal, my Brother-in-Christ.

$$A = A \ \ B \neq B \ \ C \neq C \ \ D \neq D$$

Sample of Cluster Writing

Hands Show Humanness

by J.B., 1997

There are millions of things that hands can do. <u>It is with our hands that we show love and caring, create items of practical and artistic value, and communicate who we are to others.</u> Hands are used to show much that makes us human.

<u>It is through our hands that we show compassion and love by caring for others. By touching others we let them know we are there for them.</u> Giving a long, warm <u>hug,</u> a quick, gentle <u>pat</u> on the back, or a firm <u>handshake</u>, are some ways we can do this. Even if we get blisters on our palms, by <u>sweeping</u>, <u>mopping</u> the house, or by <u>pushing</u> the lawn mower, <u>we show others our love</u>.   <u>Another way our hands can be used is to care for the needs of others.</u> Caring can be as simple as <u>putting</u> a Band-Aid <u>on</u> a scraped knee, or by <u>picking up</u> a crying baby or <u>preparing</u> a home-cooked <u>meal</u> for an ill friend.

<u>Besides showing care, our hands can create</u>. Much around us shows human creativeness though the use of hands. <u>Music is created by individuals' hands writing down the music, playing instruments, and directing orchestras.</u> Instruments from drums to harps, pianos to violins, trumpets to flutes all need talented hands to produces a clear melodic sound. <u>Art is another creative outlet that needs hands to be expressed.</u> Masterpieces in <u>painting</u>, <u>sculpturing</u>, and <u>drawing</u> are created by an artists' steady hands and insightful eyes. <u>Hands create machines that have helped make life easier</u> such as <u>cars</u>, <u>computers,</u> and <u>phones</u>.

Lastly, <u>hands help us communicate better with each other</u>. By sitting down and picking up a pen to write a <u>letter</u> to a good friend, we can keep communication lines open. We can pick up a <u>book</u> and find out about the experiences and lives of people in different times and places who used their hands to write them down. We can use our hands to <u>type</u> up <u>reports</u> on the computer. <u>Most of us use our hands to communicate emotion</u>, swing them around to <u>show excitement</u>, put our hands out with our palms up to <u>ask why</u>, or clench our fist when we are <u>mad</u>. <u>Hands can be used to instruct</u>. Putting a finger to your mouth means to <u>be quiet</u>; waving to someone means to <u>come over</u>, and in sports, such as baseball, hand signs are used to let players <u>know what to do</u> next. It is a lot more effective then trying to shout out the instructions. Probably <u>the most noted example of using hands to communicate is sign language</u>. Sign language was developed so those who are hard of hearing can still <u>share</u> their <u>thoughts, ideas,</u> and <u>dreams</u> with others.

<u>In so many ways, it is with our hands we care, create and communicate many of the best qualities about being human. Take the time and effort to use your hands wisely in all these areas.</u>

Sample of THE GARDEN OF EDEN REVISITED

The Writing Contest

by Summer Williams, 1997 (age 15)

Scene 1

(Clarrisa, Dominique and Allen are in the school hallway)

Clarrisa: (singing out cheerfully and holding up a paper) Hello, Dominique! Look at this, it's a creative writing contest. Whoever wins will receive a thousand dollars towards college. Now that is something I could use.

Dominique: Why don't you enter? Is it short stories or essays?

Clarrisa: It's short stories. I can enter the story I wrote for English class at the beginning of the year. Everyone loved it.

Dominique: (pointing to the bottom of the paper) There is a problem, look here.

Clarrisa: (scans the rules, then screams) Oh no! The rules say it is only for students ages 12 to 14. I'm already 16!

Dominique: Rissa, that doesn't have to be a problem. Turn your paper in under Allen's name. He's your brother and is young enough. (Turns towards Allen and smiles cunningly) You 'll do it, right Allen?

Allen: (Reading a book, and not really listening) Yeah, sure. Whatever you say.

Clarrisa: (Staring longingly at the contest) I don't know. I mean that would be lying.

Dominique: (Moans impatiently) Rissa, Rissa,you are so smart, if anyone deserves to go to college, it is you! Besides that, ever since your dad died, your mom been under tremendous stress. When college rolls around its going to make it that much more difficult for her. You wouldn't do that to your mother, would you?

Clarrisa: (Feeling put on the spot) Well, no, but...

Dominique: (A little impatiently) No buts. All you have to do is take it home and fill out the entry form in his name. Then staple it to your story. Then tomorrow bring it back here and drop it off. No one else will know and you will be happy knowing it took so much of the burden off your mother's shoulders.

Clarrisa: (Fiddling with the hem of her shirt, and sound uncertain) Yeah, yeah, you're right. Man, we do need a break. I'll take this home and fill it out and bring it back in the morning.

Dominique: Great, I knew you would see it my way. She made the right decision. Don't you think Allen?

Allen: (glancing up) I don't care.

Sample of THE GARDEN OF EDEN REVISITED

The Writing Contest continued

Scene 2

(It is late that night in Clarrisa's home. Allen and their Mom are in the living room. Mom picks up a set of papers.)

Mom: (a worried look on her face) Allen, why did you enter a contest using your sister's story?

Allen: Mom, it wasn't my idea, Clarrisa decided to do it and I just went along with her. I really didn't do anything wrong; it's all her fault.

Mom: Clarrisa, come here. What is this all about?

(Clarrisa enters room)

Clarrisa: Oh, Mom, I didn't mean for you to find those papers.

Mom: Clarrisa, do you want to explain to me why a story you wrote is stapled to a contest in your brother's name?

Clarrisa: Mom, I really didn't want to do it, but Dominique said that if we won the contest, and got the scholarship, it would be helping out the family. You work so hard and we barely can make ends meet. I figured this was a way I could take off some of the pressure.

Mom: Honey, it has been hard, and sometimes I am overwhelmed with it all. I miss your father, and we have so many financial expenses from his long illness. I am pleased that you want to help me out. However, the way Dominique proposed is not the way to go. Dominique took something that was wrong and twisted it so much that it may have seemed to be the good and noble thing to do. I want and I expect your help, but being deceitful and dishonest is not the way to do it. It dishonors God's faithfulness in providing for our needs. It also goes against everything your father and I stand for. It is never right to do something wrong, even for good reasons.

Clarrisa: You're right Mom. I haven't felt good about it all day. I've been sick to my stomach every time I thought about it. But I really wanted to help. Can we please just tear up the contest? I don't even want it around at all. Can you imagine the mess it would have been if I had won. It would have put Allen and me in a position where we would have had to tell more and more lies to cover up what we had done. And I would have had to worry all the time that someone would find out.

Allen: Mom, I sorry too. I guess I didn't even care enough to think about whether it was right or wrong.

Mom: I am glad we caught it now before it got out of hand. Help me tear it up and let's go out for a milk shake.

(They all help tear up the papers and head out the door, laughing and hugging each other)

The End

Samples of CHIASTIC STRUCTURE

A Necessary Move

By Emily Welser, 1996 (age 12)

A. The crops weren't growing and there is a small harvest.

B. Many people run out of food.

C. Soon people start moving away.

D. Anna writes a letter to relatives, asking to move in with them.

E. She sells her home and possessions.

F. Anna travels to her relatives' town.

G. She get reacquainted with her relatives.

H. Anna unpacks and settles in.

I. She gets a job in a store.

J. Anna does her best to fit in.

K. Anna likes her relatives a lot.

L. She gets a little homesick.

M. Anna wishes she could go back to her own town.

N. News comes that the drought is over.

M. Anna makes plans to move home.

L. She is very happy to be going back.

K. Anna is sad to be leaving her relatives.

J. She tells them she will do her best to keep in touch.

I. Anna quits her job.

H. She packs her few belongings.

G. She says good-bye to her relatives.

F. Anna goes back to her own town.

E. Anna must buy a new home and goods.

D. She writes to reassure her relatives that the move was for the best.

C. Almost all the people are coming back.

B. There is now plenty of food.

A. The crops grow well and there is an abundant harvest.

Samples of CHIASTIC STRUCTURE

A NECESSARY MOVE

by Emily Welser, 1996 (age 12)

In the small town of Percy, on the edge of a great prairie, lives a woman named Anna. The year is 1880, and it has been about ten years since Anna had moved here. Anna is troubled, for there is a drought in this area. The crops have grown very slowly. This is not good at all, for most of the people around Percy are farmers and depend on the crops for food and money. Many of her neighbors are getting low on supplies and some are even starving. A few people, like the shopkeepers are going to stick out the drought. Many others must give up, pull up roots and move away. They will try to survive elsewhere until the drought is over. Anna is one of the many people who must move away. She has relatives in the neighboring town of Nyman, that is not hit as hard by the drought.

Anna writes a letter to her relatives asking if she can live with them until after the famine. Her aunt writes back saying they would be more than happy to have her come. Anna finds and travels the dusty roads, with a wagon train to Nyman.

Anna really enjoys her aunt and uncle and settles in with them easily. With a little help, Anna finds a good job helping out at the drug store. Anna is easy to get along with and she works hard to fit in and help out. However, even though she really likes her aunt and uncle, Anna is homesick for Percy.

Then finally she hears that the famine is over. Delighted, Anna makes plans to move back to Percy. Although she is very happy to be able to go back to Percy, she is still sad to be leaving her beloved aunt and uncle.

Anna quits her job and packs up her few belongings. She says good-bye, promising to do her best to keep in touch. Her trip back to Percy is joyful, and she settles back into town. It takes some time to buy a new home and get all new supplies, but Anna is not afraid of hard work. Anna writes her aunt, reassuring her that her move was for the best.

Slowly, but steadily the farmers and townspeople return. Now the harvest is large and plentiful and there is food for everyone. Anna is pleased to be back home.

Samples of CHIASTIC STRUCTURE

CLIMBING A LIVE VOLCANO

By Wendy Mortimer, 1996 (age 16)

A. Tim and Max discuss climbing a live volcano.

B. There are no volcanoes around here.

C. They get an airplane flight to Mexico.

D. They fly to Mexico City.

E. They rent a car to go to the volcano Popocatepetl.

F. They drive to its base.

G. They put on their hiking gear and start up.

H. It gets colder and colder the higher they go.

I. They see black smoke billowing out of the volcano.

J. Max gets scared and starts running.

K. Max falls and sprains his ankle.

L. Tim finds him and tapes up his ankle.

M. It takes a long time to climb up the volcanic ash.

N. They reach the top and look into the crater.

M. They slip and slide quickly down the volcanic ash.

L. Max's ankle is hurt and needs to be re-taped.

K. Max slips easily with his sprained ankle.

J. They recognize the spot where Max had gotten lost.

I. They look back at the volcano and see a new burst of smoke.

H. Slowly it gets warmer and warmer as they desend.

G. They take off their hiking gear and head for their car.

F. They drive to their hotel.

E. They talk about Popocatepetl as they take back the rent car.

D. They prepare to fly out of Mexico City.

C. They get an airplane flight back home.

B. There are no volcanoes around here.

A. Tim and Max reminisce about climbing a live volcano.

The write-up of this story has not been included since the reader can follow the story line without it.

Samples of ALLITERATION

Barrier of Babble Blocked the Building of Babel

The building of Babel began with a bustling backslidden brotherhood of builders, who began bricking a building of baked bricks bound by bitumen. But God bolted to Babel, blocking the building by baffling the brickers' brains and boggling them with bewildering babble. Bedlam broke out and the baffled brotherhood began to break off and branch out.

Adam Smith, (age 11) and Emily Welser, (age 12) 1996

Confusion in Communication Contributes to Chaos

The Creator commanded the community to clear out to all the continents. But, in contempt, the community congregate in a country clearing.

"Come, clans, and construct a colossal construction to the clouds," came the call.

The colony commenced to collaborate on constructing a complex to the constellations. Cooked clay cubes were caulked into a colossal concrete complex. The clans carelessly continued construction, contemptuous of the Creator's command. Consequently, construction came to a catastrophic conclusion when God completely cleared out the community by confusing their capacity to communicate, causing clamor, chaos, and conflict.

A collaboration by Summer Williams, Wendy Mortimer, and Ely Kirkendall 1996

Samples of STEPPING OUT IN FAITH

Cancer Scare

by *Summer Williams, 1997 (age 15)*

(Read the numbered lines in consecutive order, starting at the bottom.)

drive home 29
talk happily 28
buy a hamburger 27
go for fast food 26
start home 25
leave doctors's office 24
call home with good news 23
in joy thank God 22
relieved, hug mother 21
"No cancer," doctor says 20
19 doctor enters
18 drum fingers
17 watch clock
16 swing legs and wait
15 go to the backroom
14 sit staring at a magazine
13 sign in
12 walk through the door
11 cry on mom's shoulder
10 park in parking lot
9 drive away
8 open the door and get in
7 walk to the car
6 drink a sip of water
5 push food around plate
4 drag feet going down steps
3 cry while putting on shoes
2 slowly get dressed
1 jump when the alarm went off

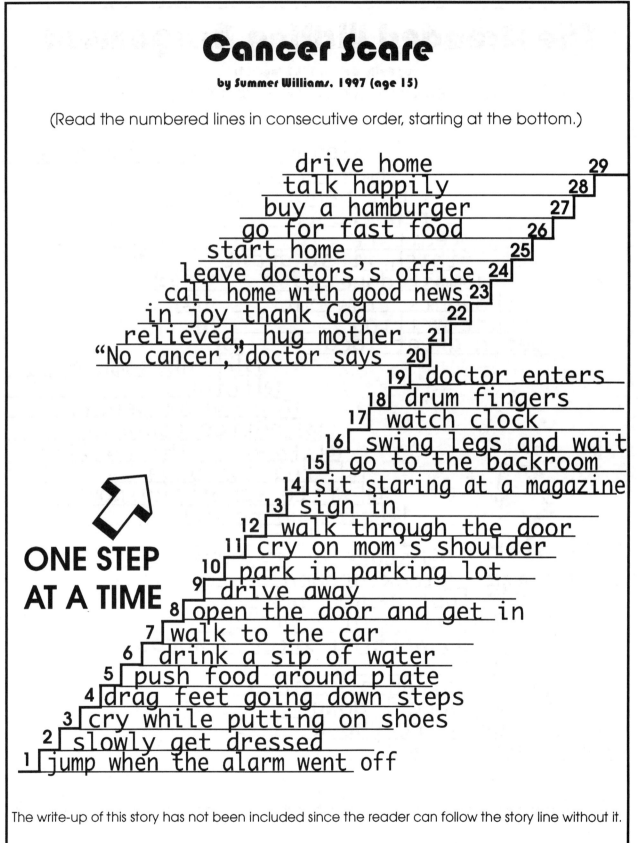

**ONE STEP
AT A TIME**

The write-up of this story has not been included since the reader can follow the story line without it.

The Dreaded Writing Assignment

by Emily Welser, 1997 (age 12)

(Read the numbered lines in consecutive order, starting at the bottom.)

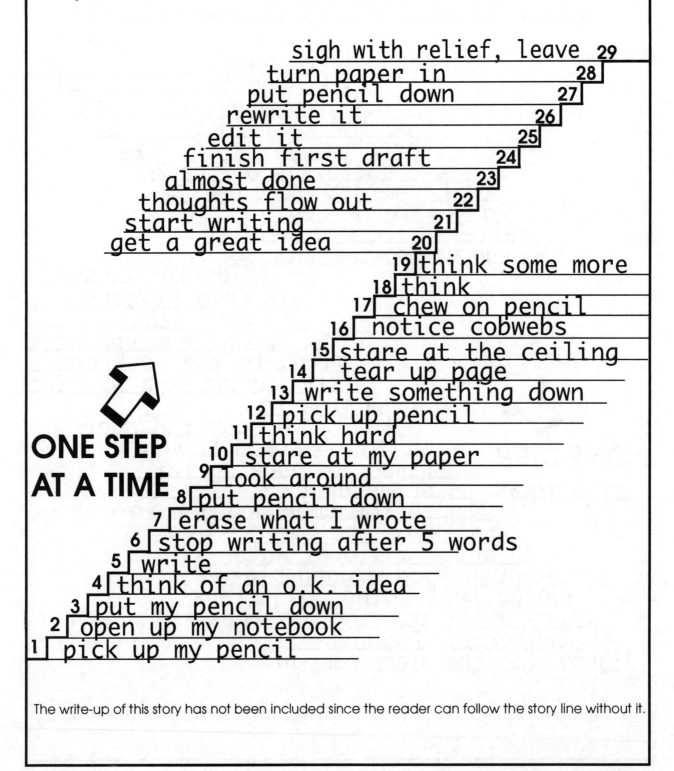

29 sigh with relief, leave
28 turn paper in
27 put pencil down
26 rewrite it
25 edit it
24 finish first draft
23 almost done
22 thoughts flow out
21 start writing
20 get a great idea
19 think some more
18 think
17 chew on pencil
16 notice cobwebs
15 stare at the ceiling
14 tear up page
13 write something down
12 pick up pencil
11 think hard
10 stare at my paper
9 look around
8 put pencil down
7 erase what I wrote
6 stop writing after 5 words
5 write
4 think of an o.k. idea
3 put my pencil down
2 open up my notebook
1 pick up my pencil

ONE STEP AT A TIME

The write-up of this story has not been included since the reader can follow the story line without it.

Samples of "THAT'S GOOD THAT'S BAD" STORIES

The Story of Succeeding at Soccer by J.B., 1997

Narrator: I was going to try out for a soccer team.
Audience: Oh, that's good!
Narrator: No, that's bad because I was small for my age.
Audience: Oh, that's bad!
Narrator: No, that's good because I tried very hard.
Audience: Oh, that's good!
Narrator: No, that's bad because I wasn't that coordinated.
Audience: Oh, that's bad!
Narrator: No, that's good because my dad practiced with me.
Audience: Oh, that's good!
Narrator: No, that's bad because I missed the ball more often than I kicked it.
Audience: Oh, that's bad!
Narrator: No, that's good because I still made the team.
Audience: Oh, that's good!
Narrator: No, that's bad because in my first game I kicked the ball the wrong way.
Audience: Oh, that's bad!
Narrator: No, that's good because I worked very hard and got better.
Audience: Oh, that's good!
Narrator: No, that's bad because the team still lost.
Audience: Oh, that's bad!
Narrator: No, that's good because I was voted most improved player.
Audience: Oh, that's good!
Narrator: No, that's was *very* good because, with God's help, our team won the next year.

The Story of Being Pulled Over (A true story) by Sheri Mortimer, (age 16)

Narrator: I had just gotten my drivers license and was driving to my friend's house.
Audience: Oh, that's good!
Narrator: No, that's bad because two police cars were behind me.
Audience: Oh, that's bad!
Narrator: No, that's good because I was driving carefully.
Audience: Oh, that's good!
Narrator: No, that's bad because the police pulled me over anyway.
Audience: Oh, that's bad!
Narrator: No, that's good because one policeman was my English teacher's husband.
Audience: Oh, that's good!
Narrator: No, that's bad because he still had to do his job.
Audience: Oh, that's bad!
Narrator: No, that's good because my best friend drove up with his parents.
Audience: Oh, that's good!
Narrator: No, that's bad because this was no way to greet him after his three-month mission trip.
Audience: Oh, that's bad!
Narrator: No, that's good because I was glad he was back.
Audience: Oh, that's good!
Narrator: No, that's bad because the policeman said my tail pipe had fallen off.
Audience: Oh, that's bad!
Narrator: No, that's good because I didn't get a ticket.
Audience: Oh, that's good!
Narrator: No, that's was *very* good because my parents decided to get me a newer car.

Sample of IF THERE WAS A PLAGUE TODAY...

Local Reporter Gives Eyewitness Account!

News has reached us of astounding events in our country. Local reporter, J.B., has this to report to our readers.

The United States, as we know it, has come to a screeching halt. Yesterday at exactly 7 o'clock a power surge swept the country. There had been warnings about the power surge for several days. Many individuals and even companies decided to unplug all their electrical appliances. However, there were not enough people did to make a big difference. Everything electrical that had been left plugged in has been irreversibly destroyed. All but the one television station is off the air, due to the power surge. Even so, there are few TVs in homes left unaffected to pick up its broadcasting.

No one is sure what caused it. Some suggest a large sun spot, but most are saying it was the hand of God. The reasoning, is that all the power stations were unaffected. However, any electrical item left plugged in was shorted out and the wires inside melted down. Another fact indicating that it was caused by supernatural intervention is the fact that there have been no reported fires caused by the massive electrical surge.

For all practical purposes, official government records have been obliterated, since the computers they were kept on were destroyed in the surge. Most businesses have shut down, with their computers and machinery disabled. The few companies who did unplug all their equipment, are still closed since the country is in a state of panic.

Stores have opened their doors for people to get food. However, much of the frozen goods has melted and is already spoiled. They are taking cash only. Without credit cards and checks, people are panic-stricken not knowing what to do. Banks will not confirm whether or not their records of bank accounts have been wiped out, but many individuals are mobbing the banks trying to withdraw their money. The military has been called in to keep control.

All emergency systems have been shut down, while many people have taken to the streets wandering around in disbelief. We will keep you informed as we get new information.

Help! How do I get started drawing?

When I teach a drawing class, I began with a short talk about how we learn how to draw.

When a small child first picks up a pencil to draw a person, he tends to draw a circle for the head with dots for eyes. Next he will add two lines coming down for the legs. This, to him, is a person.

As he gets older he will add more and more to his person, but until around nine years of age, he will be drawing symbols for objects and not really drawing the object.

What is the difference between drawing a symbol and drawing an object? Let's start with an eye. I could spell the word "eye." We know that means an eye, but it is not anyone's eye in particular, it is just a symbol that stands for the eye. Next I could draw a symbol for an eye like this.

It stands for an eye, but it is not a specific eye. This is the point where most people stop learning how to draw. They develop their symbols for a house, a tree, and a person.

What I want you to do is to go beyond the symbol stage, and start drawing what you actually see. In order to do this you will have to look at an object, for instsnce an eye, and forget that you know what the object is. View it almost as a math problem, made up of lines, angles, with variation of darks and lights. Say to yourself, as you draw, "there is a line going at this angle. It changes direction at this point and goes down to about here. This line begins about this far from my last point. Now if I did the shadow this dark here, then I need to have the same shade over there."

When I was twelve, we had an artist from Australia come down to Mexico where my parents were working as Bible translators. We had him over to eat for a meal. After I told him I was interested in drawing, he drew this drawing assignment for me. I took it to heart and began to draw on my own. As you can see in your student notebooks, your first drawing lesson is based on the assignment he gave me those many years ago.

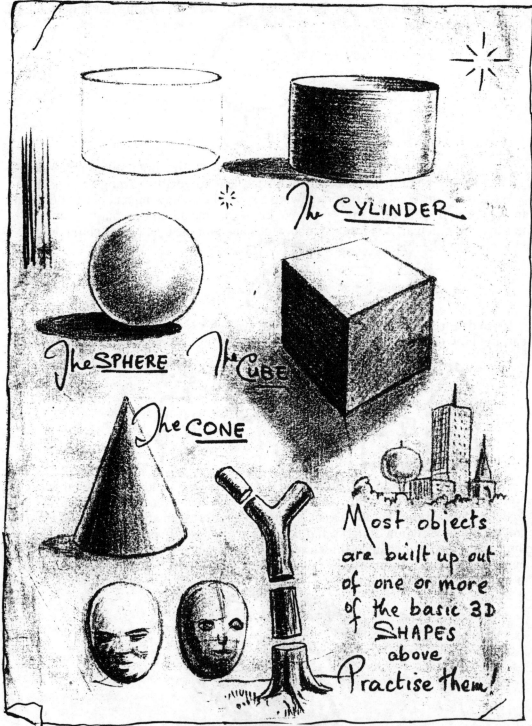

The CYLINDER

The SPHERE   The CUBE

The CONE

Most objects are built up out of one or more of the basic 3D SHAPES above Practise them!

Included in the following pages are samples of what other students have drawn. They have been reduced in size in order to have as many as possible to fit on the pages. When you draw, try to gauge your drawing to fit the space available.

DRAWING SAMPLES

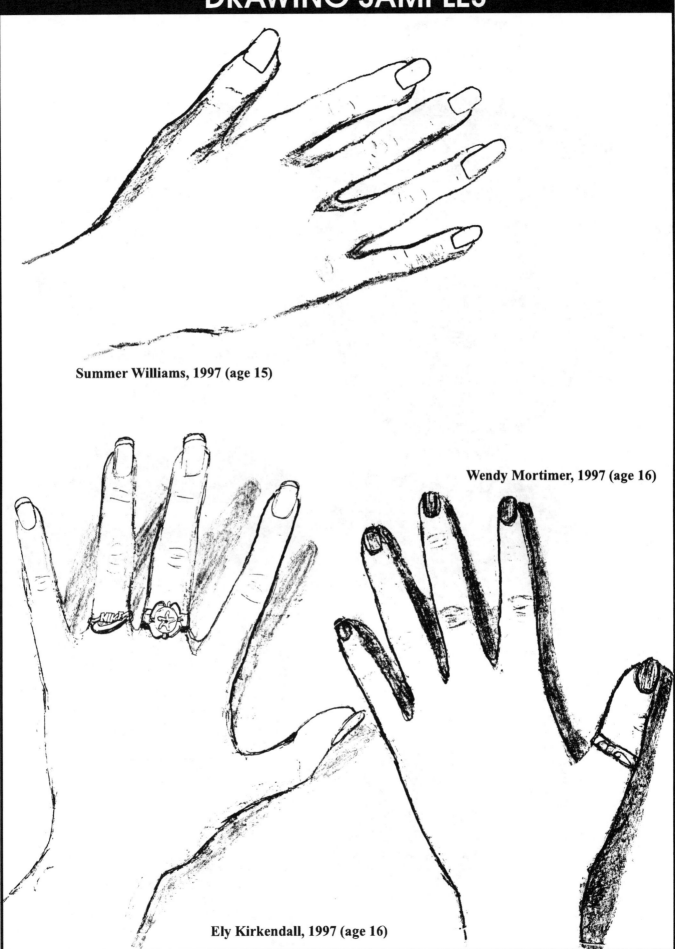

Summer Williams, 1997 (age 15)

Wendy Mortimer, 1997 (age 16)

Ely Kirkendall, 1997 (age 16)

DRAWING SAMPLES

Ely Kirkendall, 1997 (age 16)

Wendy Mortimer. 1997 (age 16)

DRAWING SAMPLES

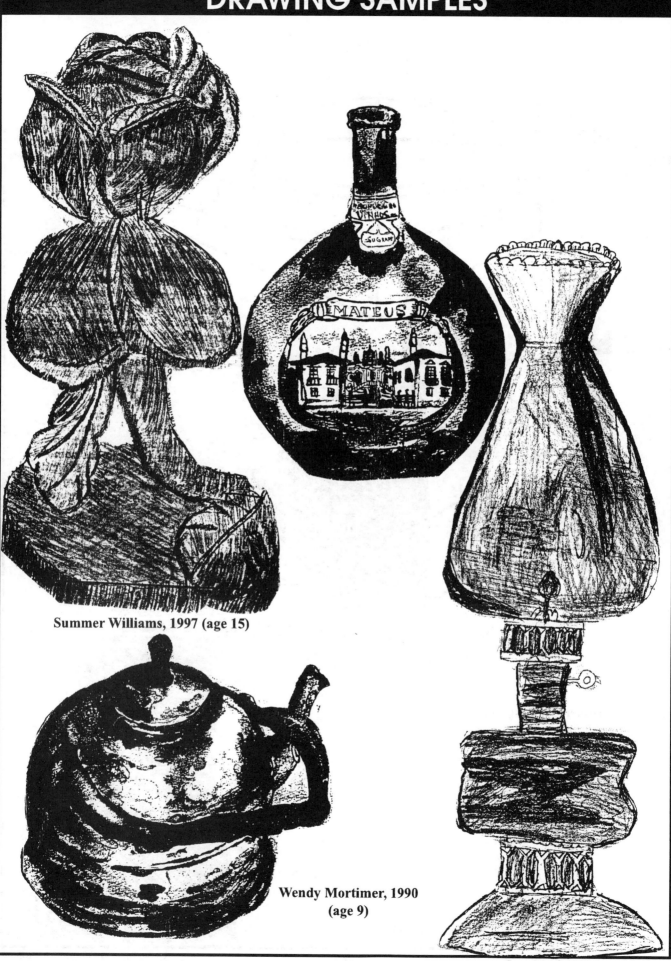

Summer Williams, 1997 (age 15)

Wendy Mortimer, 1990
(age 9)

61

DRAWING SAMPLES

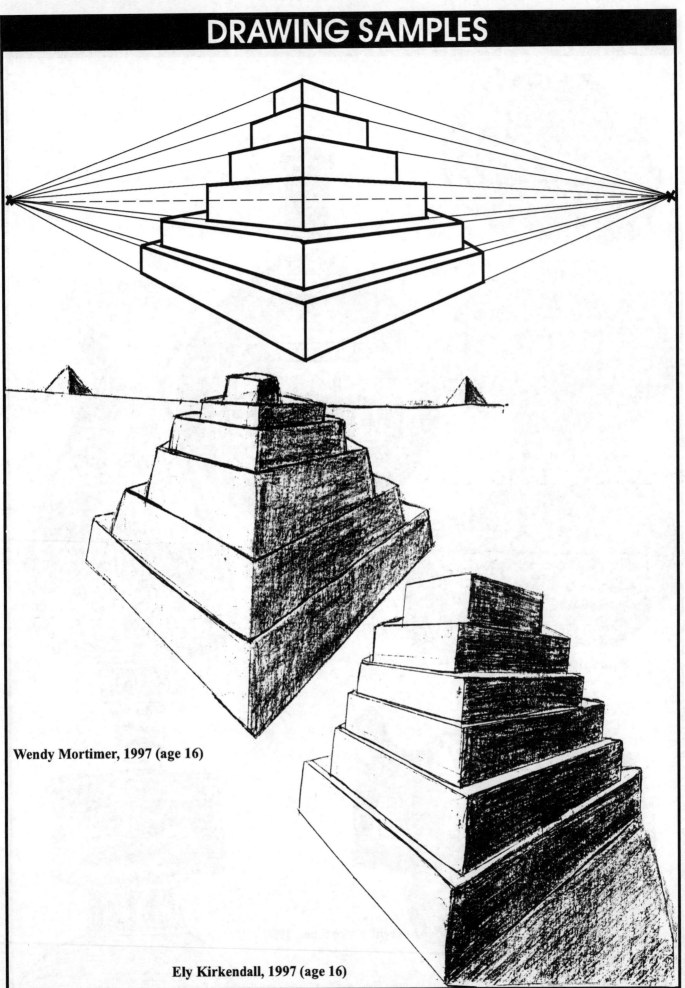

Wendy Mortimer, 1997 (age 16)

Ely Kirkendall, 1997 (age 16)

62

Diane Richart (age 18)

Wendy Mortimer, 1997 (age 16)

J.B.

Remembering God's Awesome Acts

Discussion Speech and Drama

The History of History

Preparation: You will need a large clear glass bowl, filled with clean water, red food coloring, and a dropper full of water. Read through the lesson ahead of time and then read aloud for the class.

Lesson: For events that happened long before our time, we are dependent upon those people in the past who left written accounts and upon those people who have made it their life work to study and provide us with interpretations of the information that we can read and study. When studying history, keep in mind that all historians are influenced by their perspective and prejudice, and limited by availability of information. When you read a history book, try to figure out where the author is coming from and if possible, compare several accounts of the same event. We will be studying history to have a better understanding of the Bible. And we will be studying the Bible to have a better understanding of history.

Our most important source of ancient history is the Bible. Archeological discoveries, such as the Dead Sea Scrolls, showed that the Bible has been transmitted accurately over thousands of years. Comparison of ancient scriptures showed a 95% accuracy, and of those differences, most of them were not in meaning but punctuation. Werner Keller, a skeptic who questioned the reliability of the Bible, came to this conclusion: "In view of the overwhelming mass of authentic and well-attested evidence now available, . . . there kept hammering in my brain this one sentence—'The Bible is right after all!'"

The controversy in the study of ancient civilizations is not so much actual events, but the exact dates and the interpretation of those events. These dates may vary in as much as several days to several thousands of years, depending upon the perspective and source of information. While time lines help us to gain a clearer understanding of events, we cannot be absolutely certain of most exact dates. For instance, the list of the kings of Egypt comes from two scholars quoting a long lost list. These two do not agree with each other. In addition, several kings could have ruled different areas at the same time. Prior to 800 BC, dates become increasingly unreliable.

Recognizing that the study of history is profitable for instruction in our current affairs, let's not become distracted by dates, but instead focus on the event and what we can learn from it, since from God's perspective, "a day is as a thousand years and a thousand years are as a day." Philip Yancy reminds us, "The Bible does not record history for its own sake. Rather it selects and highlights certain events that yield practical and spiritual lessons."

The humanists would say that our lives have no more impact than this drop of water in the sea of humanity. *(Drop a drop of water from the dropper into the bowl of water.)* However, if we approach history from the viewpoint that God created each of us to be a special part of a particular time and place in history, we will come to recognize that our individual lives, decision and actions have a significant impact on human history. *(Drop a drop of red food coloring into the bowl of water.)* Our lives do color and affect the whole world.

Adam and Eve

Preparation: You will need balloons; a straight pin, scotch tape, red cellophane, card stock paper, scissors, stapler, crayons, pencil. Before the class—1. Blow up two balloons. Put a piece of clear scotch tape on one of them. (Practice ahead of time.) 2. Fold a sheet of card stock paper in half lengthwise. Cut out a heart shape in the center of the paper. Staple several sheets of red cellophane over the heart opening in the page. Check out which colors of crayons will work best by marking on a scrap of paper with yellow, orange, pink and light red crayon and then placing the cellophane over the page. You will then use only the colors that can not be seen. Trace the heart on two pieces of card stock. On one heart, write in large letters (in pencil) 'RIGHT WITH GOD'. On the other heart write, 'THEY SHALL BE WHITE AS SNOW.' (Practice ahead of time)

Story: God made the first man by forming him out of dirt and breathing life into him. This man was named Adam. God placed him into a beautiful garden called Eden. This garden was wonderful. It was full of trees with fruit. God told Adam that he could eat of any tree in the garden except for one. That was the tree in the center of the garden, called the Tree of the Knowledge of Good and Evil. If he ate of it, he would die.

Adam was lonely, so God made animals and brought them to Adam to see what he would name them. But Adam was still lonely, so God put Adam to sleep. While he was asleep, God took a rib out of him and formed a woman.

Adam was very happy when he saw her. He said, "She is bone of my bone, flesh of my flesh. I will call her 'woman', for she was taken out of 'man.'"

Now the serpent did not love God. He lied to the woman and said that if she ate the fruit from the Tree of the Knowledge of Good and Evil, she would not die, but become wise like God.

The woman saw that the fruit looked good to eat and she wanted to be wise, so she ate the fruit and gave some to Adam. Adam ate it too.

Adam and the woman, Eve, knew they had disobeyed God. Their perfect relationship with God was destroyed. From that point, they began to die. It was through Adam and Eve that sin came into the world. Consequently we are all sinners and separated from God.

Some people feel that they are too evil or too worthless for God to care about them. But that is not true. God loves them and does not want anyone to be separated from Him. Other people do not feel that they are all that bad. Why, they have seen others who are much worse. They reason that God is so good and loving, He could easily overlook their few faults. What they do not take into account is that God is a righteous God and cannot tolerate sin at all. Just as this balloon *(hold up balloon)* is perfect, whole and beautiful, so was man's relationship with God before sin entered the world. I could take a large sharp knife and pop this balloon, just like murder or selling drugs seem to be huge sins that would destroy our relationship with God.

But it doesn't take something big to do the job. Something small and seemingly insignificant can do the same thing. Take this tiny, little, almost imperceptible pin for example. (Hold up pin.) This too, can destroy the balloon. In the same way, a tiny, insignificant, almost imperceptible sin can destroy our relationship with God. The Bible says if we are guilty of one sin, we are guilty of them all. It also says that we have all sinned and fall short of the glory of God. *(Pop the balloon with the pin.)* This is what any sin did to the once beautiful, full and complete relationship with God. That relationship, like the balloon, becomes shattered, broken and destroyed.

However, God did not leave us without hope. *(Take out the heart with the words "RIGHT WITH GOD" written on it.)* Once man's heart was right with God. But sin came in. Can you tell me different kinds of sin. *(Using your pre-selected crayons, write the words of sins suggested by the students all over the heart, completely covering the words "RIGHT WITH GOD".)* Now you can see that sin has soiled and ruined our relationship with God. God says that the punishment for sin is death. But wait, there is hope! For Jesus came into the world, took our sins upon himself and died to pay the price for them. All we have to do is accept Jesus and his sacrifice for us. *(Place red cellophane heart over the other heart.)* Like this red cellophane makes it so we cannot see all the sins we wrote down, so Jesus' blood covers our sins. Now, when God looks at our hearts, He no longer sees our sins, for Jesus' blood has paid for them. Once we accept Jesus Christ into our hearts, we are again right with God.

Now we have a new relationship with God . *(Take out the balloon with scotch tape on it.)* Let's see what happens when we sin. *(Take out pin, and poke it through the scotch tape on the balloon.)* The balloon didn't pop! Once we are a child of God, our relationship with Him is not destroyed when we sin, but it still grieves Him. Now we want to do what is right out of love for God *(Caution: the balloon will be slowly losing air—either put it up or have one of the students come up and pop it with a pin.)*

If anyone has not asked Jesus Christ into your life, you may do so today. Let's pray.

Take-home illustration: Isaiah 1:18 says, "Though your sins are like scarlet, they shall be white as snow." To help us remember that Jesus' blood covers our sin, we will make something special to take home. First, make a heart out of stiff paper. Then make a heart, the same size, out of red cellophane and staple it on one corner. Write "THEY SHALL BE WHITE AS SNOW" in pencil on the paper heart. Then with a light red crayon, write over it, 'THOUGH YOUR SINS ARE LIKE SCARLET." When you put the red cellophane over your paper heart, the red words will disappear, like our sins do through the blood of Jesus.

Sin, Separation, and New Life

It has invaded the world. It has seeped into every corner of our lives. It is in our homes, our schools, and our churches. No one can escape, for we still are reaping its disastrous affects. It has caused us pain, a loss of innocence, disillusionment with mankind and a shattered relationship with God. The world is filled with the hurt and the dying, with destruction, death, and decay, all because of a single event that brought sin into the world.

And what a simple event it was. It wouldn't even make the headlines today. With every kind of evil out there, an article entitled "Individuals Eat Fruit They Were Told Not To" would never make it to the front page of a newspaper. But that is what happened. It was so minor, so simple, yet so deadly to us all.

When we go over the story of how sin entered the world in the Garden of Eden, it is amazing to see how God dealt with the situation! He did not single out an individual and place all the blame on him. <u>He judged each one for his or her own part in the sin</u>. Let's look over what each one did wrong.

1. It was the serpent who took what God said, skillfully twisted it, and calmly and persistently dissuaded any arguments and fears. He made evil look harmless and inviting. So twisted was the truth, that he made sin seem like the good and noble thing to do.

2. It was Eve who, misinterpreting what God had said, put up only a feeble resistance. The fruit looked so good, so enticing, and the serpent promised her lofty ideals with no consequences. In the end, she was persuaded, for who had ever lied to her before? She was naive and gullible, unaware that she should be on the lookout for evil. And so she was taken in and sinned. She did not stop there but, in turn, convinced another to follow her example.

3. It was Adam who had heard from the very mouth of God the commandment not to eat the forbidden fruit. But he seemed to stand silently by, watching the deadly drama unfold. Here was an opportunity to really make a difference in the world. He should have loved Eve enough to stand up to her and say, "No, do not do this terrible thing, for this is a road that leads to death." However, he did nothing and said nothing to stop it. And then he, too, went along with the sin and ate the fruit.

Sin has a way of being passed on. Do you see how Adam and Eve both changed from being the seduced to being an active participant, from being a victim to being the perpetrator, and from being the fearless defender of truth to being a passive bystander?

Adam and Eve's eyes were now opened, for they now had the knowledge of Good and Evil. Their consciences were awakened, but this was not what they had expected or wanted. They felt ashamed, exposed, and naked, both physically and spiritually. They needed to cover it up and hide—even from God. Something else even more tragic had occurred: Their perfect relationship with God had been shattered. They were now spiritually dead and they, along with the whole world, began the slow and painful process of physically dying.

When God confronted them, Adam not only blamed Eve for his sins, but he also blamed God for making her in the first place. Eve couldn't stand for that, and she, in turn, blamed the serpent for deceiving her. And, as people have done ever since, they would not claim any responsibility for their own actions. They reasoned that it was not their fault because someone else had wronged them first. But just as with Adam and Eve, God still holds each person accountable for his own actions.

What a blessing that God has made a provision for freeing us from the chains of sin and death through His Son, Jesus Christ.

ANGER

Read aloud and discuss before doing <u>A Study on Anger</u> page.   Copyright © 1996 Susan Mortimer

In some ways, anger is like a temperature gauge. It is an indication that something needs to be checked out. Often we are angry because we do not have a right attitude when we do not get our own way. At other times we need to recognize that we truly have been wronged by others and use the experience to help us treat others more kindly. And still other times we are angered when we see sin or evilness which is harming others.

Since anger is like a gauge, there are three things we can check out when we are angry. First, check out our own hearts—are we in right relationship with God and others? Often we are angry because of self-centeredness. This is the time that anger often leads to sin by reacting with a selfish, unloving response.

Secondly, figure out what has been done wrong and by whom. Many people are afraid of being angry, and so suppress their anger. But if there has been a wrong done, it needs to be recognized and dealt with. Thirdly, what is the most loving thing to do in the situation . . . should we just forgive or do we need to confront?

So what should our response be when there is a need to confront something that is wrong? We need to be sure our hearts are right and that our motivation is from love. Jesus was not afraid to confront the Pharisees and money changers for their sin. Anger toward sin, coupled with love for its victims has been the motivating and driving force behind many people who have spent their lives to correct a wrong. They have turned their anger into action, realizing that their lives are worth giving for a larger cause.

Many world-changing events began with righteous anger.
♦ Angry at the indifference of Christians toward the lost and dying world, General William Booth began the Salvation Army, which has now become the first worldwide organization to provide emergency relief to victims of tragedies.
♦ Seeing the inequity in the fact that the majority of people in the world had no Bible in their own language, Cameron Townsend began what is now the Wycliffe Bible Translators. It now has thousands of members working to translate the Bible into languages around the world.
♦ Many others, such as Florence Nightingale (founder of the Red Cross), Mother Teresa (who started the City of Hope in India), have made a difference because they cared enough to confront the wrong and work for change.

In conclusion, we see that anger can often lead to sin; but we have the choice to respond with forgiveness and loving action or in sin and complacency.

Noah and the Flood

Prepare the slips from <u>Noah and the Flood</u> p. 3 as directed. Select as many as twelve or more assistants to read their slips when they are mentioned. © 1996 Susan Mortimer

Preparation: Twelve envelopes, numbered with black marker from 1-12; the twelve slips cut out from <u>Noah and the Flood</u> p. 3; (Animal crackers—optional snack.)

Story: Today we will be studying the story of a faithful man named Noah. Before there were books available to read, stories were told aloud to children. They would in turn tell their children. God knew this and so in the story of Noah, He included a way to help people remember the events in the correct order. Then the story would be told and retold accurately.

I have here twelve envelopes and twelve slips of paper. I will need volunteers to help me. Each of you will get a slip of paper and an envelope with the same number. *(If there are less than twelve, give several to each person. If there are more, have one person read the slip and seal it in the envelope, and another person open the envelope and read it.)* I will call your number. You will read the phrase on your slip of paper, place it in the envelope that has the same number and then seal it. This way you will know that they were not changed. Then we will reopen the envelopes as the story continues and see if they are the right answers.

After Adam and Eve sinned, they were sent out of the Garden of Eden. They had children and their children had children. So #1, what happens on the earth? *(Volunteer reads #1—Men increased in number.)* Please place your answer in the envelope and seal it.

There is one righteous man who was blameless among the people. He has three sons. #2, please tell us who they are. *(Volunteer reads #2—Noah, Shem, Ham and Japheth.)* Place your answer in the envelope and seal it.

But the rest of mankind does not follow God. They are not doing what God wants them to. This grieves the Lord. The earth is full of violence and corruption. How bad is mankind, #3? *(#3—Man's heart is only evil.)* Seal it up.

Now God decides to destroy the world and mankind. But what about Noah, #4? *(#4—God makes a covenant.)* Seal it up. A covenant is a promise. God tells Noah, "I am going to destroy all the people and every living thing on the earth. So make an ark. Build it 75 feet by 45 feet. Make a lower, middle and upper deck. I am going to bring floodwaters that will destroy all life. But I will establish a covenant with you. You, your wife, your sons and their wives will enter the ark. Also, bring animals of every kind onto the ark to keep alive. And bring food for you and them."

What did Noah do, #5? *(#5—Noah builds a structure.)* Seal it up. The structure was the ark.

When that was done, what happens next, #6? *(#6—God gives a commands to Noah.)* Seal it up. The command was, "Go into the ark with your family. Take all the animals—the flood will begin soon."

How long did God say there would be before the flood, #7? *(#7—Seven-day wait.)* Seal it up. How long was it before the flood began, #8? *(#8—Seven-day wait.)* Seal it up. What stepped in the ark, #9? *(#9—First animal.)* Seal it up. After Noah, his family and all the animals were on board, the Lord shuts the door to the ark. Now the floods come. How long did they last, #10? *(#10-Forty days.)* Seal it up.

The waters are rising so high the ark begins to float. Soon, the waters are so high that what is covered, #11? *(#11—Highest mountains.)* Seal it up.

Every living creature that breathes air on the land dies, both man and animal. The only ones left are Noah and those on the ark with him. The water continues to cover everything for how long, #12? *(#12—One hundred and fifty days.)* Seal it up. That was a long time to be floating in huge ocean.

Had God forgotten Noah? No! GOD REMEMBERED NOAH! He sends a wind and the waters start going down. The waters recede for how long? #12, please open your envelope. *(#12—One hundred and fifty days.)* After that amount of time, the ark comes to rest on the mountain of Ararat. Soon something becomes visible. Open your envelope, #11. *(#11—Highest mountains.)*

Noah waits how many days before opening the windows? Open your envelope, #10. *(#10—Forty days.)* He then releases something. Open your envelope #9. *(#9—First animal.)* The first animal to leave the ark is a raven that flies back and forth until the waters dry up. Then he sends out a dove. It cannot land, so it returns to Noah in the ark. How long does Noah wait before sending it out again? Open your envelope #8. *(#8—Seven-day wait.)* The dove returns in the evening with an olive leaf. Noah waits again before letting the dove out again. How long does he wait this time, #7? *(#7—Seven-day wait.)* This time the dove does not return.

By now Noah has been on the ark over a year and the earth is finally dry. What happens now, #6? *(#6—God gives a commands to Noah.)* God's command this time is for Noah, his family and the animals to leave the ark. Noah is grateful that God has protected him. What does he do, #5? *(#5—Noah builds a structure.)* The structure he builds is an altar to sacrifice offerings to God. Since God is pleased with Noah, what does He do, #4? *(#4—God makes a covenant.)* The promise or covenant is that as long as the earth endures, there will be seedtime and harvest, cold and heat, summer and winter, day and night. However, there is still a problem. What is it, #3? *(#3—Man's heart is only evil.)* God says He knows that man is still evil but even so He will never destroy the whole earth with a flood. As a sign, God puts the rainbow in the sky. This way, both God and man can remember God's promise.

After this there were only four men on the earth. Who were they, #2? *(#2—Noah, Shem, Ham and Japheth.)* God told them to scatter over the earth. What came of these men and their wives, #1? *(#1—Men increased in number.)*

How did God arrange this story to make it easy for us to remember and retell? *(The story went up point by point and then went down point by point in reverse order.)* God gives us true stories, like the story of Noah, which also illustrate events that will happen in the future. The Bible says that at the end of time, the people will be like those in the days of Noah. How were the people then? (Wicked.) God says He will destroy the world again—not with a flood but by fire. He has a special plan though, to save the righteous people. That plan is through His Son, Jesus Christ. Accepting Jesus as our Savior is like getting on the ark. We will be safe with Him. If you are not sure that Jesus is your Savior, talk with us after the meeting. Let's pray.

Noah and the Flood 3

Cut on the dotted lines. Prepare 12 envelopes by numbering 1-12. Use with <u>Noah and the Flood</u>.   © 1996 Susan Mortimer

1. **Men increased in number** (Genesis 6:1; 9:19)

2. **Noah, Shem, Ham** and **Japheth** (Jay-feth) (Genesis 6:10; 9:19)

3. **Man's heart is only evil** (Genesis 6:11; 8:21)

4. **God makes a covenant** (Genesis 6:18-20; 8:21)

5. **Noah builds a structure** (Genesis 6:22; 8:20)

6. **God gives a command to Noah** (Genesis 7:1-3; 8:15)

7. **Seven-day wait** (Genesis 7:4; 8:12)

8. **Seven-day wait** (Genesis 7:10; 8:10)

9. **First animal.** (Genesis 7:14; 8:7)

10. **Forty days** (Genesis 7:17; 8:6a)

11. **Highest mountains** (Genesis 7:19; 8:5)

12. **One hundred and fifty days** (Genesis 7:24; 8:3)

Missions

Preparation: You will need: a large map of the world; a picture of the flag of the chosen country; enough copies of "Getting to Know a Country" page for each student in the class; pencils and crayons; any souvenirs or clothing from the country (optional); a simple snack from the country (optional).

This is an opportunity to research missions and missionaries. Contact a missionary or read a missionary story. Then prepare a short one to two page oral report about the country and the missionary. Also, fill out a "Getting to Know a Country" page.

Lesson: Present the talk to your group or Sunday School class. After your report, pass out the "Getting to Know a Country" page to each child and help them fill it out. Pray for the country and the missionary. Have a simple snack from the country.

GETTING TO KNOW A COUNTRY

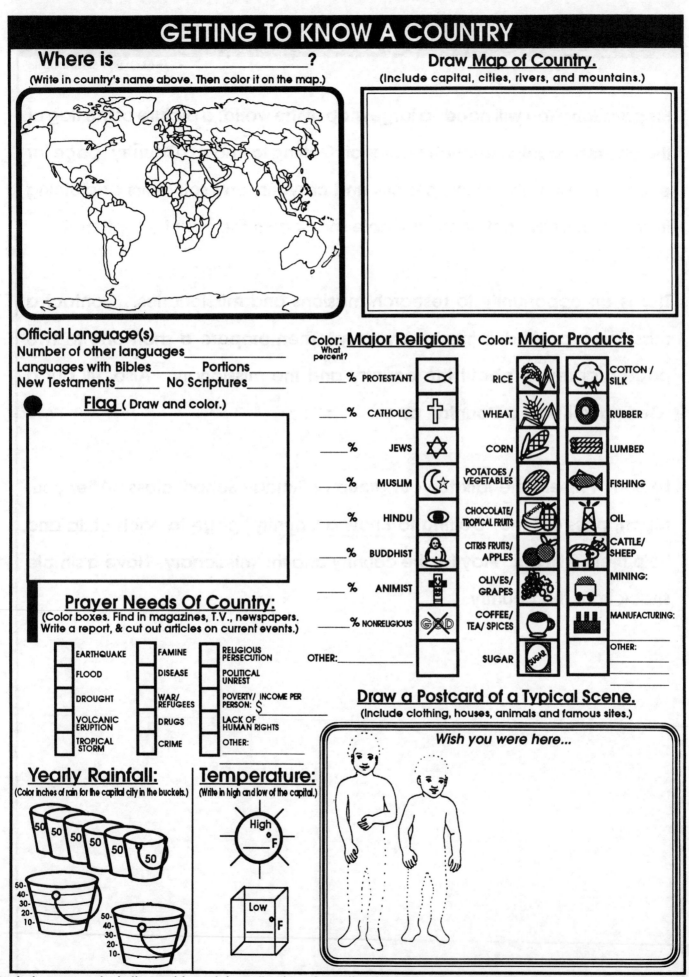

Where is _____?
(Write in country's name above. Then color it on the map.)

Draw Map of Country.
(Include capital, cities, rivers, and mountains.)

Official Language(s)_____
Number of other languages_____
Languages with Bibles_____ Portions_____
New Testaments_____ No Scriptures_____

Flag (Draw and color.)

Color: **Major Religions**
What percent?

_____% PROTESTANT

_____% CATHOLIC

_____% JEWS

_____% MUSLIM

_____% HINDU

_____% BUDDHIST

_____% ANIMIST

_____% NONRELIGIOUS

OTHER:_____

Color: **Major Products**

RICE

WHEAT

CORN

POTATOES / VEGETABLES

CHOCOLATE/ TROPICAL FRUITS

CITRIS FRUITS/ APPLES

OLIVES/ GRAPES

COFFEE/ TEA/ SPICES

SUGAR

COTTON / SILK

RUBBER

LUMBER

FISHING

OIL

CATTLE/ SHEEP

MINING:
_____

MANUFACTURING:
_____

OTHER:
_____
_____

Prayer Needs Of Country:
(Color boxes. Find in magazines, T.V., newspapers.
Write a report, & cut out articles on current events.)

EARTHQUAKE

FLOOD

DROUGHT

VOLCANIC ERUPTION

TROPICAL STORM

FAMINE

DISEASE

WAR/ REFUGEES

DRUGS

CRIME

RELIGIOUS PERSECUTION

POLITICAL UNREST

POVERTY/ INCOME PER PERSON: $_____

LACK OF HUMAN RIGHTS

OTHER:
_____

Draw a Postcard of a Typical Scene.
(Include clothing, houses, animals and famous sites.)

Wish you were here...

Yearly Rainfall:
(Color inches of rain for the capital city in the buckets.)

50 50 50 50 50 50

50- 40- 30- 20- 10-

50- 40- 30- 20- 10-

Temperature:
(Write in high and low of the capital.)

High ___°F

Low ___°F

To study any country in the world, use information from <u>Operation World</u> and Encyclopedias. Copyright © 1991, 1996 S. Mortimer

76

Three Lives and Three Choices

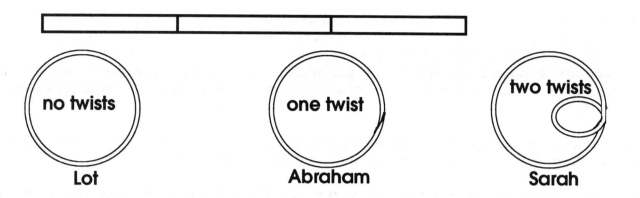

Preparation: *Practice this lesson before class. Use short loops (3 feet) to practice and extremely large loops (12 feet or more) for the class. Make strips of paper two inches wide by cutting lengths from regular typing paper. Tape or glue several strips together. Then make into a loop. Make sure that there are no twists in the paper. Write the name "Lot" on the loop.*

Make a second loop, but put one twist in it before taping it together. The best way to do this is to hold the ends of the strip together, making sure there are no twists in it. Then take hold of one end of the strip and turn it over once. Then tape the loop together and write the name "Abraham" on it.

Make a third loop, this time putting in two twists before taping. Again, the best way to do this is by holding the ends together with no twists and turning the top end over twice. Mark this loop "Sarah".

(Take the loop labeled "Lot" and as you tell his story, Slowly cut lengthwise down the center of the two-inch width. Do not take the last snip until the story is done. You should end up with two one-inch loops.)

Story: We will be studying the lives of three people over the next few weeks. Each one made choices in their lives that had long-term results. These three people were Abraham, his wife, Sarah, and his nephew, Lot.

Lot was taken into Abraham's family when his father died. When God called Abraham to leave Haran and go to Canaan, Abraham took Lot with him.

After many years, both men became wealthy with many servants and many large herds of sheep. Then trouble set in. The land was not able to sustain both herds of sheep. There was constant bickering and fighting between the servants of Lot and those of Abraham over getting water from the wells.

Abraham did not want this to go on, so he took Lot up a high mountain where they could look out over the land.

He said to Lot, "Let's not have quarreling between us. We'll go our separate ways. You choose which way you want to go and I'll go the other direction."

Lot looked out and saw that the land to the east was rich and lush. He had not asked God to help him in the decision. He did not think about what could happen in the future or the moral influence of those around him. So he picked the best for himself. It seemed like he made a great choice. He settled down and gathered more wealth. He moved to a great city, married and had two daughters. His choice was selfish, based on "what is best for me".

Well, what happened to Lot? Because of the wickedness of the city of Sodom, where Lot was living, God decided to destroy it. Abraham pleaded with God and Lot was allowed to escape. However, Lot's wife looked back and was turned into a pillar of salt. And Lot ended up humiliated and penniless, living in a cave with his two daughters. *(Make the last snip to cut the loops apart and hold up one of the separated loops.)* Lot wanted more and more and like this loop, he ended up with little.

(Take the loop marked "Sarah" and slowly cut lengthwise down the center of the two-inch width as you tell her story. Wait to make the last snip until the end of the story.)

Now let's look at Sarah's life. She was the wife of Abraham and also went with him to the land God had promised. God had told Abraham he would make of him a great nation, but there was a problem. Sarah was barren—she could not have children. Month after month, and year after year went by and still no child. Sarah was getting old and she no longer wanted to wait. So she had Abraham take her maid, Hagar, as a second wife. (This practice of having several wives was allowed in ancient times, but as you will learn in this story, it was never a good option.)

Once Hagar became pregnant, she became proud and haughty. This infuriated Sarah, and she beat Hagar. Ishmael was born to Hagar and twelve long years passed. Then the Lord came to Abraham and told him that Sarah would have a child. Sarah laughed, for she was an old woman of ninety, long passed the age she could have children. But the Lord told her, "nothing is impossible with God," and at the same time the next year, she gave birth to a son, Isaac.

Ishmael, the son of her maid, Hagar, began to taunt Isaac. Again Sarah would not tolerate it and forced Abraham to send him and his mother away.

This did not end her problem. For Ishmael grew up to become the father of many of the Arab nations. Sarah thought she knew better than God and took matters into her own hands. But because of her choice—to have Hagar have a child—the two nations raised from both women (the Jews from Sarah and the Arabs from Hagar) have been in deadly combat for over 4,000 years. *(Make the last cut. The two loops should be interlocked.)* Just as these loops are locked together, so the descendants of Sarah and Hagar have been locked in conflict ever since.

(Take the last loop, marked "Abraham". Slowly cut lengthwise down the center of the two-inch width as you tell the story. Wait to make the last cut until the end.)

Abraham, on the other hand, trusted God. By faith, he moved where God told him. God promised him that from his descendants would come someone who would bless all people of the world. *(Make the last cut. There should be one large loop.)* His choice to follow God's directions not only enlarged his own blessings, but provided a blessing for the whole world in the person of one of his descendants, Jesus Christ.

When you face choices in your life, think about the choices made by Lot, Sarah and Abraham. Are you making your choice for selfish reasons like Lot did? *(Hold up the short loop.)* Are you trying to work things out by your own means like Sarah? *(Hold up the interlocking loop.)* Or are you asking God's guidance and giving God the time and permission to take care of the needs in your life as Abraham did? *(Hold up the large loop.)* These loops will help you remember what the end results of each of those choices will be.

Rebekah-the Needle in the Haystack

Present this lesson before doing the <u>Mission Possible</u> page.   Copyright © 1996 Susan Mortimer

Preparation: Needed: 2 plastic gallon jugs filled with water, a tray, confetti, a tiny metal washer (like in an ink pen), a very small magnet or small strip of sticky-back magnetic tape. Cover the tray with confetti. Fix one piece of confetti as follows: Glue a tiny metal washer between two pieces of confetti. Write an 'R' on the confetti and glue another piece of confetti on top, that can be pulled back to see the 'R'. Before you begin the lesson, hide the 'R' piece in the tray of confetti, and tape a magnet or strip of magnetic tape to the palm of your hand, being careful not to let the class see it.

Story: Abraham was now old, and his greatest desire was to get a good wife for his son, Isaac. He told his chief servant to go back to his country and to find a wife for Isaac from among Abraham's relatives. The faithful servant was filled with questions by this command. What young girl would be willing to come back to a strange land to marry someone she had never met? And there were other problems. How could he find her in the first place? He had to travel far to find the city of Nahor. It was a long journey with ten camels and all kinds of potential problems and dangers along the way. And when he did find the place, how would he find the family? It would be as hard as finding a needle in a haystack. But Abraham's faithful servant prayed that the very first girl to come up to him would be the one Isaac was to marry.

Let's see if you can pick Rebekah on your first try. On this tray is a piece of confetti with an 'R' on it, which stands for Rebekah. See if you can pick it out. *(Have two or three children pick out a piece of confetti and see if it has an 'R' on it. Note: Odds are great that they will not pick out the right one!)* Now let's see if I can find it on the first try. *(Pat the tray with your hand. The confetti with the washer should stick to the magnet. Pull it off, keeping the magnet hidden, and show that it was the one marked with the 'R'.)*

For Abraham's servant to have traveled hundreds of miles to a far-off land, come to a large city with many people and find the very person he was looking for on the first try, showed that God had His hand in the matter. *(Turn your hand over and show the magnet.)* See, I had help too. Inside the confetti was a metal washer and on my hand is a magnet. From our human perspective, it would be nearly impossible, but with God, nothing is impossible. He knows where we are; He knows the future, and He has a plan and purpose for our lives. Just like the magnet could easily find the right confetti, so God can do what for us would seem impossible.

Abraham's servant asked God to have the first girl to come by be the one for Isaac. He wanted God to show that she was the right one by having her do a chore for him. Let's take a break now and have a relay race.

(Relay Race): Have two plastic gallon milk jugs filled with water, lids on, sitting on two chairs. Divide the class into two teams. Line them up at one end of the room. Have the first member of each team pick up a jug, put it on their shoulder, and walk with it to a chair at end of the room. They must touch the chair, then return to the other end and put the jug down on the first chair. The next member will pick up the jug and do the same. Assign someone to keep count of the number of laps. The first team to reach 30 times wins the relay.)

You are tired from walking back and forth, and you are probably wondering why we did this relay. Well, the chore Abraham's servant wanted done was to have the girl offer to water all his camels. A thirsty camel can drink between 30 to 50 gallons of water in as little as six minutes, and you have just watered one camel! Let's do some math. Abraham's servant did not have only one camel, but ten. That means Rebekah would have had to water them all. If we take the lower number, 30 gallons per camel, and there were ten camels, Rebekah would have had to draw 30 x 10 or 300 gallons. At the 50 gallons per camel, how many gallons would she have had to draw? *(500 gallons)*

This was no small task. Many times we volunteer to help out, but we get tired and give up. Abraham's servant waited to see if Rebekah would follow through with the task. If she had stopped at any point, she would not have been chosen to marry Isaac, and to have as one of her offspring, Jesus Christ—the Savior of the world.

The Struggle

This story is to be done as a play. The setting is an "Awards Banquet". Prepare the cards from <u>The Struggle</u> p. 2 as directed. Select a Narrator and four assistants (Leah, Rachel, Zilpah, and Bilhah) to read their cards when they are opened.

© 1996 Susan Mortimer

Narrator: When we say we are "pulling his leg", it means we are teasing or tricking some-one. Jacob was born grabbing the heel of his twin brother Esau and his name means, "he grasps the heel", which was a saying, even back then, that meant "pulling his leg" or deceiving someone. All through his life, Jacob is deceiving others or being deceived by them.

At first he deceives and cheats his twin brother out of his birthright and blessing. His brother is so angry that he wants to kill him. Jacob has to escape to his Uncle Laban's home.

There, Jacob falls in love with Rachel, Laban's youngest daughter. He tells Laban, "I will work for you seven years in return for your youngest daughter, Rachel."
Laban agrees. The seven years fly by as if they are a few days, so much in love is Jacob.

However, it is Laban's turn to "pull Jacob's leg". And instead of Rachel, he gives Leah, his oldest daughter to marry Jacob. He then agrees to give Jacob Rachel in exchange for another seven years of labor.

Rachel and Leah are both angry with their father for "selling" them rather than "giving" them in marriage. Rachel does not want to share Jacob, and Leah is unloved and unwanted. So an intense and bitter competition begins between the two sisters.

When the Lord sees that Leah is not loved, He allows her to become pregnant, while Rachel is barren. And so the struggle begins.

The first child is born to Leah. She names him: (Open and read "Leah 1")
The second child again is born to Leah. (Open and read "Leah 2")
And the third is born to Leah. (Open and read "Leah
The fourth child is born to Leah. (Open and read "Leah 4")

Rachel still has no children. She is so jealous of her sister, she screams to Jacob, "Give me children or I'll die."

Jacob becomes angry with her and says, "Am I in the place of God, who has kept you from having children?"

Then Rachel gives her maidservant, Bilhah, to Jacob as a wife.
And the fifth child goes to Rachel by Bilhah. (Open and read "Bilhah/Rachel 5")
The sixth child also goes to Rachel by Bilhah. (Open and read "Bilhah/Rachel 6")

Now Leah sees she is having no more children, so she gives her servant, Zilpah to Jacob as a wife. And the seventh child goes to Leah by Zilpah. (Open and read "Zilpah/Leah 7")
And the eighth child goes to Leah by Zilpah. (Open and read "Zilpah/Leah 8")

Then God listens to Leah and the ninth child is born to Leah. (Open and read "Leah 9")
And also the tenth child is born to Leah. (Open and read "Leah 10")
And the eleventh child is born to Leah. (Open and read "Leah 11")

Then God remembers Rachel and opens her womb.
And the twelfth child is born to Rachel. (Open and read "Rachel 12")
Finally, after some time, the last child is born to Rachel. (Open and read "Rachel 13")

And who is the winner? Actually, no one. For Rachel dies in childbirth, Leah is still unloved and Jacob shows favoritism to Rachel's son, Joseph. Now the struggle is passed on, for Joseph's brothers hate him so much they sell him as a slave. When relationships are filled with deceit and bitterness, competition and strife, no one is a winner.

If you are constantly fighting with someone, you can start healing that relationship by being kind and avoiding arguments. Anyone can be the one to start changing a bad relationship. The Bible says, "Be kind to one another, tenderhearted, forgiving one another..." (Eph. 4:32) Jesus also tells us to "Love your enemies, do good to them. (Luke 6:35) God is a God of love. If you are His, you will become like Him. Let us pray and ask God to help us be kinder from now on.

The Struggle 2

Cut on the dotted lines. Fan-fold on the solid lines so that the large name is on the outside. Use with <u>The Struggle</u> play.   © 1996 Susan Mortimer

Leah 1.	(Leah) **1. Reuben: "see a son"** "It is because the Lord has seen my misery. Surely my husband will love me now."
Leah 2.	(Leah) **2. Simeon: "hearing"** "Because the Lord <u>heard</u> that I am not loved, he gave me this one too."
Leah 3.	(Leah) **3. Levi: "attached"** "Now at last my husband will become <u>attached</u> to me, because I have borne him three sons."
Leah 4.	(Leah) **4. Judah: "praise Jehovah"** "This time I will <u>praise</u> the Lord."
Rachel-**Bilhah 5.**	(Rachel-Bilhah) **5. Dan: "judge"** "God has <u>vindicated</u> me; he has listened to my plea and given me a son."
Rachel-**Bilhah 6.**	(Rachel-Bilhah) **6. Naphtali: "my struggle"** "I have had a great <u>struggle</u> with my sister, and I have won."
Leah-**Zilpah 7.**	(Leah-Zilpah) **7. Gad: "good fortune"** "What <u>good fortune!</u>"
Leah-**Zilpah 8.**	(Leah-Zilpah) **8. Asher: "happy"** "How <u>happy</u> I am! The women will call me <u>happy</u>."
Leah 9.	(Leah) **9. Issachar: "one for hire"** "God has rewarded me for giving my <u>maidservant</u> to my husband."
Leah 10.	(Leah) **10. Zebulun: "presented a gift"** "God has presented me with a <u>precious gift</u>. This time my husband will treat me with honor, because I have borne him six sons."
Leah 11.	(Leah) **11. Dinah: "artistically formed"**
Rachel 12.	(Rachel) **12. Joseph: "let God add"** "God has taken away my disgrace. <u>May the Lord add</u> to me another son."
Rachel 13.	(Rachel) **13. Ben-Oni: "son of my sorrow"** for Rachel was dying. Jacob changed his name to **Benjamin**: "son of my right hand".

The Story of Joseph

Preparation: You will need a blender and the following ingredients in pre-measured containers on the table—1 egg yolk; 2 tablespoons lemon juice or vinegar; 1 teaspoon dry mustard; 1 teaspoon sugar; 1/4 teaspoon salt; pinch ground red pepper; 1 cup oil; bread; lunchmeat; and cheese. Before the story begins, give paper to the students and have them draw illustrations of the dreams in the story. Have them read the verses and then draw a picture about the dream. 1. Joseph's dream about the sheaves of grain (Genesis 37:5-7). 2. Joseph's dream about the sun, moon and eleven stars (Genesis 37:9). 3. The dream of the cupbearer (Genesis 40:9-11). 4. The dream of the baker (Genesis 10:16-17). 5. The first dream of Pharaoh (Genesis 41:1-4). 6. The second dream of Pharaoh (Genesis 41:5-7). *(Note: If there are only a few students, have each draw several dreams; if there are many, have more than one draw each dream.)*

Story: We will be using this blender to illustrate Joseph's life. Joseph's life started out quite good. He was loved by his father and mother. Life was good and sweet, like this sugar. *(Put sugar into the blender.)* His father gave him a richly ornamented robe. However, he came from a large family and his brothers hated him because his father favored him.

Joseph had two dreams where he was ruling over them. *(Hold up the students' illustrations of dream #1 and have each artist describe his picture.)* The first dream was about sheaves of grain out in a field. His brothers' sheaves all gathered around Joseph's sheave and bowed down to it. His brothers said, "Do you intend to rule over us?" And they hated him all the more.

(Hold up the students' illustrations of dream #2.) In the second dream, the sun, moon, and eleven stars were bowing down to Joseph. His father said, "Do you believe your mother and I and your brothers will bow down to you?" And his brothers became more jealous than ever.

Soon his brothers had their chance to get rid of him. They discussed killing him, but instead put him down into a dry well. This was a bitter thing to happen to a young boy, just like this mustard is bitter. *(Add mustard in blender.)*

His brothers then sold him to become a slave in Egypt. Just like this vinegar, it was like an acid, eating at his heart. How hard it was to be betrayed and taken away from his family. *(Add vinegar or lemon juice.)*

Now Joseph continued to trust God and God placed him under Potiphar. Potiphar put Joseph in charge of all his household. Soon, however, Potiphar's wife tried to seduce Joseph and when he would not go along with her, she falsely accused him of a terrible crime. For this, he was thrown in prison. Like this chili pepper burns, it burned Joseph's soul to be so falsely accused. *(Add chili pepper.)*

But Joseph trusted God and soon he was put in charge of the prison. Two of Pharaoh's servants were thrown into the same prison. Each one had a dream that they could not interpret. They told Joseph their dreams and he said that God could interpret them.

The first dream was the chief cupbearer's. *(Hold up the students' illustrations of dream #3.)* He dreamed about a vine with three branches that blossomed and developed into grapes. In the dream, the cupbearer took the grapes and squeezed the juice into Pharaoh's cup, which he then put into Pharaoh's hand.

Joseph explained to the cupbearer that this meant in three days Pharaoh would restore him to his position. He asked the man to remember him and mention him to the Pharaoh.

The chief baker then told Joseph his dream. *(Hold up the students' illustrations of dream #4.)* He was carrying three baskets of bread on his head, but birds came and ate the bread. Joseph told the man that this meant he would be hung in three days.

Both dreams came to pass just as Joseph had said they would. Three days later, Pharaoh had the chief baker executed and the chief cupbearer was restored to his position in the palace.

However, the cupbearer forgot all about Joseph. This was like salt in an open wound for Joseph, and he remained in prison. *(Add the salt.)*

Two full years later, God disturbed Pharaoh with two dreams. *(Hold up the students' illustrations of dream #5.)* In one, he saw seven fat cows come up out of the Nile and graze along the banks. Then seven gaunt cows came up and ate up the fat cows. *(Hold up the students' illustrations of dream #6.)* The second dream was about seven healthy heads of grain, growing on a single stalk. A second stalk spouted with seven thin dry heads of grain. The thin heads swallowed up the seven healthy heads of grain.

None of Pharaoh's magicians could tell him what these dreams meant. The chief cupbearer at last remembered Joseph and told the king about him. So Pharaoh sent for Joseph. Like this egg yolk symbolizes new life, Joseph had hopes for a new life. *(Add egg yolk.)* Joseph told Pharaoh that he could not tell him the meaning of the dreams, but that God could. God revealed to Joseph that both dreams were a prediction of seven years of great abundance that would be followed by seven years of famine. Joseph told Pharaoh to look for someone to prepare for the famine by collecting food during the years of abundance.

Now this looks like a mess! *(Hold up the blender.)* What can come out of sugar and salt, vinegar and eggs, pepper and mustard? To us it looks like a total disaster. Joseph's life seemed like this stuff in the blender—a total disaster. Joseph probably wondered why God had all these hard things happen to him. But the plan he had suggested seemed good to Pharaoh and no one was found to be more suited for the job than Joseph. So Joseph was appointed to be second-in-command to Pharaoh. Oil was used to anoint and heal and this oil represents the anointing and healing that God brought to Joseph's life. Watch what happens to all these strange ingredients when we turn the blender on. *(Turn on the blender and gradually add the oil. It will change color and texture to turn into mayonnaise.)*

It made something totally unexpected—and useful. What do you think it is? *(We made mayonnaise.)* God had a purpose for all the events in Joseph's life—he was being prepared for the second highest position in all of Egypt. And when the time came, he was equipped for the job. You had no idea what we were making in this blender when we started. And Joseph did not know what God was doing in his life either. But God planned for Joseph to save not only all of Egypt from starvation, but his own father and brothers as well. When your life seems to be full of unexplained questions, remember this mayonnaise and that God has something very special planned for your life. *(Make sandwiches for a snack with the mayonnaise.)*

The Way of the Cross Story

Read this story aloud using the illustrations shown on The Way of the Cross page.

Preparation: Practice this story before class. Follow the directions on The Way of the Cross page for cutting the paper. Read through the play to know the procedure. Prepare a piece of paper, folded up to Step 3. Choose a child to be "Chris". Adjust the gender in the story accordingly. Write out these Bible references on numbered slips of paper and pass out to volunteers to look up ahead and read when read when mentioned in the story.

1. James 2:19   2. Romans 3:19-20   3. Matthew 5:21-22   4. Matthew 15:8-9
5. Romans 3:9-10 6. Luke 18:10-14   7. Ephesians 2:8-9   8. Romans 3:23

NARRATOR: This is a story about a boy (girl) named Chris. Chris is not a real person—but he (she) is like many real people we see every day. Maybe in some ways he (she) is like you or one of your friends or a relative. Listen carefully to this story and see what you can learn from it.

Chris was a young boy (girl) who grew up in a loving Christian home. His (her) parents loved God and made sure they taught the Bible to Chris.

(Hold up the folded piece of paper.) This piece of paper will represent the whole 'good news' of Jesus Christ as told to us in the Bible.

Chris wants to go to heaven when he (she) dies. However, he (she) believes that he (she) can pick and choose what he (she) wants to from God's Word.

CHRIS: I BELIEVE IN GOD. It is important to believe in God, and I do. I'm sure that will get me into heaven.

NARRATOR: *(Make the first cut. Take one of the small pieces and give it to "Chris".)*
Sorry, Chris. Just believing in the existence of God won't get you into heaven. Even the demons believe in Him. *(Volunteer reads Slip 1. James 2:19)*

CHRIS: I TRY TO KEEP THE COMMANDMENTS. The ten commandments tell me what to do. I try to keep them . Surely that will get me into heaven.

NARRATOR: *(Give another small piece to "Chris".)*
No, Chris. No one can be justified or made "just-as-if-I'd-never-sinned" by observing the law. Instead, it shows us our shortcomings. *(Volunteer reads Slip 2. Romans 3:19-20)*

CHRIS: GOD WOULDN'T SEND PEOPLE TO HELL. My friends tell me God is a loving God. He wouldn't send anyone to hell.

NARRATOR: *(Give another small piece to "Chris".)*
Yes, God is a loving God, but He is also a Holy God. He will judge us not only for our actions, but also our attitudes and words. *(Volunteer reads Slip 3. Matthew 5:21-22)*

CHRIS: I'M VERY RELIGIOUS. I read the Bible often. I've memorized lots of verses and I go to church regularly. I even taught a kid's vacation Bible School once. I've been baptized and rededicated my life twice. That ought to count for something!

NARRATOR: *(Give another small piece to "Chris".)*
Chris, Jesus talked about people like you who did all the right things but whose hearts were far from Him and far from heaven. *(Volunteer reads Slip 4. Matthew 15:8-9)*

Read this story aloud using the illustrations shown on <u>The Way of the Cross</u> page.

CHRIS: I WAS BORN A CHRISTIAN. My parents are Christians and I live in a Christian country, not one of those heathen places!

NARRATOR: *(Make the second cut. Give another small piece to "Chris".)*
The Jews too, thought they were righteous because they were the "chosen people", but Paul had something to say about that. *(Volunteer reads Slip 5. Romans 3:9-10)*

CHRIS: I'M BETTER THAN MOST PEOPLE. Look at the newspaper. I don't do all the bad things that other people do. I'm better than they are. Thank God, I'm not like them.

NARRATOR: *(Give another small piece to "Chris".)*
Someone else said those same words, Chris, and it didn't work for them either. *(Volunteer reads Slip 6. Luke 18:10-14)*

CHRIS: I CAN BUY OR WORK MY WAY INTO HEAVEN. I give money to good causes all the time. I tithe regularly and even give extra in the mission offerings. God surely would appreciate all my sacrifices.

NARRATOR: *(Give another small piece to "Chris".)*
Wrong again, Chris. Salvation is a gift—we can't work hard enough to earn it or pay for it. *(Volunteer reads Slip 7. Ephesians 2:8-9)*

CHRIS: MY GOOD DEEDS OUTWEIGH THE BAD. If you put them on a scale, my good deeds would outweigh the bad deeds.

NARRATOR: *(Give another small piece to "Chris".)*
Chris, where sin is concerned, a little puts you in the same place as a lot—falling short of God's perfection. *(Volunteer reads Slip 8. Romans 3:23)*

Fortunately for Chris, a good friend comes to him (her) one day and asks, "Chris, do you know where you are going to spend eternity?"

"Of course," says Chris, "See all of these things I believe?" And he (she) holds up all the pieces of the good news he (she) had chosen.

"But do you see what these result in?" says the friend.
(Rearrange the pieces to form the word 'Hell', as shown.)

"You can't just believe there is a God; you can't be good enough or follow certain formulas; you can't compare yourself to others; you can't buy your way into heaven. In short, you've missed the whole point of the Good News," continues the friend. "These things by themselves are worthless. You are still heading to hell. You've overlooked the only things that truly counts—Jesus, and your relationship to Him." *(Open up the remaining piece of paper into a cross. Immediately read the following pre-marked verses: Romans 6:23, 10:9, and 8:1-4)*

Chris had a chance to see what he (she) almost missed. Are you in the same position as Chris was—almost missing the most important thing? Let's pray together. *(Pray.)*

Let's go over this story again, so that you can be prepared to share it with your friends and relatives when God gives you the opportunity. *(Review the major points of the story and show children how to cut the paper.)*

The Way of the Cross

Use these directions when you tell The Way of the Cross Story.

1. Get an 8 1/2" by 11" piece of paper. Fold one corner down.

2. Now fold the other corner over.

3. Next fold in half length-wise.

4. When the story dictates, cut two strips, each about 1 1/2" wide.

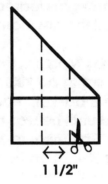

1 1/2"

5. There will be eight small pieces you have cut off. Use one each time the story dictates.

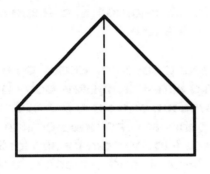

6. Rearrange them like this to spell 'Hell'.

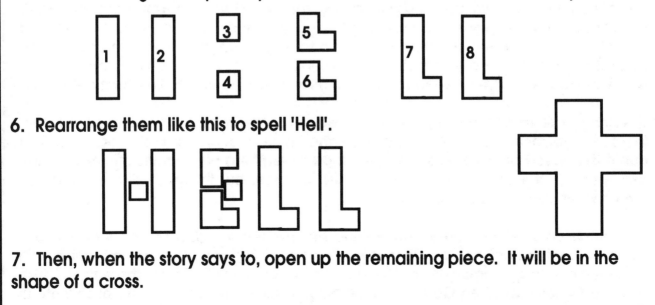

7. Then, when the story says to, open up the remaining piece. It will be in the shape of a cross.

Moses Learns the Power of God

Preparation: This lesson is a little complex but very effective. Gather all your supplies and lay them out, in order, ahead of time on a table. Then you will be able to move smoothly from one to the next. Practice the objects lessons ahead of time.

Supplies: a small piece of cotton string; a small heat-proof saucer; a small plate; a candle; matches; a straw with paper wrapper; a glass of water; a sauce pan with lid; uncooked popcorn; cooking oil; a large clear glass mixing bowl half full of water; a large cake pan; 1/3 cup of white vinegar; red food coloring; 20 or more pennies; a flat serving bowl with water; black and red pepper; oregano; liquid detergent; 1/3 cup baking soda; sugar cubes; rubbing alcohol; white paper; 1 sheet of black construction paper.

Story: After 400 years in Egypt, the number of Israelites had multiplied greatly. A new king came into power who did not know about Joseph. He was afraid that the Israelites would join his enemies and fight against him.

Thus began the oppression of God's people. They were forced to build stone cities and work in the fields. Harsh treatment made the Israelites' lives bitter—but they still flourished and thrived. Pharaoh then commanded the Hebrew midwives to kill all the baby boys at birth. The midwives feared God and would not do it. Finally Pharaoh, in a desperate act, ordered all the newborn baby boys to be thrown into the Nile.

The story of baby Moses in the basket is familiar to even young children. Moses' parents did not want him to be killed by the Pharaoh, so they hid him. This Hebrew baby boy was placed in a basket, made of papyrus and coated with tar, and set in the Nile. His sister watched until he was discovered by an Egyptian princess. She adopted him as her own child. The miracle was that his natural mother was hired to care for him for the first part of his life. Then he was raised in the courts of Pharaoh and educated to the highest levels of the day.

It was likely that he could read and write hieroglyphics and was probably being groomed to assume a leadership position in the Egyptian government. However, when he identified himself with the Hebrew people and wanted to help them out in his own strength, he burned out in a day! He saw their mistreatment, and in a rash act, killed an Egyptian who was beating a slave. Because he had been seen, he had to flee for his life.

This string represents Moses. *(Light a small piece of cotton twine on a heat-proof saucer.)* In his own power he became nothing more than a heap of ashes. Forty years of hiding out in the desert brought Moses to the place of realizing his own insufficiency. After forty years in the desert, Moses saw a bush burning, but the bush did not burn up! Moses went up to inspect the bush.

This candle wick has the same type of string we used before. *(Light a candle.)* But now, when we light this candle, the string doesn't burn up! The string keeps on burning with its source of energy coming from the wax. The encounter with God in the burning bush showed Moses that when God is in something, it does not burn up. The bush without God would have burnt up in no time. It was the presence of God that kept it burning.

This lesson gave him the faith to be able to trust God no matter what. Consequently, God was able to mightily use this humble man, who had realized his own insufficiency and was ready to trust fully in his God.

Moses went back to Egypt, and with his brother Aaron, confronted the new Pharaoh about letting the Israelites go.

Their first encounter with the king made him indignant. Instead of allowing them to go, he forced the Israelites to work even harder and beat them harshly. Moses and Aaron went back to Pharaoh again. This time Pharaoh asked them to perform a miracle.

Aaron took his staff and threw it down. This straw represents Aaron's staff. When Aaron threw it down, something happened. The staff became a serpent! *(Have a volunteer do Aaron's Staff visual.)*

AARON'S STAFF

1. (Practice ahead of class.) You will need a straw with the wrapper on it, a glass of water and a small plate.

2. Have the student push the wrapper down the straw while holding it upright on the table. It will be tightly wrinkled (see picture). Take wrapper off and place it on a small plate.

3. Place the straw in a glass of water and put your finger over the top. This will keep water in the straw when you lift it out of the glass. Put the straw directly over the wrapper and take your finger off the top, so that the water falls on the wrapper.

The wrapper wiggles about as if it were alive. This is to represent the staff becoming a live snake.

Pharaoh's magicians were able to do the same thing. But Aaron's staff swallowed all of theirs up. There was no contest! How did the Pharaoh react? *(Have a volunteer read Exodus 7:13.)*

PHARAOH'S HARD HEART

1. You will need a sauce pan with a lid to cook popcorn, and uncooked popcorn.
2. Every time you talk about Pharaoh's heart being hardened, have a volunteer drop a piece of popcorn into the pan. At the end of the class you will add oil and pop it. There will be a further explanation at that time.

This popcorn represents Pharaoh's heart—hard and unyielding. *(Have a volunteer drop a piece of popcorn into a pan.)*

Moses then went to Pharaoh in the morning, and when he would not listen, Aaron struck the Nile River with his staff and something happened. *(Have a volunteer add red food coloring to the prepared water.)*

WATER INTO BLOOD

1. Prepare ahead of lesson: a clear glass bowl half-full of water with 1/3 cup of white vinegar added to it. (The vinegar is necessary for the 'plague of boils'.)
2. Have a volunteer put red food coloring in it to make it "turn into blood." (Save for 'plague of boils'.)

The water in all of Egypt turned into blood and it stank. *(Have the students smell the red water.)* It was everywhere—in the streams and canals, and in the ponds and reservoirs. Even the water already drawn out in buckets turned to blood!

How did Pharaoh respond? *(Have a volunteer read Exodus 7:22 and drop a kernel of popcorn into the pan.)*

Several days passed. God now sent frogs when the Pharaoh steadfastly refused to let the people go. Frogs were everywhere!

FROGS

1. Pass out several pennies to each person.
2. Hold one tightly between your thumb and index finger, and press on the edge of another one on a stable hard surface (table). The one on the table will 'hop'. *(Have everyone 'hop' their 'frogs'. Enjoy a short time of 'hopping frogs'.)*

Frogs covered the land. They were in the palace, hopping into the bedroom and even into the beds. They hopped into the Egyptians ovens and into their bread troughs.

How did Pharaoh react? *(Have a volunteer read Exodus 8:8 and drop a kernel of popcorn into the pan.)*

Then Moses cried out to the Lord and all the frogs died. They stacked up all their dead bodies, and the stench of them was great. *(Have volunteers stack up all the pennies into piles.)*

How did Pharaoh react? *(Have a volunteer read Exodus 8:15 and drop a kernel of popcorn into the pan.)*

So God sent several plagues of insects.

FLIES AND MORE

1. Get a large serving bowl and fill it with water.
2. Have volunteers sprinkle the water with red pepper for gnats, black pepper for flies and oregano for locust until the top of the water is covered as was the land of Egypt.
3. Have a volunteer drop a few drops of pure water into the bowl. *(Nothing will happen.)*
4. Next use water prepared ahead of time with a quarter teaspoon of clear liquid detergent in it. Put a few drops in the center of the bowl. *(All the flies, locust, and fleas will flee to the edges.)*

First came the gnats—Aaron struck the dust of the ground and it became gnats, covering the land. *(Have a volunteer sprinkle red pepper all over a bowl of water.)*

How did Pharaoh react? *(Have a volunteer read Exodus 8:19 and drop a kernel of popcorn into the pan.)*

Next came biting flies, swarming into their houses and bugging the people and animals. *(Have a volunteer sprinkle black pepper onto the water.)*

How did Pharaoh react? *(Have a volunteer read Exodus 8:32 and drop a kernel of popcorn into the pan.)*

Later, God sent locust to devour every plant. There had never been so many locust before. *(Have a volunteer sprinkle oregano on the water.)*

Pharaoh's magicians could not produce any insects, but could they make them go away? *(Have a volunteer drop a few drops of clean water into the center of the bowl. Nothing will happen.)* No!

Let's see what Moses and Aaron did. *(Have a volunteer drop a few drops of the soap/ water solution in the center of the bowl—all the 'insects' will scatter.)* When Moses prayed, the insects left.

How did Pharaoh react? *(Have a volunteer read Exodus 10:19-20 and drop a kernel of popcorn into the pan.)*

Then God caused all the livestock of the Egyptians to become ill and drop dead. However, God protected the livestock of the Israelites.

How did Pharaoh react? *(Have a volunteer read Exodus 8:32 and drop a kernel of popcorn into the pan.)*

God gave him another opportunity to change his mind.

BOILS

1. Use the same bowl of red vinegar solution that you used for the water to blood plague. Place the bowl on a large cake pan.
2. Have a volunteer sprinkle 1/3 cup baking soda into liquid.
3. It will "boil" up just as the Egyptians' bodies were so covered with sores that they seemed to boil over.

Moses took soot and threw it into the air. *(Have a volunteer slowly sprinkle the vinegar water with the soda.)* God sent boils on the people. Boils are like huge festering pimple-like sores that can cover the whole body. The Egyptians looked like their skin was boiling and bubbling with all the sores and infection.

How did Pharaoh react? *(Have a volunteer read Exodus 9:11-12 and drop a kernel of popcorn into the pan.)*

Now God sent a storm, the likes of which the Egyptians had never seen.

HAIL

1. Place a sugar cube on a heat-proof saucer.
2. Pour 1/4 teaspoon of rubbing alcohol on it.
3. Light it carefully with a match.

Thunder and lightning, hail and fire poured down on the Egyptians, killing everyone and every animal that was out in it. *(Light the sugar cube. DO NOT use a volunteer. Have an adult do this.)*

Pharaoh begged Moses to pray for God to stop it. But when it ended, how did Pharaoh react? *(Have a volunteer read Exodus 9:34-35 and drop a kernel of popcorn into the pan.)*

Next Moses stretched out his hands and God sent darkness to Egypt. *(Have a volunteer do the <u>Darkness</u> visual.)*

DARKNESS

1. Get a sheet of typing paper and a black sheet of construction paper.
2. Roll up the typing paper to make a cylinder and hold it up to one eye. Hold the black paper 6-8 inches in front of the other eye.
3. Look through the roll at the paper, using one eye. Now open the other eye, focusing on the far side of the room. *(A hole of light will appear in the black paper.)*

It appears that there is light in the center of the blackness—just as the sun shone in Goshen although the rest of Egypt was enveloped in pitch blackness. *(Allow several volunteers to try this and describe what they see.)* The land of Egypt was so dark that the Egyptians could not even see their hands in front of their faces. However, where the Israelites were, there was light.

How did Pharaoh respond? *(Have a volunteer read Exodus 10:27 and drop a kernel of popcorn into the pan.)*

God had one final blow for the Egyptians. God warned them ahead of time, but those who would not listen had something terrible in store for them. At midnight, the Lord went through the land of Egypt and struck down all the firstborn of the land, from the firstborn son of Pharaoh to the firstborn of the prisoner in the dungeon. There was wailing throughout Egypt.

What was Pharaoh's response now? *(Have a volunteer read Exodus 12:31-32.)* Later, Pharaoh went after the Israelites to try to bring them back. Over and over again, Pharaoh's heart was hardened against the Lord, just like this popcorn is hard and unyielding. Many people are like this too. They see God's hand but they stubbornly refuse to yield to him and end up in more trouble. God does not want it to be like this. If we submit ourselves to God, there can be a total change in our hearts. *(Add more popcorn and some oil to the pan. Pop the corn.)* Our lives will be fuller and our hearts warm and soft. All by just coming into the warmth of God's love. If you have not accepted God's gift of love to you, which is Jesus, you may want to do so today. Let's pray. *(Pray and then enjoy the popcorn!)*

Remembering God's Awesome Acts

Answer Pages

Remembering God's Awesome Acts: Answer Page

The History of History

At the bottom of the page, draw lines to connect the contrasting idea from the Atheistic side to the Theistic side.   © 1996 Susan Mortimer

WHAT IS HISTORY?
⇒It is an account of events in the order they happened. However, the cause and effect of the events always reflect the opinions of the recorder.

WHAT KIND OF PEOPLE TAKE THE TROUBLE TO RECORD THESE ACCOUNTS?
An early Jewish historian, Josephus, suggested that there are three main motivations for historians—
⇒Those who write to gain recognition for their scholarly achievements.
⇒Those who write to glorify a particular group of people.
⇒Those who try to preserve the facts and truth of our past.

HOW DO WE FIT INTO THE SCHEME OF HISTORY FROM GOD'S PERSPECTIVE?
⇒God created each of us with a plan and purpose.
⇒We are not just one out of billions and billions of people living in a world that is billions and billions of years old.
⇒Our individual lives, decisions and actions have a significant impact on human history.
⇒We were created to be a special part of a particular time and place in history.

Two basic world views that *color* history:

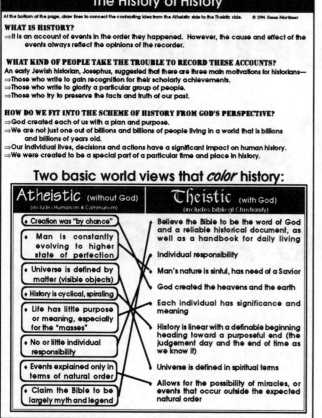

Atheistic (without God) (includes Humanism & Communism)	*Theistic* (with God) (includes biblical Christianity)
• Creation was "by chance"	Believe the Bible to be the word of God and a reliable historical document, as well as a handbook for daily living
• Man is constantly evolving to higher state of perfection	Individual responsibility
• Universe is defined by matter (visible objects)	Man's nature is sinful, has need of a Savior
• History is cyclical, spiraling	God created the heavens and the earth
• Life has little purpose or meaning, especially for the "masses"	Each individual has significance and meaning
• No or little individual responsibility	History is linear with a definable beginning heading toward a purposeful end (the judgement day and the end of time as we know it)
• Events explained only in terms of natural order	Universe is defined in spiritual terms
• Claim the Bible to be largely myth and legend	Allows for the possibility of miracles, or events that occur outside the expected natural order

5

Genesis 1: In the Beginning

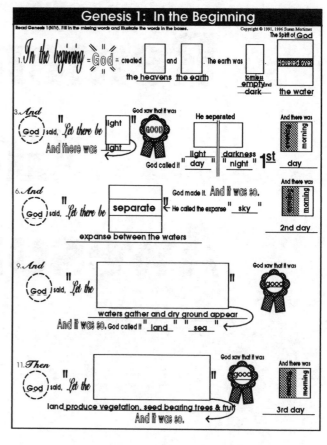

6

Genesis 1: In the Beginning Page 2

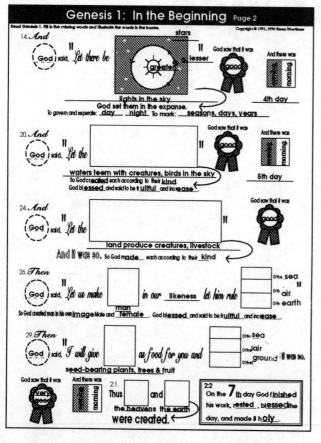

7

The God of Creation

Check which answer is correct.   Copyright © 1996 Susan Mortimer

1. God
☑ is eternal, with no beginning.
☐ had a beginning.

2. God
☐ was created.
☑ created the universe.

3. God
☐ is a part of nature, like the sun, or sky.
☑ is over and greater than all of nature.

4. God
☑ set rules and boundaries on nature.
☐ let nature develop randomly.

5. God
☐ created stars and planets to rule over the destiny of man (Astrology).
☑ created stars and planets to mark seasons, days, and years.

6. God
☐ let animals evolve from one creature to another.
☑ made each reproduce after its own kind.

7. God
☑ created the universe by His words.
☐ started the process, then left it alone.

8. God
☑ created man in His own image.
☐ created man like all other creatures.

9. God
☐ made man a part of the animal world.
☑ made man to rule over the animal world.

10. God
☐ named the animals.
☑ let man name the animals.

11. God
☑ saw that creation was very good.
☐ thought creation needed improvement.

12. God
☐ told every detail about creation.
☑ summarized it in two chapters.

Write a paragraph about what you learned about God from His creation of the universe.

<u>Answers will vary, but should include some of the</u>
<u>above elements.</u>

10

*ANSWERS MAY VARY.

PALEONTOLOGY QUIZ

Copyright © 1996 Susan Mortimer

Write your reasons for why these questions are important to ask about reconstructions of ancient bones said to be the ancestors of man.

1. BONES, IN DIFFERENT LAYERS OF ROCKS, MEAN THAT THERE ARE SEVERAL ANIMALS FROM DIFFERENT TIME PERIODS.

2. IT MAY MEAN THAT BONES FROM DIFFERENT ANIMALS ARE PUT TOGETHER TO FORM A "MANLIKE CREATURE."

3. ANY HUMAN BONES, ON THE SITE, WOULD MEAN THAT ANYTHING FOUND THERE COULD NOT BE AN ANCESTOR OF MAN.

4. RECONSTRUCTIONS DONE ON JUST A FEW BONE FRAGMENTS SUGGEST THAT MOST OF IT IS GUESS WORK.

Check which items would have to be guessed at in the reconstruction process.
- ✔ The thickness of the muscle tissue.
- ✔ The shape and width of the lips.
- ✔ The size of the ears.
- ✔ The color of the hair.
- ✔ The body build.
- ✔ The shape of the nose.
- ✔ The eye color.
- ✔ The amount of body hair.
- ✔ The skin texture and color.
- ❑ The size and shape of teeth.

Even with the most advanced modern techniques, the results of reconstructions can turn out radically different, as shown by the two drawings on the Neanderthal Update page. What does this demonstrate?
THERE IS A LOT OF ARTISTIC LICENCE IN WHAT IS PROMOTED AS 'SCIENCE'. ONE PERSON LOOKS LIKE A TROLL WHILE THE OTHERS LOOK VERY NORMAL.

Write what you conclude about the Neanderthal reconstructions.
ANSWERS MAY VARY, BUT BASICALLY THESE RECONSTRUCTIONS ARE NOT VERY SCIENTIFIC.

Since there are far fewer remains of the so-called earlier ancestors of man than those of the Neanderthal man, what is your conclusion about their reconstructions? THERE IS TOO MUCH GUESS WORK TO BE RELIABLE.

21

PRACTICING HEBREW POETRY

A = A
B > B
C = C
D ≠ D

23

The POETRY of MAN and WOMAN

A
B
B
C
A
D
E
F
G
G
E
D
C
H
H
I
I
J
F
K
K
L
L
J
M
M

A = A
B > B
C ≠ C
D = D
E = E
F = F
G = G
H = H
I > I
J > J
K = K
L = L
M > M

24

Versatile Hands

Look up each verse, then fill in the blanks with the best answer from the word bank.   Copyright © 1996 Susan Mortimer

Almost any aspect of man that is unique from the animal world can be expressed through the hand. The Bible uses the hand to show our humanity.

In Psalms 119:73, the hand is used to f o r m.

In James 4:8, the hand is used to show p u r i t y.

In Exodus 6:1, the hand is used to show m i g h t.

In Genesis 16:12, the hand is used to show w a r i n g.

In John 10:29, the hand is used to show p r o t e c t i o n.

In Genesis 4:11, the hand is used to m u r d e r.

In Psalms 119:48, the hand is used to show p r a i s e.

In Exodus 33:22, the hand is used to c o v e r.

In Genesis 5:29, the hand is used to f a r m.

In Exodus 18:10, the hand is used to show o p p r e s s i o n.

In Genesis 3:22, the hand is used to p i c k.

In Proverbs 21:25, the hand is used to w o r k.

In Matthew 8:3, the hand is used to h e a l.

In Deuteronomy 27:15, the hand is used to c a r v e.

In 1 Samuel 18:10-11 the hand is used to t h r o w.

In Galatians 6:11, the hand is used to w r i t e.

Place the letters in the boxes on the lines below. Keep them in the order found above.

m y   h a n d s   c a n   c r e a t e .

WORD BANK

farm	write	oppression	cover
might	pick	carve	work
murder	purity	heal	protection
praise	form	throw	waring

27

Remembering God's Awesome Acts: Answer Page

TWISTING THE TRUTH IS WRONG

Look at each definition, then fill in the blanks with the best answer from the word bank.   Copyright © 1996 Susan Mortimer

Words that begin with the letter combination 'wr' carry with them a meaning of 'twisted'.

A twisted ring of leaves, flowers, or pine branches. w r e a [t] h

To twist and turn, to squirm. [w] r i g g l e

A twist or pucker in material that should be smooth. w r [i] n k l e

To twist out of your opponent's various holds. w r e [s] t l e

Twisted lines that form words. w r [i] [t] i n g

Twisted metal caused by a collision. w r [e] c k

A violent twist to a joint that caused it to be injured. w r e n c h [e d]

A joint that can twist, located above the hand. w r [i] s [t]

To twist around or enclose a gift in paper. w r a p

To have twisted or squeezed water out of a rag. w r [u] n g

Twisted thinking due to intense anger, rage or fury. w r a [t] h

To twist and turn in agony. w r [i] t [h] e

Twisted or distorted justice, morality or truth. [w] [r] [o] [n] [g]

Place the letters in the boxes on the lines below. Keep them in the order found above.

t w [i] s t e d   t r [u] t h   is   w r [o] n [g].

31

TWISTED TRUTH

Genesis 3:1-4 (NIV)
"Did <u>God</u> really say, '<u>you must not eat from any tree in the garden?</u> You will not surely die. For <u>God</u> knows that <u>when you eat of it</u> your eyes will be opened and <u>you will</u> be like <u>God</u> knowing <u>good and evil.</u>'"

32

The Author of Lies

Copyright © 1996 Susan Mortimer

Satan uses the same types of ways to deceive today as he did in the garden of Eden through the serpent. All false religions have similar elements in them because they were created by the same author. Satan is known as the author of lies. Match the quotes with what false religions say or do.

What SATAN said through the serpent:		What false religions say and do:
1. "Did God really say...?"	4	There are ways to receive Enlightenment and Secret Knowledge.
2. " You must not eat from <u>any</u> tree in the garden?"	3	Calls God a liar, by claiming one can have life outside of God.
3. "You will not surely die."	1	Makes you question God's Word.
4. "For God knows when you eat of it your eyes will be opened,"	5	Says you can become a 'god'.
5. "You will be like God, knowing good and evil." Genesis 3 NIV	2	Misquotes God to make Him seem restrictive, unreasonable and uncaring.

Religious groups fall under different categories. First figure out what each religious group means, then write the name under the illustration that best depicts it.

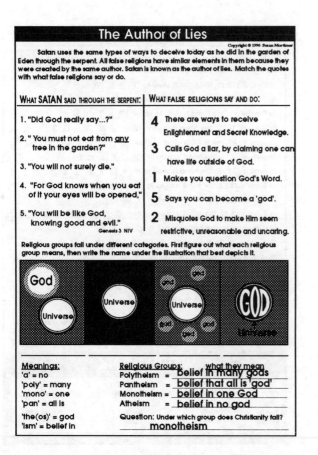

Meanings:
'a' = no
'poly' = many
'mono' = one
'pan' = all is
'the(os)' = god
'ism' = belief in

Religious Groups: what they mean
Polytheism = belief in many gods
Pantheism = belief that all is 'god'
Monotheism = belief in one God
Atheism = belief in no god

Question: Under which group does Christianity fall?
monotheism

33

Religions of the World

Fill in the name of each religious group. Read about each group and check each item that applies.   Copyright © 1996 Susan Mortimer

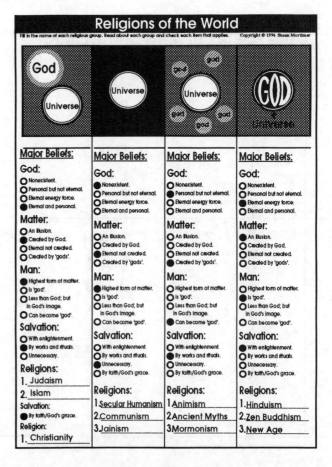

Major Beliefs:	Major Beliefs:	Major Beliefs:	Major Beliefs:
God:	**God:**	**God:**	**God:**
○ Nonexistent.	● Nonexistent.	○ Nonexistent.	○ Nonexistent.
● Personal but not eternal.	○ Personal but not eternal.	● Personal but not eternal.	○ Personal but not eternal.
● Eternal energy force.	○ Eternal energy force.	○ Eternal energy force.	● Eternal energy force.
● Eternal and personal.	○ Eternal and personal.	○ Eternal and personal.	● Eternal and personal.
Matter:	**Matter:**	**Matter:**	**Matter:**
○ An illusion.	○ An illusion.	○ An illusion.	● An illusion.
● Created by God.	○ Created by God.	○ Created by God.	○ Created by God.
○ Eternal not created.	● Eternal not created.	● Eternal not created.	○ Eternal not created.
○ Created by 'gods'.	○ Created by 'gods'.	● Created by 'gods'.	○ Created by 'gods'.
Man:	**Man:**	**Man:**	**Man:**
● Highest form of matter.	● Highest form of matter.	○ Highest form of matter.	○ Highest form of matter.
○ Is 'god'.	○ Is 'god'.	○ Is 'god'.	● Is 'god'.
○ Less than God; but in God's image.	○ Less than God; but in God's image.	○ Less than God; but in God's image.	○ Less than God; but in God's image.
○ Can become 'god'.	○ Can become 'god'.	● Can become 'god'.	○ Can become 'god'.
Salvation:	**Salvation:**	**Salvation:**	**Salvation:**
○ With enlightenment.	○ With enlightenment.	○ With enlightenment.	● With enlightenment.
● By works and rituals.	○ By works and rituals.	○ By works and rituals.	○ By works and rituals.
○ Unnecessary.	● Unnecessary.	● Unnecessary.	○ Unnecessary.
	○ By faith/God's grace.	○ By faith/God's grace.	○ By faith/God's grace.
Religions:	**Religions:**	**Religions:**	**Religions:**
1. Judaism	1 Secular Humanism	1 Animism	1. Hinduism
2. Islam	2. Communism	2 Ancient Myths	2. Zen Buddhism
Salvation:	3. Jainism	3 Mormonism	3. New Age
● By faith/God's grace.			
Religion:			
1. Christianity			

35

Remembering God's Awesome Acts: Answer Page

Poetic Justice

In the Bible, the poetry is not based on rhyme words, but on repeating or rewording a line, expanding on a thought or stating the opposite. For the following verses, mark the lines with the letter from the line that it rewords or expands on. The line B is not seen again until God talks to Adam.

Copyright © 1996 Susan Mortimer

Genesis 3: 14-19 (NIV)

So the Lord God said to the serpent,
"Cursed are you above
A   all livestock
A   and all the wild creatures!
You will crawl on your belly and
B   you will eat dust all the days of your life.
I will put enmity (hatred)
C   between you
D   and the woman,
C   and between your offspring
D   and hers;
E   he will crush your head
E   and you will strike his heel."

To the women he said,
F   "I will greatly increase your pains in childbirth;
F   with pain you will give birth to children.
G   Your desire will be to your husband,
G   and he will rule over you."

To Adam he said,
H   "Cursed is the ground because of you;
I   through painful toil
B   you will eat of it all the days of your life.
H   It will produce thorns and thistles for you
J   You will eat the plants of the field.
I   By the sweat of your brow
J   you will eat your food
K   until you return to the ground
L   since from it you were taken;
L   for dust you are
K   and to dust you will return."

In the boxes, mark the relationship of each pair of letters using these symbols:

= (reword/repeat)
> (expand upon)
≠ (opposite)

A [>] A
B [=] B
C [>] C
D [>] D
E [≠] E
F [=] F
G [>] G
H [>] H
I [>] I
J [=] J
K [=] K
L [=] L

36

QUESTIONS ON THE FALL

Copyright © 1996 Susan Mortimer

1. The act of disobedience by Adam and Eve is known as the fall of man. Although they did not physically die immediately, their precious relationship with God was destroyed. As a holy and just God, He could not allow sin into His presence. However He did have a plan to restore fellowship with mankind. What does Romans 6:23 say about the consequences of sin? THE WAGES OF SIN IS DEATH

2. When Adam and Eve sinned, God provided the first sacrifice for sin when He killed an animal to make a covering for them. Under the old covenant (or old testament) the blood of sacrificed animals continued to provide a temporary answer to cover the price of sin. Hebrews 9:14-15 and I John 1:7 tell us why we no longer have to have animal sacrifices. Summarize these verses. CHRIST DIED ONCE FOR ALL

3. As God pronounced His sentence on the serpent, He revealed the first part of His plan. Genesis 3:15 is the first prophesy about Jesus coming as the Messiah. The serpent is Satan, and Galations 3:16 tells us the offspring of the woman is JESUS. This prophesy is continuing to be fulfilled today. Read Romans 16:17-20. How does Satan try to use the same tactics with us as he used in the garden? HE USES PEOPLE TO FLATTER AND DECEIVE BY SMOOTH TALK
What are we to be like and do? BE WISE ABOUT GOOD AND INNOCENT ABOUT EVIL
What will soon happen to Satan? GOD WILL CRUSH HIM UNDER OUR FEET

4. Adam's name comes from the Hebrew word 'adamah' which means ground. The punishment of Adam is interesting, for instead of becoming like a god as the serpent had said, God keeps emphasizing that Adam is but dust. To better get a feel for what God was saying, rewrite Genesis 3:16-19 changing Adam's name to 'Dusty' and change the words 'ground' and 'it' to 'dust'. Also, read about the contrast between the two Adams and answer the questions about the last Adam.

The First Adam
To DUSTY he said,
"Cursed is the DUST because of you; through painful toil you will eat of DUST all the days of your life.
DUST will produce thorns and thistles for you,
And you will eat the plants of the field.
By the sweat of your brow you will eat your food
until you return to the DUST, since from DUST you were taken;
for DUST you are and to DUST you will return." (Genesis 3:16-19)

The Last Adam
Read Romans 5:12-21 and 1 Corinthians 15:45-49. Who was the man through whom sin entered the world? ADAM
Who was the man who brought eternal life to the world? JESUS
Why would he be called the "last Adam"? HE WAS THE OPPOSITE OF THE FIRST ADAM
Write out and learn Romans 5:19.

37

ANSWER KEY: REVIEW OF WORDS

41

A Study on Anger

Fill in the missing words and answer the questions.

Copyright © 1996 Susan Mortimer

Genesis 4:2-5 Now Abel kept flocks, and Cain worked the soil. In the course of time Cain brought some of the fruits of the soil as an offering to the Lord. But Abel brought fat portions from some of the firstborn of his flock. The Lord looked with favor on Abel and his offering, but on Cain and his offering he did not look with favor. So Cain was very angry, and his face was downcast.
1. Abel's offering was "the fat portions of the firstborn" or "the best of the first." Cain, on the other hand, "in time... brought some." What does this show us about their heart attitudes?
_____

Genesis 4:6-7 Then the Lord said to Cain, "Why are you angry? Why is your face downcast? If you do what is right, will you not be accepted? But if you do not do what is right, sin is crouching at your door; it desires to have you, but you must master it."
WHAT CAN WE LEARN ABOUT ANGER?

A. ANGER NEVER JUSTIFIES SIN.
Some people think anger justifies sin. They say, "Well, he made me angry" to explain why they felt free to do wrong and why it really wasn't their fault. Give an example.
_____

In Genesis 4:6-7 and James 1:19-20, what does God say about individual response?
_____

B. ANGER ITSELF IS NOT SIN, BUT CAN LEAD TO SIN.
Some people think anger itself is a sin, and try to avoid any confrontation because they are afraid they will get angry or others will get angry. They want "peace at any cost" and so allow sin to continue rather than confronting the issue. Give an example.
_____

What should our attitude and response be to our own feelings of anger (Ephesians 4:26)?
_____

What should our attitude and response be toward sin in others' lives (Galatians 6:1-2)?
_____

C. ANGER CAN MOTIVATE CHANGE.
Many people who have made significant changes in society have been motivated by an anger at injustice. They turned their anger into action. Anger against evil coupled with love for people has resulted in many effective efforts to feed the poor, help the needy and heal the sick. Righteous anger "hates the sin and loves the sinner". What is something you should be angry about? _____ What can you do to change it? _____
_____
_____

42

Remembering God's Awesome Acts: Answer Page

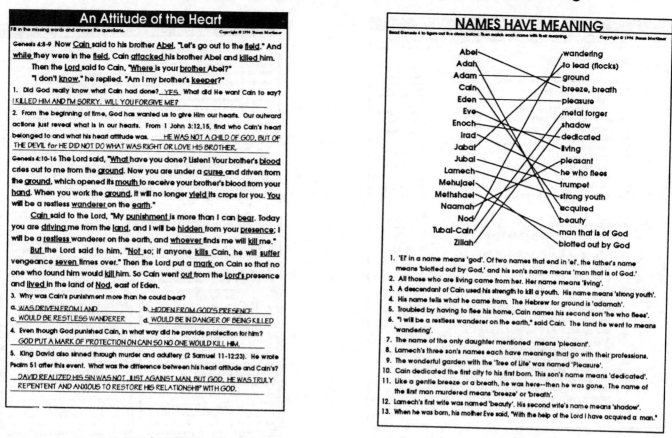

An Attitude of the Heart

Fill in the missing words and answer the questions. Copyright © 1994 Susan Mortimer

Genesis 4:8-9 Now <u>Cain</u> said to his brother <u>Abel</u>, "Let's go out to the <u>field</u>." And <u>while</u> they were in the <u>field</u>, Cain <u>attacked</u> his brother Abel and <u>killed</u> him.

Then the <u>Lord</u> said to Cain, "<u>Where</u> is your <u>brother</u> Abel?"

"I don't <u>know</u>," he replied. "Am I my brother's <u>keeper</u>?"

1. Did God really know what Cain had done? <u>YES</u> What did He want Cain to say?
<u>I KILLED HIM AND I'M SORRY. WILL YOU FORGIVE ME?</u>

2. From the beginning of time, God has wanted us to give Him our hearts. Our outward actions just reveal what is in our hearts. From 1 John 3:12,15, find who Cain's heart belonged to and what his heart attitude was. <u>HE WAS NOT A CHILD OF GOD, BUT OF THE DEVIL for HE DID NOT DO WHAT WAS RIGHT OR LOVE HIS BROTHER.</u>

Genesis 4:10-16 The Lord said, "<u>What</u> have you done? Listen! Your brother's <u>blood</u> cries out to me from the <u>ground</u>. Now you are under a <u>curse</u> and driven from the <u>ground</u>, which opened its mouth to receive your brother's blood from your <u>hand</u>. When you work the <u>ground</u>, it will no longer <u>yield</u> its crops for you. <u>You</u> will be a restless <u>wanderer</u> on the <u>earth</u>."

<u>Cain</u> said to the Lord, "My <u>punishment</u> is more than I can <u>bear</u>. Today you <u>are</u> <u>driving</u> me from the <u>land</u>, and I will be <u>hidden</u> from your <u>presence</u>; I will be a <u>restless</u> wanderer on the earth, and <u>whoever</u> finds me will <u>kill</u> me."

<u>But</u> the Lord said to him, "<u>Not</u> so; if anyone <u>kills</u> Cain, he will <u>suffer</u> vengeance <u>seven</u> times over." Then the Lord put a <u>mark</u> on Cain so that no one who found him would <u>kill</u> him. So Cain went <u>out</u> from the <u>Lord's</u> presence and <u>lived</u> in the land of <u>Nod</u>, east of Eden.

3. Why was Cain's punishment more than he could bear?
a. <u>WAS DRIVEN FROM LAND</u>   b. <u>HIDDEN FROM GOD'S PRESENCE</u>
c. <u>WOULD BE RESTLESS WANDERER</u>   d. <u>WOULD BE IN DANGER OF BEING KILLED</u>

4. Even though God punished Cain, in what way did he provide protection for him?
<u>GOD PUT A MARK OF PROTECTION ON CAIN SO NO ONE WOULD KILL HIM.</u>

5. King David also sinned through murder and adultery (2 Samuel 11-12:23). He wrote Psalm 51 after this event. What was the difference between his heart attitude and Cain's?
<u>DAVID REALIZED HIS SIN WAS NOT JUST AGAINST MAN BUT GOD. HE WAS TRULY REPENTENT AND ANXIOUS TO RESTORE HIS RELATIONSHIP WITH GOD.</u>

43

NAMES HAVE MEANING

Read Genesis 4 to figure out the clues below. Then match each name with that meaning. Copyright © 1994 Susan Mortimer

Abel	wandering
Adah	to lead (flocks)
Adam	ground
Cain	breeze, breath
Eden	pleasure
Eve	metal forger
Enoch	shadow
Irad	dedicated
Jabal	living
Jubal	pleasant
Lamech	he who flees
Mehujael	trumpet
Methshael	strong youth
Naamah	acquired
Nod	beauty
Tubal-Cain	man that is of God
Zillah	blotted out by God

1. 'El' in a name means 'god'. Of two names that end in 'el', the father's name means 'blotted out by God,' and his son's name means 'man that is of God.'
2. All those who are living came from her. Her name means 'living'.
3. A descendant of Cain used his strength to kill a youth. His name means 'strong youth'.
4. His name tells what he came from. The Hebrew for ground is 'adamah'.
5. Troubled by having to flee his home, Cain names his second son 'he who flees'.
6. "I will be a restless wanderer on the earth," said Cain. The land he went to means 'wandering'.
7. The name of the only daughter mentioned means 'pleasant'.
8. Lamech's three son's names each have meanings that go with their professions.
9. The wonderful garden with the 'Tree of Life' was named 'Pleasure'.
10. Cain dedicated the first city to his first born. This son's name means 'dedicated'.
11. Like a gentle breeze or a breath, he was here--then he was gone. The name of the first man murdered means 'breeze' or 'breath'.
12. Lamech's first wife was named 'beauty'. His second wife's name means 'shadow'.
13. When he was born, his mother Eve said, "With the help of the Lord I have acquired a man."

50

THE BIBLICAL FAMILY TREE OF MAN
Student is to color in the life-span on the graph as well.

NOAH -950
LAMECH-777   JAPHETH
METHUSELAH-969   HAM
ENOCH-365   SHEM-600
JARED-962   ARPHAXAD-438
MAHALALEL-830   SHELAH-433
KENAN-910   FLOOD LASTED   EBER-464
ENOSH-905   1 Year   PELEG-239
SETH-912   1 Month   REU-239
ADAM-930   27 Days   SERUG-230
CAIN   *Noah entered ark at age 600 (Gen. 7:6). Noah left*   NAHOR-148
MEHUJAEL   *the ark at 601 and 27 days, 2cd month (Gen. 8:14).*   TERAH-205
METHUSHAEL   JABAL   ABRAM (ABRAHAM)-175
LAMECH WIFE-ADAH   JUBAL
WIFE-ZILLAH   NAANAH
TUBAL-CAIN

49

51

ANSWER KEY: GENESIS—BEGINNINGS

A chiasmus is an inversion of parallel phrases, clauses, sentences or paragraphs. The writer builds to an apex or focal point (which is the turning point of his story), and then recedes to an ending, matching each point. Here are two examples.

In the Hebrew word order, this is how Genesis 6: 8-9 would read.

A. Noah
  B. found favor in the eyes of the LORD
    C. these are the generations of Noah
      D. Noah was a righteous man
      D. perfect he was
    C. in his generation
  B. with God walked
A. Noah

Genesis 7:21-22

A. Every living thing that moved on earth perished
  B. birds,
    C. livestock, wild animals, all the creatures that swarmed over the earth
      D. and all mankind
        E. everything on dry land that had the breath of life in its nostrils died
        E. everything on the face of the earth was wiped out
      D. men
    C. and animals and the creatures that moved along the ground
  B. and the birds of the air
A. were wiped from the earth

In the first selection, the focal point is "Noah was a righteous man, perfect he was." Then each beginning and ending point are matched. What phrase matches "these are the generations of Noah"?
IN HIS GENERATION

What phrase matches "with God walked"?
FOUND FAVOR IN THE EYES OF THE LORD

What is the focal point of the second selection?
EVERYTHING ON DRY LAND THAT HAD THE BREATH OF LIFE IN ITS NOSTRILS DIED
EVERYTHING ON THE FACE OF EARTH WAS WIPED OUT

What phrase matches "and the birds of the air"?
BIRDS

What phrase matches "Every living thing that moved on earth perished"?
WERE WIPED FROM THE EARTH

Now draw lines connecting each matching point in the second selection.

BEFORE ABRAHAM WAS BY ISAAC KIKAWADA AND ARTHUR QUINN, ABINGDON PRESS NASHVILLE © 1985, PG. 86-95

53

54

CHIASTIC STRUCTURE OF THE FLOOD

A. (6:1) Men increased in number on the earth
  B. (6:10) Noah and his three sons, Shem, Ham, and Japheth
    C. (6:12-13) Since man's heart is only evil, earth will be destroyed (by flood)
      D. (6:18-20) God makes a covenant with Noah
        E. (6:22) Noah builds ark
          F. (7:1-3) God commands to enter ark
            G. (7:4) 7 days wait until God sends rain
              H. (7:10) 7 days wait before flood came
                I. (7:14) Last animal enters the ark
                  J. (7:16) The Lord shuts the door
                    K. (7:17) 40 days and 40 nights the floods come
                      L. (7:19) Highest mountains covered
                        M. (7:24) 150 days waters prevails
                          N. (8:1) BUT GOD REMEMBERED NOAH
                      M. (8:3) 150 days waters recedes
                    L. (8:5) Mountain tops become visible
                  K. (8:6a) 40 days water abates
                J. (8:6b) Noah opens window of the ark
              I. (8:7) First creature (a raven) leaves the ark
            H. (8:10) 7 days wait to send out dove
          G. (8:12) 7 days wait to send out dove again
        F. (8:15-16) God commands to leave ark
      E. (8:20) Noah builds altar
    D. (8:21) God makes a covenant with Noah and all life on earth
    C. (8:21) Though man's heart only evil, earth will NOT be destroyed (by flood)
  B. (9:19) Noah and Shem, Ham and Japheth
A. (9:19) People increase and scatter over the earth

55

NOAH'S ZOO

AMPHIBIANS	3,000
MAMMALS	4.500
REPTILES	6,000
BIRDS	8,600
FISH	20,000
INVERTEBRATES	1,150,000

12% > SHEEP
32% BETWEEN RATS & SHEEP
56% < RATS

HOW BIG WAS THE ARK?

IT COULD HOLD AT LEAST
125,280 SHEEP-SIZE ANIMALS

59/62

Remembering God's Awesome Acts: Answer Page

EVALUATING THE SUMERIAN/BABYLONIAN GODS & GODDESSES

Check one in each group of two. Give an examples from the Epic of Gilgamish that demonstrates your choice. © 1996 Susan Mortimer

Sumerian & Babylonian gods and goddesses:

- ☐ are holy.
- ■ are sinful. Example: ANY EXAMPLE FROM THE EPIC OF GILGAMISH WHICH ILLUSTRATES THE CHARACTERISTIC OF THE SUMERIAN & BABYLONIAN GODS AND GODDESSES IS CORRECT.
- ■ are vengeful. Example:
- ☐ are loving.

- ☐ are long-suffering. Example:
- ■ are quick to anger.

- ■ have limited power. Example:
- ☐ are all powerful.

- ☐ have nothing to fear. Example:
- ■ can be frightened.

- ■ are upset with the truth. Example:
- ☐ are lovers of truth.

- ■ can be outwitted. Example:
- ☐ have the final word.

- ☐ formed man with great care and purposefulness. Example:
- ■ formed man haphazardly and carelessly.

- ■ behavior is deceiving, demanding and devastating. Example:
- ☐ behavior is considerate, caring and consistent.

Look at the choices you did not check. Do they describe the God of the Bible?
Write a sentence comparing the gods of Sumer with the God of the Bible.
_____
_____

69

Truth and Twisted Truth in the Epic of Gilgamish

Answer each section correctly. © 1996 Susan Mortimer

Truth about the flood in the Gilgamish Epic:
What kind of man was saved? RIGHTEOUS MAN
What happened to all mankind not on the ship? THEY PERISHED
What besides people was saved on the ship? ANIMALS
What was offered after the flood? AN OFFERING

Where the flood stories differ, check which account is believable.

The Gilgamish Account:	The Biblical Account:
☐ The ship was built in seven days.	■ The ark took 120 years to build.
☐ The ship was a square cube. (A square ship would tumble over and over in high waves)	■ the ark was built like a barge. (A barge like the ark is stable in waves over 200 feet.)
☐ A six day flood covered the earth.	■ It took 40 days and nights of rain plus underground water to cover the earth.
☐ In no time at all the water receded.	■ It took nearly a year for the water to dry.

Truth about Promiscuous Sex in One of the Earliest Civilizations.
(Circle the correct word in the parentheses)

It is surprising that throughout early civilizations in the fertile crescent, with their goddesses of (promiscuity, faithfulness), and temple (prostitutes, virgins) the story of Gilgamish is the (least, most) told epic.

In the Epic, Ishtar is not (respected, rejected). She is shown not as the goddess of 'love,' as most scholars call her, but as the goddess of 'lust'. Ishtar (did, did not) promise eternal love to Gilgamish, but power and wealth. Even with those as bribes, he (was, was not) enticed, for he had seen the wake of (disaster, benefits) she had left behind her. She showed (no love, great love) towards others, choosing them only for their beauty and what she could (get from, give to) them. She (gave to, used) them, (helped, ruined) them, and then (stayed with, deserted) them. With example after example, Gilgamish gave (little, overwhelming) evidence to show that Ishtar (destroyed, benefited) men by her involvements with them.

Gilgamish himself left a trail of (hope, pain) behind him. The mothers, husbands and fathers of the women he (protected, took) were (angry and distraught, pleased and happy). Regardless of any other redeeming qualities he may have had, they wanted him (severely punished, profoundly rewarded).

In a culture where sexual impurity was (rampant, rare), by their own admission they recognized it as "(good, stinking) deeds", and a "(fragrance of loveliness, stench and foulness)". The Epic of Gilgamish clearly shows the universal truth that promiscuous behavior (destroys, benefits) others and is always (right, wrong).

70

Comparing the Bible with the Gilgamish Myth

Question	Genesis	Gilgamish Epic
Compare how man was created in both accounts.	GOD CREATED IN HIS IMAGE FROM DUST OF EARTH AND BREATHED LIFE INTO HIM	FORMED DEFECTIVELY FOR THE GODS' ENTERTAINMENT
Compare what Matt. 19:4-6 says about a wife versus the kind of wife Ishtar was.	MARRIAGE SHOULD BE A PERMANENT JOINING OF TWO PEOPLE AS ONE	ISHTAR WENT FROM MAN TO MAN, USING, DESTROYING AND LEAVING THEM
What was the purpose of mankind?	CREATED TO HAVE FELLOWSHIP WITH GOD	TO DO THE WORK FOR THE GODS
What was the reason for the flood?	TO DESTROY THE WICKED PEOPLE	BECAUSE A GOD'S SLEEP WAS DISTURBED BY THEIR NOISE
Why were Noah and Utnapishtim warned?	NOAH WAS A RIGHTEOUS MAN	UTNAPISHTIM WAS GOOD AND HUMBLE
Describe the ships. (Length, height, number of floors, its stability)	450 X 75 X 45 3 STORIES VERY STABLE	120 X 120 X 120 6 STORIES UNSTABLE
How long did it take to build the ships?	120 YEARS	7 DAYS
What was saved?	NOAH, WIFE, 3 SONS, THEIR WIVES, AND ANIMALS	FAMILY, KIN, AND ANIMALS
Where did the water come from?	SPRINGS FROM DEEP AND FLOOD GATES OF HEAVEN	STORM
How long did it rain?	40 DAYS AND NIGHTS	7 DAYS
Where did they come to land?	MOUNTAINS OF ARARAT	MOUNT NITISI
Name the birds in the order they were sent out.	RAVEN, DOVE, DOVE	DOVE, SWALLOW, RAVEN
What was the reason for the offerings?	TO THANK GOD FOR HIS PROTECTION	TO APPEASE THE GODS
How long did each man live after the flood?	350 YEARS	ETERNALLY
How did the serpent affect man's destiny?	LIED TO EVE IN THE GARDEN TO ENTICE HER TO DISOBEY GOD	ATE THE PLANT SO MAN COULD NOT HAVE ETERNAL LIFE

71

NAMES HAVE MEANING 2

Read Genesis 5, 9 & 10 to figure out the clues below. Then match each name with their meaning. Copyright © 1996 Susan Mortimer

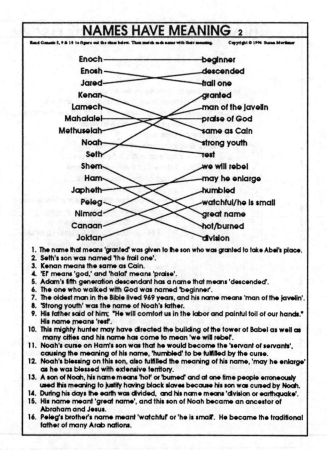

Enoch — beginner
Enosh — descended
Jared — frail one
Kenan — granted
Lamech — man of the javelin
Mahalalel — praise of God
Methuselah — same as Cain
Noah — strong youth
Seth — rest
Shem — we will rebel
Ham — may he enlarge
Japheth — humbled
Peleg — watchful/he is small
Nimrod — great name
Canaan — hot/burned
Joktan — division

1. The name that means 'granted' was given to the son who was granted to take Abel's place.
2. Seth's son was named 'the frail one'.
3. Kenan means the same as Cain.
4. 'El' means 'god,' and 'halal' means 'praise'.
5. Adam's fifth generation descendant has a name that means 'descended'.
6. The one who walked with God was named 'beginner'.
7. The oldest man in the Bible lived 969 years, and his name means 'man of the javelin'.
8. 'Strong youth' was the name of Noah's father.
9. His father said of him; "He will comfort us in the labor and painful toil of our hands." His name means 'rest'.
10. This mighty hunter may have directed the building of the tower of Babel as well as many cities and his name has come to mean 'we will rebel'.
11. Noah's curse on Ham's son was that he would become the 'servant of servants', causing the meaning of his name, 'humbled' to be fulfilled by the curse.
12. Noah's blessing on this son, also fulfilled the meaning of his name, 'may he enlarge' as he was blessed with extensive territory.
13. A son of Noah, his name means 'hot' or 'burned' and at one time people erroneously used this meaning to justify having black slaves because his son was cursed by Noah.
14. During his days the earth was divided, and his name means 'division or earthquake'.
15. His name meant 'great name', and this son of Noah became an ancestor of Abraham and Jesus.
16. Peleg's brother's name meant 'watchful' or 'he is small'. He became the traditional father of many Arab nations.

80

Remembering God's Awesome Acts: Answer Page

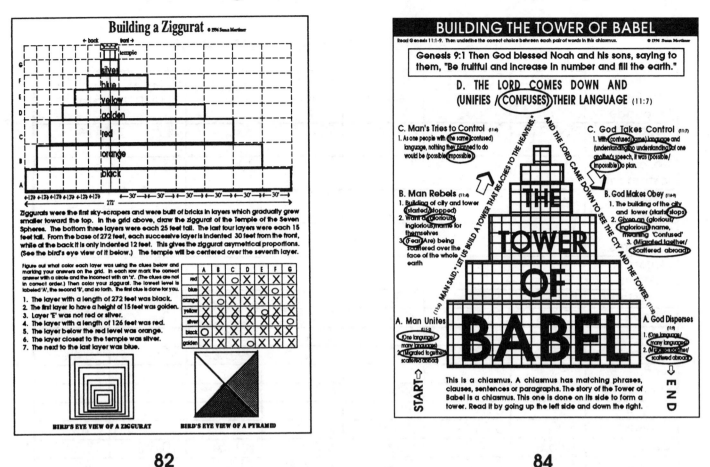

82

84

A WORLD OF LANGUAGES

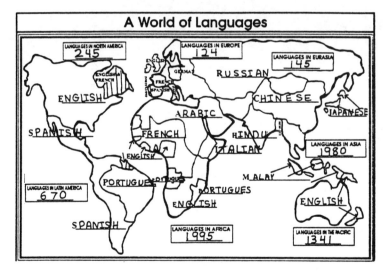

91

ANSWER KEY: DELUGE AND DISPERSION

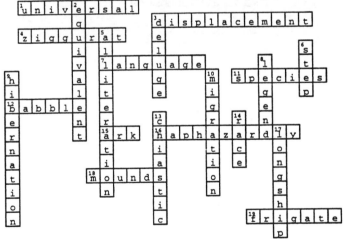

92

Information for <u>Getting to Know a Country</u> pages.

Statistics	Mexico	Ecuador	Vietnam	Australia	Turkey	Nigeria	Egypt
Official language	Spanish	Spanish	Vietnamese	English	Turkish	English	Arabic
No. of languages	234	22	88	234	35	427	11
No. of New testaments	93	10	16	8	10	55	3
Portions of Bible	39	5	20	26	13	57	3
No. of scriptures	132	15	36	34	23	112	6
Major religions							
Protestant	5.2%	3.8%	0.8%	39.6%	0.03%	26.5%	0.85%
Catholic	87.5%	93.3%	8.9%	26.3%	0.02%	13%	0.32%
Jews	0.1%	0.01%		0.5%	0.04%		
Muslim	0.05%		0.2%	1.5%	99.8%	40%	85.4%
Hindu							
Buddhist			52%	0.8%			
Animist		0.5%	3%			10%	
Nonreligious	5.3%	0.74%	29.8%	26.6%			0.4%
Other	1.85%	1.65%	5.3%	4.7%	0.11%	10.5%	13.03%
Income per person	$1,990	$1,040	$189	$14,400	$1,360	$319	$790

Information from Operation World, 5th Ed., Zondervan Publishing House, 5300 Patterson Ave. SE, Grand Rapids, MI, © 1993 Patrick J StG Johnstone.

VIETNAMESE LANGUAGE STUDY

Λwŋ=you   ŋu = sleep
zë = hours   lΛw = long

1. I STUDY
2. YOU STUDY
3. I SLEEP
4. YOU SLEEP TWO HOURS
5. YOU STUDY HOW MANY HOURS
6. I STUDY HOW LONG
7. TWO HOURS I SLEEP
8. HOW LONG YOU SLEEP
9. HOW LONG I STUDY

96

MEXZQUITAL OTOMI LANGUAGE PROBLEM

FANI = HORSE
CATYO= DOG

MIŠI = CAT

4. CHASE THE HORSE
5. FOLLOW YOUR CAT
6. RESCUE MY DOG
7. CHASE MY DOG
8. RESCUE THE HORSE
9. FOLLOW MY LITTLE DOG
10. CHASE YOUR WHITE CAT
11. FOLLOW YOUR HORSE
12. CHASE MY BIG HORSE

100

WAORANI LANGUAGE STUDY

D. daddy rainforest goes
C. 1. daddy rainforest goes
   2. doggy goes
   3. daddy trail goes
   4. doggy doesn't trail goes
   5. just rainforest goes
   6. doesn't fast goes
B. 7. red monkey comes
   8. fast goes
   9. daddy then shoots
  10. red monkey then rainforest falls
  11. doesn't trail falls

102/103

WAORANI LANGUAGE STUDY

A. 12. doggy then fast rainforest goes
  13. takes
  14. doesn't eats
  15. just fast takes
  16. daddy then takes
  17. doesn't rainforest eats
  18. just home comes
  19. cones
  20. then eats
  21. fast eats
  22. doggy then home eats

102/103

Remembering God's Awesome Acts: Answer Page

WAORANI LANGUAGE STUDY

3. Daddy goes on the trail.
4. The doggy doesn't go on the trail.
5. The doggy goes through the rainforest.
6. He doesn't go fast.
8. He goes fast.
10. Then the red monkey falls in the rainforest.
11. He doesn't fall on the trail.
12. Then the doggy goes quickly into the rainforest.
14. But he doesn't eat it.
15. He gets it fast.
16. Then daddy takes it.
17. But he doesn't eat it in the rainforest.
19. When he comes home,
20. he eats the monkey
21. and he eats it fast.
22. The doggy comes home and eats too.

IGALA LANGUAGE STUDY
(Pages 275 and 277 are yellow.)

F. cut + weeds = <u>cut</u> the weeds
   du + igbala = <u>d'igbala</u>
   ko + una = <u>k'una</u>
   <u>ne + opia</u> = n'opia
   ñmo + omi = <u>ñm'omi</u>
   drank + water = <u>drank the water</u>
   ne + ukoche = <u>n'ukoche</u>

E. e + da = <u>eda</u>
   e + la = <u>ela</u>
   -ing + buy = <u>buying</u>
   e + ta = <u>eta</u>
   e + ra = <u>era</u>

IGALA LANGUAGE STUDY
(Note: Articles such as 'a', 'the' are optional.)

D. 1. Mother went to the farm.
2. She carried the machete.
3. Father went to the farm.
4. He carried the big hoe.
5. The child went to the farm.
6. He carried fire and water.
C. 7. Mother used the machete to cut weeds.
8. She began sweating.
9. The child gave water to (mother) to drink.
10. Father used the big hoe to build mounds.
11. He began sweating.
12. Mother gave water to (father) to drink.
B. 13. Mother gave the machete to the child.
14. The child used the machete to cut firewood.

IGALA LANGUAGE STUDY

15. He built a fire.
16. He put firewood into the fire.
17. The firewood ran out.
18. The child put the yam into the fire.
19. The child began sweating.
20. He drank water. The yam was cooked.
21. The child gave the yam to mother to eat.
22. He gave the yam to father to eat.
23. Father ate the yam.
24. He drank the water.
25. Mother ate the yam.
26. She drank the water.
27. The child ate the yam.
28. He drank the water.
29. The yam ran out.
30. The water ran out.

Remembering God's Awesome Acts: Answer Page

Turkish Language Problem

Fill in the lines under the Turkish sentences with the English word or picture for each word. Fill in the spaces on page 2 with the correct words. Read over the helpful hints on page 2 before you start.
© 1991, 1996 Susan Mortimer

1. The eighth man gave five apples.
sekizinji | adam | beš | elma | verdi
8th | 🚹 | 5 | ♂ | he gave

2. Ten men gave five apples (on the) fifth day.
on adam bešinji gŭnde beš elma verdiler
10 | 🚹 | 5th | day | 5 | ♂ | they gave

3. He gave ten apples (in the) eighth month.
sekizinji ayda on elma verdi
8th | month | 10 | ♂ | he gave

4. Nine men gave ten apples to five of us.
dokuz adam bešimize on elma verdiler
9 | 🚹 | 5 of us | 10 | ♂ | they gave

5. The fifth man took eight of us apples.
besinji adam sekizimize elma aldi
5th | 🚹 | 8 of us | ♂ | he took

6. The man gave ten of us five apples apiece.
adam onumuza bešer elma verdi
🚹 | 10 of us | 5 apiece | ♂ | he gave

7. He took nine of us eight apples apiece.
dokumuza sekizer elma aldi
9 of us | 8 apiece | ♂ | he took

8. Ten of us took the man eight apples (on the) ninth day.
onumuz dokuzunju gŭnde adama sekiz elma aldik
10 of us | 9th | day | 🚹 | 8 | ♂ | we took

9. Nine of us gave eight men ten apples apiece.
dokuzumuz sekiz adama onar elma verdik
9 of us | 8 | 🚹 | 10 apiece | ♂ | we gave

A lesson taught to college students learning to be Bible Translators. Taken from *Laboratory Manual for Morphology and Syntax*, S.I.L.

113

Turkish Language Problem (page 2)

© 1991, 1996 Susan Mortimer

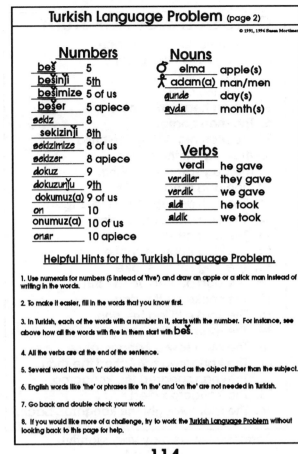

Numbers
beš	5
besinji	5th
bešimize	5 of us
bešer	5 apiece
sekiz	8
sekizinji	8th
sekizimize	8 of us
sekizer	8 apiece
dokuz	9
dokuzunju	9th
dokumuz(a)	9 of us
on	10
onumuz(a)	10 of us
onar	10 apiece

Nouns
♂ elma	apple(s)
🚹 adam(a)	man/men
gunde	day(s)
ayda	month(s)

Verbs
verdi	he gave
verdiler	they gave
verdik	we gave
aldi	he took
aldik	we took

Helpful Hints for the Turkish Language Problem.

1. Use numerals for numbers (5 instead of 'five') and draw an apple or a stick man instead of writing in the words.

2. To make it easier, fill in the words that you know first.

3. In Turkish, each of the words with a number in it, starts with the number. For instance, see above how all the words with five in them start with beš.

4. All the verbs are at the end of the sentence.

5. Several word have an 'a' added when they are used as the object rather than the subject.

6. English words like 'the' or phrases like 'in the' and 'on the' are not needed in Turkish.

7. Go back and double check your work.

8. If you would like more of a challenge, try to work the Turkish Language Problem without looking back to this page for help.

114

OOLDEA LANGUAGE STUDY

C. child camp sat
dog ground sat
dog child bit
child cried
man child heard
man came
man child picked up

B. dog camp left
dog echidna saw
dog an ambush made
echidna dog speared
echidna hole dug
dog cried

118

OOLDEA LANGUAGE STUDY

A. dog snake heard
dog snake saw
dog snake picked up
snake dog bit
snake dog killed

man camp left
man kangaroo saw
kangaroo man scratched
man kangaroo speared
kangaroo died
man kangaroo brought back

119

Remembering God's Awesome Acts: Answer Page

OOLDEA LANGUAGE STUDY

1. The child sat in the camp.
2. A dog sat on the ground.
3. The dog bit the child.
4. The child cried.
5. A man heard the child.
6. The man came.
7. The man picked up the child.
8. The dog left the camp.
9. The dog saw an echidna.
10. The dog ambushed it.
11. The echidna speared the dog.
12. The echidna dug a hole.
13. The dog cried.
14. The dog heard a snake.
15. The dog saw a snake.
16. The dog picked up the snake.
17. The snake bit the dog.
18. The snake killed the dog.
19. The man left the camp.
20. The man saw a kangaroo.
21. The kangaroo scratched the man.
22. The man speared the kangaroo.
23. The kangaroo died.
24. The man brought the kangaroo back.

Correct answers may vary slightly!

121

INDO-EUROPEAN LANGUAGES-ROUNDABOUT AND BACK AGAIN

(LEFT TO RIGHT)
quintet
cinquefoil
five
pentagon
punch

125

INDO-EUROPEAN LANGUAGE WHEEL

The sequence within each language family may vary.

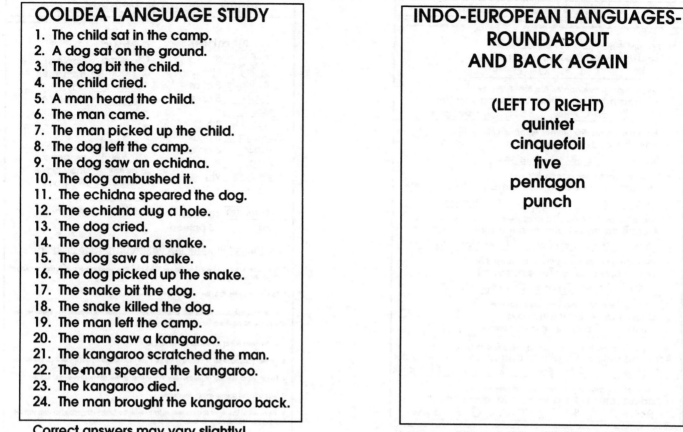

Answers at bottom of workbook page.

128

127

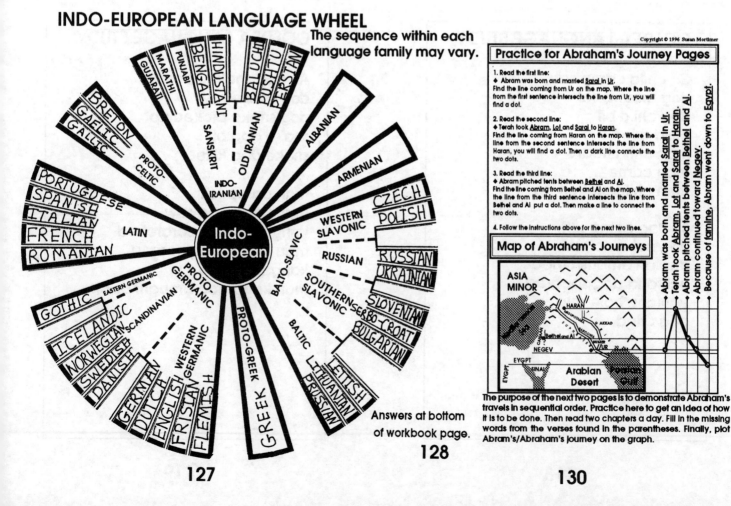

Copyright © 1996 Susan Mortimer

Practice for Abraham's Journey Pages

1. Read the first line:
◆ Abram was born and married <u>Sarai</u> in <u>Ur</u>.
Find the line coming from Ur on the map. Where the line from the first sentence intersects the line for Ur, you will find a dot.

2. Read the second line:
◆ Terah took <u>Abram</u>, <u>Lot</u> and <u>Sarai</u> to <u>Haran</u>.
Find the line coming from Haran on the map. Where the line from the second sentence intersects the line from Haran, you will find a dot. Then a dark line connects the two dots.

3. Read the third line:
◆ Abram pitched tents between <u>Bethel</u> and <u>Ai</u>.
Find the line coming from Bethel and Ai on the map. Where the line from the third sentence intersects the line from Bethel and Ai put a dot. Then make a line to connect the two dots.

4. Follow the instructions above for the next two lines.

Map of Abraham's Journeys

The purpose of the next two pages is to demonstrate Abraham's travels in sequential order. Practice here to get an idea of how it is to be done. Then read two chapters a day. Fill in the missing words from the verses found in the parentheses. Finally, plot Abram's/Abraham's journey on the graph.

130

Remembering God's Awesome Acts: Answer Page

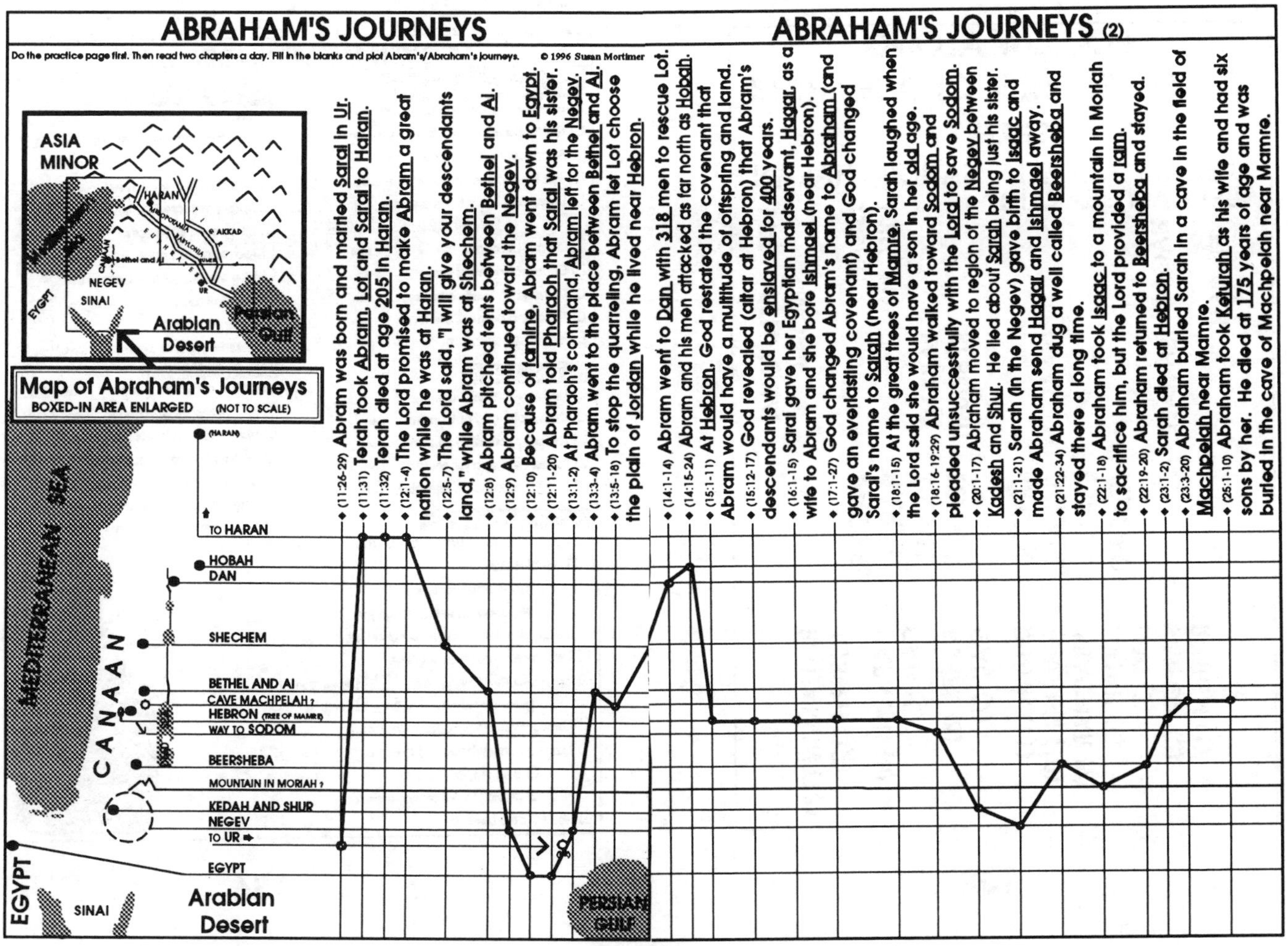

ABRAHAM'S JOURNEYS   ABRAHAM'S JOURNEYS (2)

Do the practice page first. Then read two chapters a day. Fill in the blanks and plot Abram's/Abraham's journeys. © 1996 Susan Mortimer

Map of Abraham's Journeys
BOXED-IN AREA ENLARGED (NOT TO SCALE)

Map labels: ASIA MINOR · HARAN · AKKAD · Bethel and Ai · NEGEV · SINAI · EGYPT · Arabian Desert · MEDITERRANEAN SEA · CANAAN · PERSIAN GULF

Y-axis labels: (HARAN) · TO HARAN · HOBAH · DAN · SHECHEM · BETHEL AND AI · CAVE MACHPELAH? · HEBRON (TREE OF MAMRE) · WAY TO SODOM · BEERSHEBA · MOUNTAIN IN MORIAH? · KEDAH AND SHUR · NEGEV · TO UR → · EGYPT

- (11:26-29) Abram was born and married Sarai in Ur.
- (11:31) Terah took Abram, Lot and Sarai to Haran.
- (11:32) Terah died at age 205 in Haran.
- (12:1-4) The Lord promised to make Abram a great nation while he was at Haran.
- (12:5-7) The Lord said, "I will give your descendants land," while Abram was at Shechem.
- (12:8) Abram pitched tents between Bethel and Ai.
- (12:9) Abram continued toward the Negev.
- (12:10) Because of famine, Abram went down to Egypt.
- (12:11-20) Abram told Pharaoh that Sarai was his sister.
- (13:1-2) At Pharaoh's command, Abram left for the Negev.
- (13:3-4) Abram went to the place between Bethel and Ai.
- (13:5-18) To stop the quarreling, Abram let Lot choose the plain of Jordan while he lived near Hebron.
- (14:1-14) Abram went to Dan with 318 men to rescue Lot.
- (14:15-24) Abram and his men attacked as far north as Hobah.
- (15:1-11) At Hebron, God restated the covenant that Abram would have a multitude of offspring and land.
- (15:12-17) God revealed (altar at Hebron) that Abram's descendants would be enslaved for 400 years.
- (16:1-15) Sarai gave her Egyptian maidservant, Hagar, as a wife to Abram and she bore Ishmael (near Hebron).
- (17:1-27) God changed Abram's name to Abraham (and gave an everlasting covenant) and God changed Sarai's name to Sarah (near Hebron).
- (18:1-15) At the great trees of Mamre, Sarah laughed when the Lord said she would have a son in her old age.
- (18:16-19:29) Abraham walked toward Sodom and pleaded unsuccessfully with the Lord to save Sodom.
- (20:1-17) Abraham moved to region of the Negev between Kadesh and Shur. He lied about Sarah being just his sister.
- (21:1-21) Sarah (in the Negev) gave birth to Isaac and made Abraham send Hagar and Ishmael away.
- (21:22-34) Abraham dug a well called Beersheba and stayed there a long time.
- (22:1-18) Abraham took Isaac to a mountain in Moriah to sacrifice him, but the Lord provided a ram.
- (22:19-20) Abraham returned to Beersheba and stayed.
- (23:1-2) Sarah died at Hebron.
- (23:3-20) Abraham buried Sarah in a cave in the field of Machpelah near Mamre.
- (25:1-10) Abraham took Keturah as his wife and had six sons by her. He died at 175 years of age and was buried in the cave of Machpelah near Mamre.

131/133

UR OF THE CHALDEANS

- ❏ Wheat and barley, dates and vegetables were grown.
- ■ Goats, donkeys and cattle had been domesticated.
- ❏ Pigs and sheep were raised for meat and wool.
- ❏ Sacred prayers were sung to the gods by large choirs.
- ■ The wheel was made from three pieces of wood.
- ■ Musical instruments like the lyre and harps were used.
- ■ Fish was caught to expand their diet.
- ❏ Many houses were made with sun-baked bricks.
- ❏ Protective walls were placed around the cities.
- ❏ Houses did not have windows.
- ❏ Cattle were used to plow fields.
- ■ Rope was used to lead animals.
- ❏ There were frequent wars against city-states.
- ■ Chariots were used in battles.
- ■ There were chairs to sit in.
- ❏ The clothing was made out of wool.
- ❏ Poor houses were made out of reeds.
- ■ Nobles and priests shaved their heads.

135

UR OF THE CHALDEANS (2)

- ■ There were no horses, only domesticated donkeys.
- ❏ Town grew and became self-governing as city-states.
- ❏ Houses were often built around a open courtyard.
- ■ People carried items in a bundle on their backs.
- ❏ They had instruments like flutes and oboes.
- ■ People in the art from Ur have large eyes.
- ❏ Important buildings were made of fired-baked bricks.
- ❏ Farmers gave one-third of what they grew to the priest.
- ❏ Royal graves in Ur had dozen of bodies.
- ❏ Farms were outside the walls.
- ■ The wheel had been invented.
- ❏ Each town had its own god.
- ❏ Fields were watered by irrigation.
- ■ Cuneiform writing was invented.
- ❏ There was little wood and few stones.
- ❏ Summers were warm and winters were cool.
- ❏ Cattle were the most prized possessions.
- ❏ Temples were built in the middle of town.

137

FOLLOW ALONG
THE FAMILY TREE OF ABRAHAM

TERAH

ABRAM   SARAI   NAHOR   HARAN
(ABRAHAM) (SARAH)

KETURAH   HAGAR   ISHMAEL   ISCAH   MILCAH   LOT   BEN-AMMI   MOAB

ISAAC   REBEKAH   LABAN

JACOB (ISRAEL)   ESAU (EDOM)   LEAH   ZILPAH   BILHAH   RACHEL   NAPHTALI (6)   DAN (5)   JOSEPH (12)   BENJAMIN (13)

DINAH (11)   ZEBULUN (10)   ISSACHAR (9)   JUDAH (4)   LEVI (3)   SIMEON (2)   REUBEN (1)   ASHER (8)   GAD (7)

132

COVENANT WITH ABRAHAM

Fill in the chapters and verses described by each statement as you study the life of Abraham. There may be more than one reference. © 1996 Susan Mortimer

COMMANDS AND CONDITIONS:
- Look north, south, east and west: Gen. _13:14_
- Go to the land I will show you: Gen. _12:1_
- Sacrifice your son Isaac: Gen. _22:2_
- Walk the length and breath of the land: Gen. _13:17_
- Leave your ☐ country and people: Gen. _12:1_
  - ☐ father's household: Gen. _12:1_
- Do not be afraid: Gen. _15:1_
- Circumcise every male: Gen. _17:10-14_
- Do not lay a hand on the boy: Gen. _22:12_
- Take and possess the land: Gen. _15:7_
- Bring a heifer, pigeon, ram, dove, goat: Gen. _15:9_

PROMISED LAND:
- I will give the land: Gen. _12:7; 13:14,17; 15:7, 18_
- The whole land of Canaan: Gen. _17:8_
- Everlasting possession/covenant: Gen. _17:7, 8_
- Possess the cities of you enemies: Gen. _22:17_
- From Egyptian river to Euphrates: Gen. _15:18_

BLESSINGS AND CURSES:
- Is anything too hard for the Lord?: Gen. _18:14_
- I will bless ☐ you: Gen. _12:2, 22:17_
  - ☐ those who bless you: Gen. _12:3_
  - ☐ all people on earth through you: Gen. _12:3_
  - ☐ all nations through your offspring: Gen. _22:18_
- I will make your name great: Gen. _12:2_
- I am your ☐ God Almighty: Gen. _17:1_ ☐ shield: Gen. _15:1_
  - ☐ great reward: Gen. _15:1_ ☐ Lord: Gen. _15:7_
- I brought you out of Ur of the Chaldeans: Gen. _15:7_
- I will ☐ curse whoever curses you: Gen. _12:3_
  - ☐ be your/their God: Gen. _17:7, 8_
  - ☐ punish the nation that enslaves: Gen. _15:14_
- You will be a blessing: Gen. _12:2_

DESCENDANTS WILL BE:
- Strangers in a country: Gen. _15:13_
- Like sand on the seashore: Gen. _22:17_
- Enslaved: Gen. _15:13_
- Like stars in the heavens: Gen. _15:5, 22:17_
- Greatly increased in numbers: Gen. _17:2_
- Mistreated 400 years: Gen. _15:13_
- Too many to count: Gen. _13:16, 15:5_
- Like the dust of the earth: Gen. _13:16_
- Very fruitful: Gen. _17:6_
- Given this land: Gen. _13:15, 17:8_
- Returned here in 4th generation: Gen. _15:16_

PROMISE OF A SON:
- Father of many nations: Gen. _17:5_
- My covenant will be with Isaac: Gen. _17:19_
- Make you into a great nation: Gen. _12:2_
- Sarah will bear Isaac/son: Gen. _17:16, 19; 18:10, 14_
  - ☐ be mother of nations/kings: Gen. _17:16_
- Kings will come from you: Gen. _17:6_
- A son from your own body: Gen. _15:4_

136

Melchizedek and Jesus Compared

The verses listed below contain many similarities found in the lives of Melchizedek and Jesus Christ. Read these verses and write each reference in the correct box. Also answer the question below the grid.
Copyright © 1996 Susan Mortimer

Similarities	Melchizedek	Jesus
Name is title meaning "King of Righteousness". (Melek="king", Zedek="righteousness")	Hebrews 7:2b	I Corinthians 1:30
Was called "King of Peace". (Salem=Peace)	Hebrews 7:2c	Isaiah 9:6
Was made high priest by "the most high God".	Hebrews 7:1	Hebrews 5:10
Was not descendant of priestly line of Levi.	Hebrews 7:6	Hebrews 7:14-17
Was given tithes out of love and obedience and not because of law.	Hebrews 7:4	2 Corinthians 9:7
Brought out bread and wine.	Genesis 14:18-19	Matthew 26:26-29
Was without beginning of days or end of life.	Hebrews 7:3	Hebrews 7:23-25

Hebrews 7:23-25   Hebrews 7:2b   Hebrews 7:14-17   Hebrews 7:6
I Corinthians 1:30   Hebrews 7:4   2 Corinthians 9:7   Genesis 14:18-19
Isaiah 9:6   Hebrews 7:2c   Matthew 26:26-29   Hebrews 7:3
Hebrews 5:10   Hebrews 7:1

Read Hebrews 4:14-16 and briefly tell what kind of a high priest Jesus is.

JESUS UNDERSTANDS OUR WEAKNESSES AND HAS BEEN TEMPTED LIKE WE ARE, YET WITHOUT SIN.

HE IS APPROACHABLE AND READY TO GIVE US MERCY AND GRACE IN OUR TIMES OF NEED.

146

God Rescues the Righteous

Fill in the missing words as you read 2 Peter 2:4-9a NIV.
Copyright © 1996 Susan Mortimer

For _If_ God did not _spare_ angels when they _sinned_, but sent them to _hell_, putting them into gloomy _dungeons_ to be held for _judgment_;

_If_ he did not _spare_ the _ancient_ world when he brought the _flood_ on its _ungodly_ people, but _protected_ Noah, a preacher of _righteousness_, and _seven_ others;

_If_ he _condemned_ the cities of _Sodom_ and _Gomorrah_ by _burning_ them to _ashes_, and _made_ them an _example_ of what is going to _happen_ to the _ungodly_;

and _If_ he _rescued_ Lot, a _righteous_ man, who was _distressed_ by the _filthy_ lives of _lawless_ men (for that _righteous_ man, _living_ among them _day_ after day, was _tormented_ in his _righteous_ soul by the _lawless_ deeds he saw and _heard_)—

_If_ this is so,

Then the _Lord_ knows how to _rescue_ godly men from _trials_ and to hold the _unrighteous_ for the day of judgment....
2 Peter 2:4-9a NIV

The Coming Day of Judgment

What is God's perspective of time? (2 Peter 3:8b)
One day is like a thousand years, & a thousand years are like a day.

Why does God seem slow to keep His promise to return? (2 Peter 3:9)
He is patient, not wanting anyone to perish.

What will happen when He returns? (2 Peter 3:10)
The heavens will disappear, and everything will be destroyed by fire.

How are we to live today in an unrighteous world? (2 Peter 3:11b-14)
We ought to live holy and godly lives so that we will be found spot-less, blameless and at peace with Him, and be looking forward to a new heaven and new earth.

147

Remembering God's Awesome Acts: Answer Page

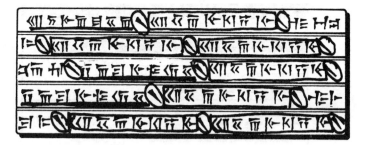

148

(Note: Vowels in parentheses do not have to be included to be correct.)

1. G. Guess: D-A-R-H-E-U-SH
MODERN: D(a)-A-R(a)-Y(a)-W(a)-U-SH(a)

2. G. Guess: KH-SH-H-E-R-SH-E
MODERN: H(a)-SH(a)-Y(a)-A-R(a)-SH(a)-A

3. G. Guess: G-O-SH-T-A-S-P
MODERN: W(i)-I-SH(a)-T(a)-A-S(a)-P(a)

4. G. Guess: KH-SH-E-H-I-O-H
MODERN: H(a)-SH(a)-A-Y(a)-TH(a)-I-Y(a)

150

Firsts from Ur: The First Known Spoiled and Lazy Son

Read the story. Give examples of what the son does to show the father's mistakes in fathering.   Copyright © 1994 Susan Mortimer

Father to Son in Ur

Son, all you do is wander about the public square.
Why don't you go to school?
My heart is weary because of you.
I keep away from you, for your grumbling and clamoring
has brought me to the point of death.
I am angry with you because you don't have any human kindness.
I never in my life made you carry reeds.
I never sent you to work as a laborer.
I never said, "Go to work and support me."
Other sons support their parents.
Other sons multiply the barley, maintain the oil and wool.
But not you!
You're not a man at all. You don't labor like them.
I don't make you work like them.
All night and day I am tortured because of you.
You have wasted away in pleasures.
You have expanded far and wide. You are fat and puffed-up.
All your family is waiting for your misfortune.
They will rejoice in it for you are not kind.

The father in this story from Ur did not seem to realize that he had not fulfilled his own responsibilities as a father. King Solomon addressed this issue in his book of Proverbs. Look up each verse and find the missing word. 1) He did not **discipline** the son. (Proverbs 13:24)

2) He did not teach the son to **work**. (Proverbs 12:11)

3) He did not instruct and **train** him as a child. (Proverbs 22:6)

At the same time, the son was not a wise son. King Solomon also deals with this issue many times in his book of Proverbs. Look up each reference and sort them into columns of wise and foolish.

Wise	Foolish
1:7(a)	1:7(b)
3:7	1:22
9:8-9	10:5(b)
10:5(a)	13:1(b)
11:30	13:20(b)
13:1(a)	15:20(b)
13:20(a)	17:21
15:20(a)	17:25
19:8	18:1
	18:9
	24:30-34

All verses are from Proverbs
((a)=1st part of verse; (b)-2nd part of verse)

3:7	1:22	17:21
9:8-9	18:9	11:30
10:5(a)	15:20(b)	24:30-34
17:25	1:7(a)	13:20(a)
19:8	1:7(b)	15:20(a)
18:1	13:1(b)	13:1(a)
10:5(b)	13:20(b)	

151

ABRAHAM STEPS OUT IN FAITH

The Lord called Abraham to do a very hard thing—sacrifice his son Isaac. The story is told in a painful step-by-step account of what Abraham had to do. When we are asked to do something hard, we need to take it one step at a time. Put the steps in order on the lines below, following what the Bible says in Genesis 22:3-19.   Copyright © 1994 Susan Mortimer

Then God said, "Take your son, your only son, Isaac, whom you love, and go to the region of Moriah. Sacrifice him there as a burnt offering on one of the mountains I will tell you about." Genesis 22:2   NIV

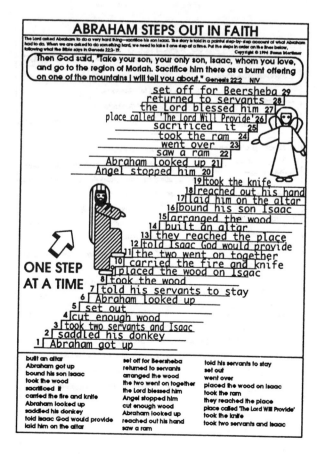

ONE STEP AT A TIME

29 set off for Beersheba
28 returned to servants
27 the Lord blessed him
26 place called 'The Lord Will Provide'
25 sacrificed it
24 took the ram
23 went over
22 saw a ram
21 Abraham looked up
20 Angel stopped him
19 took the knife
18 reached out his hand
17 laid him on the altar
16 bound his son Isaac
15 arranged the wood
14 built an altar
13 they reached the place
12 told Isaac God would provide
11 the two went on together
10 carried the fire and knife
9 placed the wood on Isaac
8 took the wood
7 told his servants to stay
6 Abraham looked up
5 set out
4 cut enough wood
3 took two servants and Isaac
2 saddled his donkey
1 Abraham got up

built an altar
Abraham got up
bound his son Isaac
took the wood
sacrificed it
carried the fire and knife
Abraham looked up
saddled his donkey
told Isaac God would provide
laid him on the altar

set off for Beersheba
returned to servants
arranged the wood
the two went on together
the Lord blessed him
cut enough wood
Abraham looked up
reached out his hand
saw a ram

told his servants to stay
set out
went over
placed the wood on Isaac
took the ram
they reached the place
place called 'The Lord Will Provide'
took the knife
took two servants and Isaac

152

Camels—the Desert's 'Beast of Burden'

Answer the questions below in complete sentences. Use all the information from The Beast of Burden page.   Copyright © 1994 Susan Mortimer

Camels—The Desert's 'Beast of Burden'
There are two kinds of camels. Dromedaries are swift camels found in India, Arabia and Africa. They have only one hump. The Bactrian is a woollier, two-humped camel found in Asia. Camels are ill-tempered and tend to bite, spit and kick. They groan, whine and grunt when made to do work, but they are indispensable to desert people. How do camels help man?

Answers will vary but should include transportation, food, shelter, clothing, plow fields.

When extremely thirsty, a camel can drink up to 35 gallons of water in six minutes. It can drink 50 gallons of water a day but only like to drink clean water and will actually turn down dirty water. What enables a camel to go days without food or water?
Answers will vary. The camel does not sweat, so it does not require a lot of water. It stores fat in its hump to use when food is not available.

How do the different features of a camel's head protect it in a harsh environment? Answers will vary. Three layers of eyelids keep out sand, ears go back with lots of hair to keep out sand, and nostrils can close to slits to keep out sand.

How is the body of a camel suited for walking and kneeling in the sand?
Answers will vary. Wide pads on feet, leathery knees, very strong.

To conserve water, a camel's body temperature can rise eleven degrees without ill effect. If your temperature goes up two or three degrees what does it mean?
You are ill with a fever or overheated.

156

Remembering God's Awesome Acts: Answer Page

MISSION POSSIBLE

Read Genesis 24. Then fill in the number that matches each aspect of the mission of Abraham's chief servant. © 1996 Susan Mortimer

5	The mission:	1. "I will go."
10	The stipulations for a wife:	2. A wife to Isaac and his comfort
8	Release of oath:	3. Daughter of nephew of Abraham
12	The number of camels:	4. Before finished praying
9	The destination:	5. Find a wife for Isaac
7	Specific prayer request:	6. Ten times fifty equals five hundred
4	Prayer answered:	7. First girl asked to give a drink will offer to water camels
6	Formula showing maximum number of gallons of water Rebekah drew:	8. Woman unwilling to come
11	Servant's prerequisite for giving gifts:	9. Nahor
3	Relationship of the girl:	10. Not among the Canaanites
1	Rebekah's decision:	11. Completion of task
2	What Rebekah became:	12. Ten

Write a paragraph about how God's timing in answering prayer differed between Sarah and Abraham wanting a son and Abraham's servant wanting to find a wife for Isaac.

_____
_____
_____
_____
_____
_____
_____
_____
_____
_____

158

ISAAC AND JESUS COMPARED

Check the box under Jesus or mankind to show what different events in the life of Isaac represent. Copyright © 1996 Susan Mortimer

ISAAC	JESUS	MANKIND
He was announced and promised long before his birth.	✔	
He was named before his birth.	✔	
His mother could not believe she could have a child.	✔	
He had an earthly father and mother.		✔
He was born with a sin nature.		✔
He was born at the very time God had promised.	✔	
He was the only beloved son of his father. (Only one by Sarah—see Genesis 22:2)	✔	
He was to die on a mountain.	✔	
He was obedient to the point of death.	✔	
He was promised that God himself would provide the offering.		✔
He had to carry the wood for his own death.	✔	
God provided another to die in his place.		✔
He was told the whole earth would be blessed because he obeyed God.	✔	

God knows that we, as humans, are very visual and tactile; we need to see, hear, touch, taste and feel abstract spiritual truths in order to understand them. From the beginning to the end of the Bible, every story is pointing to Jesus and what He has done for us. If we do not see Jesus in all the stories of the Old Testament, we are missing the point. In the times of Abraham, human sacrifice was found all over the world as a means of appeasing the 'gods'. If God had wanted human sacrifices, it most certainly would have been Isaac, so loved and longed for by his father. But God was just testing Abraham to see if he was willing to sacrifice his beloved son and to point out that sinful mankind is not good enough to meet God's high standard for a sacrifice. In this encounter, God was showing us that He does not want human sacrifice. Instead He shows us a picture of what Jesus Christ, the perfect and sinless sacrifice, did for us by dying in our place.

Write out Romans 12:1 to see how God wants us to present ourselves to Him.

_____
_____
_____

159

Abraham's Sons

Write in the names and the birth order on the chart below. Then read each clue. Mark an "X" in any box that is not correct, a "C" in any box it could be and an "O" in the boxes that are correct. Copyright © 1996 Susan Mortimer

Abraham had eight sons. Their names are Medan, Ishmael, Zimran, Shuah, Jokshan, Ishbak, Midian and Isaac. Their names meant 'he will leave', 'judgement', 'he will hear', 'a trap or snare', 'strife and discord', 'sunken', 'he will laugh' and 'mountain goat'. Figure out the order each one was born and what their names mean.

1. Abraham's 3rd, 5th and 7th sons were Medan, Ishbak and Zimran. One of their names means 'judgment'.
2. The 7th-born son's name means 'he will leave'.
3. Zimran's name does not mean 'judgment' or 'a trap or snare'.
4. Midian and Medan were not the 4th or 7th child, nor do their names mean 'a trap or snare'.
5. The 2nd and 4th-born's names mean 'he will laugh' and 'a trap or snare'.
6. The names starting with 'Is' or 'Ish' have 'he will' in their meaning.
7. Zimran, the 3rd-born, doesn't mean 'strife and discord' or 'sunken'.
8. The 1st-born's name means 'he will hear'.
9. Midian and Ishbak were born 6th and 7th.
10. Isaac and Shuah are not 1st or 4th. One of their names means 'sunken' the other means 'he will laugh'.

Meaning of Names / Birth Order

Names	'he will leave'	'judgement'	'he will hear'	'a trap or snare'	'strife and discord'	'sunken'	'he will laugh'	'mountain goat'	1	2	3	4	5	6	7	8
Medan		O											O			
Ishmael			O						O							
Zimran					O						O					
Shuah				O												O
Jokshan			O									O				
Ishbak	O													O		
Midian						O								O		
Isaac							O			O						

160

LEAH AND RACHEL'S STRUGGLE

Read Genesis 29:31 to 30:25, and 35:17-18. Fill in the correct number to match the name with the mother's statement. Also, put the initial of the mother next to each son. © 1996 Susan Mortimer

1. Reuben: 'see a son'
   Mother is _L_
2. Simeon: 'hearing'
   Mother is _L_
3. Levi: 'attached'
   Mother is _L_
4. Judah: 'praise Jehovah'
   Mother is _L_
5. Dan: 'judge'
   Mother is _R/B_
6. Naphtali: 'my struggle'
   Mother is _R/B_
7. Gad: 'good fortune'
   Mother is _L/Z_
8. Asher: 'happy'
   Mother is _L/Z_
9. Issachar: 'one for hire'
   Mother is _L_
10. Zebulun: 'presented a gift'
    Mother is _L_
11. Joseph: 'let God add'
    Mother is _R_
12. Benjamin: 'son of my right hand'
    Mother is _R_

KEY for MOTHER
L= Leah
R=Rachel
R/B=Rachel/Bilhah
L/Z=Leah/Zilpah

__9__ "God has rewarded me for giving my maid-servant to my husband."

__7__ "What good fortune!"

__10__ "God has presented me with a precious gift. This time my husband will treat me with honor, because I have borne him six sons."

__3__ "Now at last my husband will become attached to me, because I have borne him three sons."

__12__ His mother named him Ben-Oni: 'son of my sorrow' as she was dying. Jacob changed his name to this.

__11__ "God has taken away my disgrace. May the Lord add to me another son."

__5__ "God has vindicated me; he has listened to my plea and given me a son."

__2__ "Because the Lord heard that I am not loved, he gave me this one too."

__1__ "It is because the Lord has seen my misery. Surely my husband will love me now."

__4__ "This time I will praise the Lord."

__6__ "I have had a great struggle with my sister, and I have won."

__8__ "How happy I am! The women will call me happy."

161

Remembering God's Awesome Acts: Answer Page

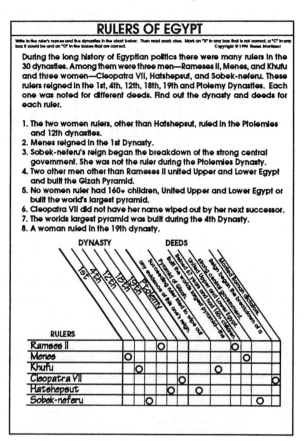

162

165

Key to Egyptian Sites on the Nile River

1. FERTILE NILE VALLEY
2. WESTERN DESERT
3. EASTERN DESERT
4. BOATS ON THE NILE
5. STEP PYRAMID
6. THE GREAT SPHINX
   THE GREAT PYRAMID
   (OF KHAFE)
7. VALLEY OF THE KINGS
8. COLOSSI OF RAMESES II
9. ROSETTA STONE
10. BENT PYRAMID
11. TEMPLE OF RAMESES II

168

169

Remembering God's Awesome Acts: Answer Page

The Rise and Fall of the Nile River

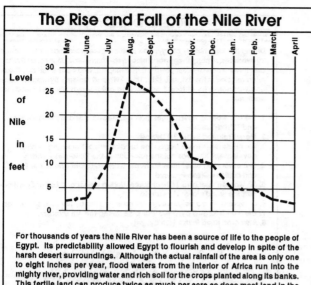

For thousands of years the Nile River has been a source of life to the people of Egypt. Its predictability allowed Egypt to flourish and develop in spite of the harsh desert surroundings. Although the actual rainfall of the area is only one to eight inches per year, flood waters from the interior of Africa run into the mighty river, providing water and rich soil for the crops planted along its banks. This fertile land can produce twice as much per acre as does most land in the United States. Cotton is a major cash crop. Several types of grains and fruits are also grown. Cattle, water buffalo and sheep graze along the river.

Ninety-five out of a hundred Egyptians live along the narrow strip of fertile land along the banks of the Nile River, just as their ancestors did for thousands of years before them. Many of the ancient Egyptians worshiped the Nile River as their source of life, and this was reflected in the gods that they created.

Plot the level in feet of the Nile for each month on the graph.

2 feet--April, May	12 feet--November
3 feet--March, June	20 feet--October
5 feet--January, February	25 feet--September
10 feet--December, July	27 feet--August

170

FAMILY FEUD

After you have studied Abraham, Isaac, Jacob, and Joseph, fill in the blanks with the correct names. Then match the correct letter of the response to each deception.

The Deception and Betrayal

1. [K] Ishmael mocked his half-brother Isaac.
2. [L] When she became pregnant, Hagar became proud and haughty toward her mistress Sarah.
3. [A] Abraham loved Isaac and sent his seven other sons away.
4. [B] Rebekah and Jacob conspired to deceive Isaac and receive the blessing meant for Esau.
5. [D] Jacob would not feed his famished brother Esau.
6. [I] Laban gave Leah, the oldest sister to Jacob instead of Rachel.
7. [C] Leah was unloved, but had children.
8. [J] Jealous of her sister's children, Rachel got her handmaiden, Bilhah to have children for her.
9. [E] Jacob was treated poorly and was made to pay for any injured animals, as well as suffer exposure to the heat and cold.
10. [F] Laban changed Jacob's wages ten times.
11. [H] Laban regarded Leah and Rachel as foreigners by selling them for fourteen years of wages to Jacob.
12. [G] Jacob showed favoritism to Joseph by buying him a coat.

The Resentful Response

A. Because his own father had shown favoritism, Isaac and his wife Rebekah each had a favorite son.
B. Esau held a grudge and vowed to kill his twin.
C. Leah stopped having children, so she got her handmaiden Zilpah to have children for her.
D. Esau is angered for having to sell his birthright for a pot of red stew.
E. Jacob felt that Laban would send him away empty-handed.
F. Jacob bred strong sheep and goats for himself and weak ones for his father-in-law Laban.
G. Rachel cried to Jacob, "Give me children of I'll die!"
H. The family of Jacob snuck off in the middle of the night.
I. Leah and Rachel were in constant competition for their husband's love.
J. Angered and jealous, Joseph's brothers refrained from killing him, but sold him into slavery.
K. Abraham sent Ishmael and his mother away permanently.
L. Hagar was beaten for her bad attitude and ran away from her mistress Sarah.

171

SOLVING THE HIEROGLYPHIC MYSTERY

(Under the Rosetta Stone and with the hieroglyphics, answers are the same.)

1. Ptolemlios
4. Cleopadra
5. Alksendrs
6. Rameses
7. Thothmes

177

The Deceit of the Devil

Look over the words below. Think about what you want to write. You may choose to use only a few key words that start with 'd' or you may want to see how many 'd' words you can get into your paper. Either way, make sure you focus on having a well-written, meaningful paper that gives a clear picture on how the devil tries to deceive us. Do a rough draft. Copy your polished paper on the next page.

dagger	deceit	dejection	destitute	disappoint	disturb
damage	deceive	delinquent	destroy	disarm	divergent
damnation	deception	delusion	destruction	disaster	divert
danger	decline	demean	deteriorate	disclaim	divide
dark	decoy	demoralize	detestable	discomfort	doom
darkness	decrease	deny	deviate	discourage	doubt
dart	deep-seated	deplete	devold	discredit	downhearted
dash	defame	deploy	die	disdain	downhill
dead	defeat	depraved	difficult	disgrace	drag
dead end	defiance	depressed	digress	dishonest	dragon
deadly	deficit	deprive	dilemma	dispute	drain
deaf	defilement	derail	dilute	disregard	dreadful
dealer	defraud	desert	dim	disrespectful	dumb
death	defy	despair	diminish	disrupt	dump
debauchery	degenerate	desperate	dirty	dissuade	dungeon
debt	degrade	despise	disable	distract	duped
decay	dehumanize	despondant	disagree	distrust	dysfunctional

Draw a line to the definition. Use a dictionary to help.

dysfunctional — unable to function properly
desperate — hopeless
dilemma — predicament
detestable — hateful
disrespectful — rude
disarm — remove defenses
defame — slander
defilement — made filthy
deception — fraud, trickery
dehumanize — to deprive of human kindness
desert — leave

divergent — turn from the norm
dishonest — not truthful
dissuade — persuade against
duped — deceived by trickery
deteriorate — become worse
defiance — open opposition to authority
despondant — disheartened, depressed
decoy — something to lure or tempt to danger
discredit — cast doubt on
disregard — neglect, ignore
depraved — perverted, corrupt

178

HIEROGLYPHIC DETERMINERS IN ENGLISH

NILE	QUEEN ELIZABETH	BLIND
CANADA	LIVING ROOM	BLOND
SPAIN	SUNSET	SHARK
PUDDLE	MOTHER	WINTER
PADDLE	NEW YORK	BORN
POODLE	WHITE HOUSE	BARN
CATTLE	GOLDFISH	BURN
TULIPS	DOOR KEEPER	ENEMY
LONDON	GREYHOUND	LIVING
DINNER	GRANDSON	LIBRARY
TIGER	PRESIDENT	DARK
SUMMER	VICTORY	HURRICANE
LOOK	CLOTHES WASHER	HONEST

184

PYRAMID STRUCTURE OF EGYPTIAN GOVERNMENT

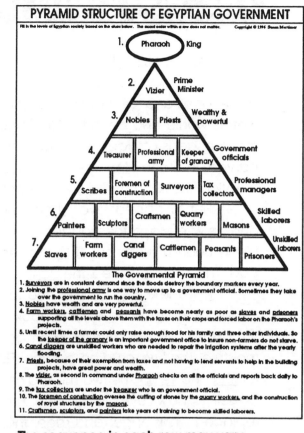

Fill in the levels of Egyptian society based on the clues below. The exact order within a row does not matter. Copyright © 1996 Susan Mortimer

1. Pharaoh — King
2. Vizier — Prime Minister
3. Nobles, Priests — Wealthy & powerful
4. Treasurer, Professional army, Keeper of granary — Government officials
5. Scribes, Foremen of construction, Surveyors, Tax collectors — Professional managers
6. Painters, Sculptors, Craftsmen, Quarry workers, Masons — Skilled laborers
7. Slaves, Farm workers, Canal diggers, Cattlemen, Peasants, Prisoners — Unskilled laborers

The Governmental Pyramid

1. Surveyors are in constant demand since the floods destroy the boundary markers every year.
2. Joining the professional army is one way to move up to a government official. Sometimes they take over the government to run the country.
3. Nobles have wealth and are very powerful.
4. Farm workers, cattlemen and peasants have become nearly as poor as slaves and prisoners supporting all the levels above them with the taxes on their crops and forced labor on the Pharaoh's projects.
5. Until recent times a farmer could only raise enough food for his family and three other individuals. So the keeper of the granary is an important government office to insure non-farmers do not starve.
6. Canal diggers are unskilled workers who are needed to repair the irrigation systems after the yearly flooding.
7. Priests, because of their exemption from taxes and not having to lend servants to help in the building projects, have great power and wealth.
8. The vizier, as second in command under Pharaoh checks on all the officials and reports back daily to Pharaoh.
9. The tax collectors are under the treasurer who is an government official.
10. The foremen of construction oversee the cutting of stones by the quarry workers, and the construction of royal structures by the masons.
11. Craftsmen, sculptors, and painters take years of training to become skilled laborers.

The sequence in each row may vary.

185

Second-in-Command to Pharoah

Fill in the numbers on the matching sentences. Copyright © 1996 Susan Mortimer

Pharaoh appointed viziers to run Egypt. In most of Egypt's history there were two viziers, one to run Upper Egypt and the other to run Lower Egypt. They were often chosen from royal princes or nobility. Therefore it was highly unusual that Joseph, a foreigner, slave and prisoner, was the one appointed vizier, second in command only to Pharaoh. It was the vizier who ran the country. He would report every morning to the king on the events from the day before and receive new orders. Then he would have thirty meetings and functions to attend that day. Before his day was done, he examined written reports and dictated replies. To get an idea what his multitude of responsibilities were, read his titles and connect them with the obligations that would have come with the title.

The vizier had dozens of titles besides being called a PRINCE and COUNT:

1. SEALBEARER OF THE KING
2. SOLE COMPANION OF THE KING
3. OVERSEER OF THE FIELDS
4. JUDGE PRESIDING OVER HIGHEST COURTS OF JUSTICE
5. OVERSEER OF GRANARIES
6. STEWARD OF THE KING
7. OVERSEER OF ROYAL RESIDENCE
8. CONTROLLER OF CRAFTS
9. CONTROLLER OF CONSTRUCTION
10. CHIEF OFFICER OF THE STATE
11. MINISTER OF WAR
12. CHIEF OF POLICE
13. CHIEF TREASURER

- 13 Supervised collection of taxes.
- 4 In law cases must be fair and equitable to all people from the nobles to the slaves.
- 11 Above temple and military officials.
- 10 Could stand in for the king or act as his spokesman in civil matters.
- 3 Checked on gardens, cows, serfs and farmers.
- 5 Supervised movement of food.
- 7 Insured smooth running of the palace.
- 9 Checked the progress of royal and irrigation building projects.
- 12 Made sure civil laws were upheld.
- 8 Oversaw the carving of statues and the painting of murals.
- 6 In charge of stewardship or management of all the king's resources.
- 2 Reported every morning to the king.
- 1 Could imprint the Royal seal to any written command to make it law.

186

Joseph as Vizier of All of Egypt

Fill in the correct job title for what Joseph did from the list below. You might use the same answer more than once. © 1996 Susan Mortimer

Pharaoh told Joseph, "You shall be *in charge of my palace*, (OVERSEER OF ROYAL RESIDENCE) and all my people are to submit to your orders (VIZIER). I am Pharaoh, but *without your word no one will lift hand or foot in all Egypt* (CHIEF OFFICER OF STATE). Only with respect to the throne *will I be greater* than you (VIZIER)." Pharaoh gave his *signet ring (seal)* to Joseph (SEALBEARER OF THE KING). He dressed him in *royal robes and put a gold chain* around his neck (PRINCE /COUNT). He rode in his chariot as his *second-in-command* (VIZIER). Joseph traveled throughout the fields of Egypt, (OVERSEER OF THE FIELDS). He collected a *fifth* (CHIEF TREASURER) of all the food grown and storing it in *granaries* (OVERSEER OF GRANARIES) in the cities.

When the famine came and the people had no food left, Joseph *sold the grain* to the people (CHIEF TREASURER). The famine was so severe that there was no food growing in the whole region, even as far away as Canaan. When his brothers came to buy food, Joseph charged them with being spies and *put them under arrest* (JUDGE OF HIGHEST COURT).

By selling the stored grain of Egypt, Joseph collected all the *money* (CHIEF TREASURER) that was found in Egypt and Canaan. When the money was gone the people bought grain by selling their livestock. When that was gone, Joseph bought all the land of Egypt for Pharaoh in exchange for food, and reduced the people to servitude. However, he did not buy the land of the priests because they received regular food allotments from Pharaoh. Joseph established it as *law* (SEALBEARER OF THE KING) that a fifth of the produce belonged to Pharaoh.

Based on Genesis 41, 42, 46 and 47 NIV

VIZIER: Second only to Pharaoh, gave orders.
CHIEF OFFICER OF THE STATE: Could stand in for king and act as his spokesman; word must be obeyed.
SEALBEARER OF THE KING: Could imprint the royal seal on any written command and make it law.
OVERSEER OF THE FIELDS: Checked on farmers and their farms.
JUDGE OF HIGHEST COURT: Able to judge, convict and put in prison.
OVERSEER OF GRANARIES: Controled the collecting and moving of grain.
OVERSEER OF ROYAL RESIDENCE: Insured smooth running of the palace.
CHIEF TREASURER: In charge of collecting taxes and all moneys or goods.
PRINCE /COUNT: Had royal privileges, wealth and fine clothes.

187

THE EGYPTIAN STORY OF CREATION

Fill in the name of the correct god in each space, using the information from The gods of Egypt page.

© 1996 Susan Mortimer

From before time, there existed a boundless mass of water. This watery mass was a god named Nu. Nu was both male and female. From Nu sprang forth all the gods and all creation. Nu placed his live-giving waters into the Nile. These waters would also be in the Nile River in the afterlife . Put in charge of the Nile were the dual gods of Hapi, who were called the hidden gods and were never to be carved in stone. Nu, the water god, was considered to be the source of all creation, the sustainer of life on earth and the giver of eternal life after death.

First to appear was Thoth, the divine intelligence that created the world, and his wife Maat, the goddess of truth. By Thoth's word, four elements (fire, water, air and earth) arose out of Nu. For each element there was a male and a female god. These were called the Eight. They had the heads of frogs and of serpents.

Ra, the sun god, was the force that gives warmth and life to the earth. (Many of the gods, over time, took on attributes of Ra and were also considered sun gods.) Ra had two children: Shu, the god of air, and Tefnut, the goddess of moisture. The two children got lost. Ra took out one of his eyes to go and search for Shu and Tefnut, his two missing children. The search took so long that Ra made himself a new eye. When the first eye returned, it found that it had been replaced. In its anger and rage, the eye burst into flames. Ra turned the eye into a snake which could spit flames of fire to scorch his enemies. This fire-spitting eye of Ra became the sun. Ra, the sun god, was highly revered for he conquered night and darkness, clouds and mists.

Now Shu, the air god and Tefnut, the goddess of moisture gave birth to Nut, the goddess of the sky, and Seb, the god of the earth. Nut and Seb became husband and wife. Jealous of them, Ra, the sun god, became so angry with Nut the sky god that he separated her forever from Seb, the earth god, by putting Shu, the god of the air, between them. Nut, the mother of the gods, was already pregnant, but Ra put a curse her that she could not give birth in any day of any month of any year. Another god felt sorry for her, and in a betting game won a seventh part of every day. All the parts added up to five whole days which he claimed as holidays that were to be separate from any month. With the curse thus broken, Nut gave birth to five children, one on each of the five holidays.

Osiris, the god of vegetation, was born on the first day. Next was Isis, the nature goddess who became Osiris' wife. The third day was a day to dread, for the evil Set, god of the desert sand storms, cut his way out of his mother's womb. Then came Horus, who is seen again as the child of Isis and Osiris. Last came Nephthys, the sister and helper of Isis.

Another story about how the sun was made, where Ra is now the CHILD of Nut.

Nut, the sky goddess, bends over the earth. On her belly are the stars. Her husband Seb, the earth god, lies beneath her. The sky goddess, Nut gives birth daily to the sun god Ra. Time began when he first appeared in the eastern sky. The sun god travels across the sky in the sun boat and is swallowed by his mother Nut in the west, at sundown. He then travels unseen through his mother's body at night to be born again every morning.

Remembering God's Awesome Acts: Answer Page

SPELL AND FIGURE

1. th-s-m; dog-plural=dogs
2. n-e-s; fire, light=the flames
3. nether (land)/lands=Netherlands
4. b-h-n-t-u; dog=hyenas
5. m-a-u; cat=cat
6. heart/the, one/my=my heart
7. s-t; fire=fire
8. p-t; sky=sky
9. ch-r-s-n; fall/plural=fallen
10. mouth/the, one/his=his mouth
11. p-s-t; shine=shining
12. ne-f-r; good, beautiful=happy
13. h-h; sun, day=eternity
14. mother/female/his=his mother
15. sky/star=night
16. i-k-u-a; the, one/come=one has come
17. give; ta-t-u-n-k; thou, thee=given to thee
18. a-n-ch-u; life/me, my/plural=lives
19. Amen-t-t; land=Amenta
20. s-t; land=mountain

190

MYTH OF RA'S DAILY REBIRTH

BORN IS HE (or HE IS BORN) AS RA, SHINING IN THE SKY/ HEAVENS. THOU GOES (TO) THY MOTHER NUT. PRAISES TO THEE SHINING AS GOLD SHINING ON THE TWO (or DOUBLE) LANDS/EARTH IN THE DAY OF HIS BIRTH.

195

Joseph - The Original 'That's Good, No That's Bad' Story (1)

Cut out the sentences on the 'That's Good That's Bad' page and place them in sequencial order on the following pages. Read the story to see if you did it correctly before you glue them down.
Copyright © 1996 Susan Mortimer

Narrator: 'The Story of Joseph.'
Audience: Oh, that's good! | Joseph's father loved him very much and gave him an beautiful coat.

Narrator: No, that's bad because
Audience: Oh, that's bad! | his brothers were so jealous, that they could not speak one kind word to him.

Narrator: No, that's good because
Audience: Oh, that's good! | Joseph had two dreams in which God revealed that his family would honor him.

Narrator: No, that's bad because
Audience: Oh, that's bad! | his brothers hated him all the more because of the dreams and wanted to kill him.

Narrator: No, that's good because
Audience: Oh, that's good! | Reuban said, "Let's not take his life."

Narrator: No, that's bad because
Audience: Oh, that's bad! | Instead, they thew him in a dry cistern.

Narrator: No, that's good because
Audience: Oh, that's good! | later, Reuban came back to rescue Joseph from the cistern.

Narrator: No, that's bad because
Audience: Oh, that's bad! | his brothers had already sold Joseph and covered his coat with blood so his father would believe him dead.

Narrator: No, that's good because
Audience: Oh, that's good! | the Lord was with Joseph. Potiphar bought him, and put him in charge of his whole household.

Narrator: No, that's bad because
Audience: Oh, that's bad! | day after day, Potiphar's wife tried to get Joseph to sleep with her.

Narrator: No, that's good because
Audience: Oh, that's good! | Joseph would not do such a wicked thing, and stayed away from her.

Narrator: No, that's bad because
Audience: Oh, that's bad! | she got him alone, grabed his coat and said, " Come to bed with me!"

Narrator: No, that's good because
Audience: Oh, that's good! | Joseph ran out of the house.

Narrator: No, that's bad because
Audience: Oh, that's bad! | Potiphar's wife accused him of trying to rape her and her husband put Joseph in prision.

198

Joseph - The Original 'That's Good, No That's Bad' Story (2)

Cut out the sentences on the 'That's Good That's Bad' page and place them in sequencial order on the following pages. Read the story to see if you did it correctly before you glue them down.
Copyright © 1996 Susan Mortimer

Narrator: No, that's good because
Audience: Oh, that's good! | the Lord was with Joseph in prision and he was put in charge of all the prisoners.

Narrator: No, that's bad because
Audience: Oh, that's bad! | two of the prisoners, Pharoah's cupbearer and baker were dejected for no one could interpret their dreams.

Narrator: No, that's good because
Audience: Oh, that's good! | God showed Joseph that the cupbearer's dream meant that in 3 days, he would get back his position.

Narrator: No, that's bad because
Audience: Oh, that's bad! | God also showed Joseph that the baker's dream meant that in 3 days, he would be executed.

Narrator: No, that's good because
Audience: Oh, that's good! | on the third day, Pharoah had a birthday and restored the chief cupbearer to his position.

Narrator: No, that's bad because
Audience: Oh, that's bad! | on that same day, Pharaoh hung the chief baker.

Narrator: No, that's good because
Audience: Oh, that's good! | it was the chief cupbear who Joseph had asked to help get him out of prision.

Narrator: No, that's bad because
Audience: Oh, that's bad! | the chief cupbear forgot all about Joseph for two years.

Narrator: No, that's good because
Audience: Oh, that's good! | when Pharaoh had two dreams no one else could interpret, Joseph was taken to him.

Narrator: No, that's bad because
Audience: Oh, that's bad! | Joseph told Pharaoh that he could not interpret the dreams.

Narrator: No, that's good because
Audience: Oh, that's good! | Joseph said God knew, and that the dreams meant there would be seven good years.

Narrator: No, that's bad because
Audience: Oh, that's bad! | those seven good years would be followed by seven years of famine.

Narrator: No, that's good because
Audience: Oh, that's good! | Pharoah put Joseph in charge of storing up food for the coming bad years.

Narrator: No, that's bad because
Audience: Oh, that's bad! | the famine came to all the world, and all the people were crying out for food.

201

THE STORY OF OSIRIS AND ISIS

Fill in the name of the correct god in each space, using the information from <u>The gods of Egypt</u> page.

© 1996 Susan Mortimer

<u>Thoth</u>, the supreme intelligence, had the god <u>Khnum</u>, the potter, create humans out of clay on his potter's wheel. This potter, <u>Khnum</u>, was kept busy because every human ever born must be molded out of clay by him.

When <u>Thoth</u>, the distributor of knowledge, saw that mankind were babbling like animals and no wiser than monkeys. He went down to them in the form of an ape and taught them words and concepts so they could communicate. He also taught them how to read and write in hieroglyphics. Then he gave them music, math, and science. <u>Thoth</u>, the creator of the world, then sent <u>Osiris</u>, the vegetation god, down to rule Egypt.

<u>Osiris</u>, the god of civilization, came to Egypt with his wife and sister <u>Isis</u>. There he taught men how to grow cotton, wheat, and grapes, thus saving them from cannibalism.

When Osiris, the rightful ruler of Egypt, had brought civilization and prosperity to Egypt, he went away to teach other people how to grow crops. He left his wife, <u>Isis</u>, in charge of Egypt.

His brother <u>Set</u>, the god of the desert and sand storms, wanted to rule Egypt. He became so angry and jealous that he devised a scheme along with 72 other gods to do away with his brother <u>Osiris</u>. Set secretly got the measurements of his brother <u>Osiris</u>. Then he made a magnificent, custom-fit, gold inlaid coffin for his brother <u>Osiris</u>.

Osiris returned, bearing all kinds of gifts and animals from the other lands he had visited. A great banquet was given to celebrate the triumphant return of <u>Osiris</u>, the rightful ruler of Egypt. <u>Set</u>, the evil one, now had his chance to get rid of his brother once and for all. He announced to all the guests at the party that whoever could fit into the magnificent coffin would be able to keep it. Thus he tricked <u>Osiris</u>, the brother he so hated, to lie down in the coffin. The minute he laid down, <u>Set</u>, the murderer, killed <u>Osiris</u>, his brother. Then he closed the coffin and sealed it with his fiery breath. He hurled the coffin into the Nile River. There the friendly Nile god, <u>Hapi</u>, floated the body out into the Mediterranean Sea to the city of Byblos in Lebanon. Lebanon is noted for its gigantic trees and it did not take long for a magnificent tree to grow up around the coffin, encasing it completely.

Meanwhile <u>Set</u>, the murderer, became the ruler of Egypt. <u>Isis</u>, the frightened wife of Osiris, fled up the Nile and hid in tall papyrus reeds with seven scorpions to guard her. In her deep sorrow, she cut her hair, put on mourning clothes, and wept. Her outburst of tears caused the Nile to overflow its banks and flood the land. Thus began the yearly inundation (flooding) of the land by the Nile.

Isis found out that her sister <u>Nephthys</u> was carrying a child of her now-dead husband, <u>Osiris</u>. When her sister gave birth to <u>Anubis</u>, the jackal-headed god, <u>Isis</u>, his aunt, took him as her own. Together they went in search of the coffin containing the body of <u>Osiris</u>.

She found out that the body of her dead husband had been encased in a tree, which the king of Lebanon had since cut down to make a pillar for his palace. <u>Isis</u>, the protector of children, went to the palace and took a job as a nanny for the child of the king. At night in the palace, Isis turned herself into a swallow and flew around the pillar that encased the coffin and body of Osiris. During the day she nursed the king's child with her finger and put him in the fire to burn off his humanness and make him immortal. However the queen thwarted these plans by coming in on them. She screamed and pulled her child out of the fire, ruining his chance to become immortal. Isis, his nanny, then revealed her story and the coffin was cut out of the pillar.

Isis, the sorrowing widow, and her nephew, Anubis, took the body and hid it in the desert. Isis opened the coffin and, in the form of a hawk, hovered over the body of her dead husband. She became pregnant and gave birth to Horus the hawk-headed god.

Meanwhile Set, the god of night, was now ruling Egypt. He went out hunting by moonlight when he stumbled on the coffin. In his rage, he cut the body of his dead brother, Osiris, into fourteen pieces and scattered them to the four winds. Just as the wind carries away the chaff of wheat, so it carried away the pieces of Osiris, the vegetation god.

Osiris' wife, Isis, and his son Horus went across the land gathering up his pieces. They then wrapped the pieces together in long sheets of fine linen. The god of creation, Thoth, had pity on them and came down, touched Osiris with the ankh, the symbol of life, and brought him back to life. Just as plants die during the yearly Egyptian drought and return to life the following year during the flooding or inundation of the Nile, so Osiris, the god of vegetation, comes back to life each year. Because he conquered death, he became the ruler of the Netherland, or afterworld.

During this time, Horus, the son of Osiris, grew up and became strong. He married Hathor, the frog and cow-headed goddess. Later, he challenged his uncle Set to gain back his rightful throne of Egypt. Four times they fought. One time Set the evil one, tore to pieces the hawk-eye of Horus. Horus was able to put the pieces back together, but there was no life in it. So Thoth, the giver of life, put a drop of magical glue on it, restoring its vision. Thus the 'Eye of Horus' symbolized healing.

In another battle, Horus' mother Isis was watching. She had a chance to spear her bother Set, murderer of her husband, but she hesitated. In a rage, her son Horus turned into a leopard and tore off her head. Thoth gave her a cow's head to replace her own.

Still, Isis, the mother of Horus, wanted him to rule Egypt. Disguising herself as a beautiful woman, she wept bitterly. Set, her donkey-headed brother, came by but did not recognize her. She told him that the rightful inheritance of her son had been taken away from him. Set, the evil one, agreed that the land that had belonged to her husband should be given to her son. The other gods heard this and claimed that, by his own words, Set, the unlawful ruler of Egypt, should give back the land to his nephew Horus.

Since Horus, son of Osiris, was the rightful ruler of Egypt, then all pharaohs were the embodiment of Horus and took a Horus' name. Then when a Pharaoh died, he became Osiris, god of the dead, and the son who took his place as the new king, became Horus, ruler and god of Egypt.

Joseph - The Original 'That's Good, No That's Bad' Story (3)

Cut out the sentences on the 'That's Good That's Bad' page and place them in sequential order on the following pages. Read the story to see if you did it correctly before you glue them down.
Copyright © 1996 Susan Mortimer

Narrator: No, that's good because Audience: Oh, that's good!	Joseph opened up the store house for all the Egyptians.
Narrator: No, that's bad because Audience: Oh, that's bad!	Joseph's family were not in Eygpt and they were starving.
Narrator: No, that's good because Audience: Oh, that's good!	Jacob, Joseph's father sent several of his sons down to Egypt to get grain.
Narrator: No, that's bad because Audience: Oh, that's bad!	they did not recognize Joseph, and as he did not trust them, he kept Simeon as a prisioner.
Narrator: No, that's good because Audience: Oh, that's good!	Joseph sent the rest of the brothers back with grain to last several months.
Narrator: No, that's bad because Audience: Oh, that's bad!	the food ran out and they had to return, against Jacob's will, with Benjamin as Joseph commanded.
Narrator: No, that's good because Audience: Oh, that's good!	Joseph treated them to a banquet, giving double portions to Benjamin.
Narrator: No, that's bad because Audience: Oh, that's bad!	Benjamin was falsely accused by Joseph of stealing a cup and was to be kept as a slave.
Narrator: No, that's good because Audience: Oh, that's good!	Reuben offered to take Benjamin's place out of love for his father and remorse for the past.
Narrator: No, that's bad because Audience: Oh, that's bad!	Joseph wept loudly, startling his brothers, and sending his frightened servants away.
Narrator: No, that's good because Audience: Oh, that's good!	Jospeh revealed to them that he was their long-lost brother and moved them all to Egypt.
Narrator: No, that's bad because Audience: Oh, that's bad!	Jacob died, and Joseph's brothers worried that he would enslave them.
Narrator: No, that's good because Audience: Oh, that's good!	Joseph forgave them saying, "You meant it for evil, but God meant it for good!"
Narrator: No, that's **very good**	because the God of Joseph is still alive and works good out of difficult events in our lives.

202

DETERMINERS DETERMINE MEANING

A.	10	N.	20
B.	13	O.	3
C.	8	P.	2
D.	15	Q.	22
E.	6	R.	21
F.	11	S.	12
G.	19	T.	7
H.	5	U.	24
I.	14	V.	23
J.	9	W.	26
K.	17	X.	1
L.	25	Y.	4
M.	16	Z.	18

204

MYTHOLOGY AND MATH

(BOXES 'A-F' FORM THE EYE OF HORUS.)

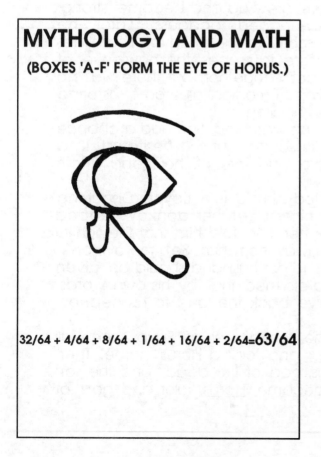

32/64 + 4/64 + 8/64 + 1/64 + 16/64 + 2/64 = **63/64**

207

THE FATHER REJOICES

Read Genesis 45:25–46:1. Circle the correct choice of the words in parentheses. Then mark the parallel/contrasting statements, with A, B, C and so forth. Then draw a line connecting the 'A' to 'A' and so on.
Copyright © 1996 Susan Mortimer

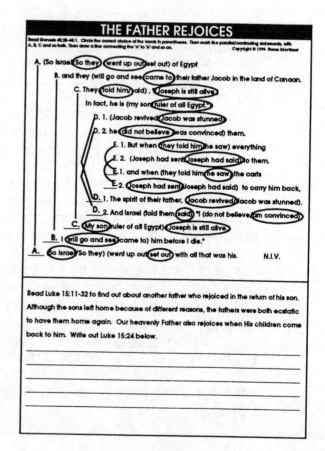

A. (So Israel, ~~So they~~) (~~went up out~~, set out) of Egypt

B. and they (will go and see, ~~came to~~) their father Jacob in the land of Canaan.

C. They (~~told him~~, said), "Joseph is still alive

In fact, he is (my son, ~~ruler of all Egypt~~.")

D. 1. (Jacob revived, ~~Jacob was stunned~~)

D. 2. he (~~did not believe~~, was convinced) them.

E. 1. But when (~~they told him~~, he saw) everything

E. 2. (Joseph had sent, ~~Joseph had said~~) to them.

E. 1. and when (they told him, ~~he saw~~) the carts

E. 2. (~~Joseph had sent~~, Joseph had said) to carry him back,

D. 1. The spirit of their father, (Jacob revived, ~~Jacob was stunned~~).

D. 2. And Israel (told them, ~~said~~) "I (do not believe, ~~am convinced~~)

C. (My son, ~~ruler of all Egypt~~) Joseph is still alive

B. I (will go and see, ~~came to~~) him before I die."

A. (So Israel, ~~So they~~) (went up out, ~~set out~~) with all that was his.

N.I.V.

Read Luke 15:11-32 to find out about another father who rejoiced in the return of his son. Although the sons left home because of different reasons, the fathers were both ecstatic to have them home again. Our heavenly Father also rejoices when His children come back to him. Write out Luke 15:24 below.

_____

_____

_____

_____

208

Remembering God's Awesome Acts: Answer Page

JESUS FULFILLS PROPHESY TO JUDAH

Fill in the letter of the correct meaning of these figures of speech used in Israel's blessing of Judah.

- __h__ will not depart
- __e__ hand on the neck of enemies
- __i__ he comes to whom it belongs
- __f__ obedience of the nations is his
- __d__ lion
- __g__ scepter
- __a__ staff
- __b__ donkey/colt
- __c__ wash robes in blood of grapes

a. used by shepherds—shows protection and guidance of people
b. peaceful kings ride colts not war horses
c. royal color and cleansing by blood
d. unquestioned 'king' (king of beasts)
e. win over, overpower
f. the whole world will obey
g. held by ruler—symbol of authority
h. forever
i. prediction of Jesus as rightful heir

(Match the letter of the verse that shows how Jesus fulfilled the blessing given to Judah. The underlined words will help you.)

The Prophesy about Judah: Genesis 49:8-11 NIV

1. __B__ Judah ('praise'), your brothers will praise you;
2. __A__ your hand will be on the neck of your enemies; your father's sons will bow down to you.
3. __H__ You are a lion's cub, O Judah; you return from the prey, my son. Like a lion he crouches and lies down; like a lioness—who dares to rouse him?
4. __D__ The scepter will not depart from Judah.
5. __C__ nor the ruler's staff from between his feet,
6. __F__ until he comes to whom it belongs and the obedience of the nations is his.
7. __G__ He will tether his donkey to a vine, his colt to the choicest branch;
8. __E__ he will wash his garments in wine, his robes in the blood of grapes.

Fulfilled by Jesus

A. Revelation 17:14a
B. Revelation 5:12
C. Revelation 7:17
D. Revelation 1:5
E. Revelation 19:13
F. Revelation 7:9
G. Mark 11:4-7
H. Revelation 5:5

Satan felt he had won when Jesus was to be crucified. Write four ways Satan mocked Jesus because he thought the prediction given to Judah was not going to be fulfilled. (Mark 15:16-20, John 19:9)

1. PURPLE ROBE (ROYAL ROBE)   2. CROWN OF THORNS
3. KNELT AND PAID MOCKING HOMAGE   4. SIGN ON CROSS: KING OF THE JEWS

Read Revelation 12:7-11 and write who came out the winner. JESUS CHRIST

209

Joseph and Jesus Compared

The verses listed below contain many similarities found in the lives of Joseph and Jesus Christ. Read these verses and write each reference in the correct box. Also answer the detail questions in the grid below.   Copyright © 1996 Susan Mortimer

Similarities	Joseph	Jesus
Beloved son of his Father	Genesis 37:3	Matthew 3:17
Pointed out the sins of others	Genesis 37:2	John 8:44
Revealed to others that he would be exalted and was hated for it	Genesis 37:5-8	Matthew 26:64-68
Was plotted against	GENESIS 37: 18-20	Luke 22:26
Betrayed for pieces of silver	Genesis 37:28 How many? 20	Matthew 26:15 How many? 30
Was tempted but did not sin	Genesis 39:7-10	Hebrews 4:15
Was wrongfully punished	Genesis 39:20	Luke 23:40-41
Forgave those who wanted him dead	Genesis 50:18-21 Who? his brothers	Luke 23:34-35 Who? his enemies
Was acknowledged as the savior and ruler of the people	Genesis 41:41,57	Philippians 2:9-11
Gave all that he gained to the one over him	Genesis 47:23	I CORINTHIANS 15: 23-24

John 8:44	Matthew 26:64-68	Luke 23:34-35	Genesis 39:20
Genesis 37:2	I Corinthians 15:24	Luke 22:2-6	Luke 23:40-41
Matthew 3:17	Genesis 50:18-21	Genesis 47:23	Genesis 37:5-8
Genesis 37:3	Genesis 41:41, 57	Genesis 37: 19-20	Hebrews 4:15
Matthew 26:15	Philippians 2:9-11	Genesis 39:7-10	Genesis 37: 28

Adapted from Through the Bible in One Year by Alan B. Stringfellow, © 1980.

212

213/216

217

NAMES IN HIEROGLYPHICS

RULER
OF ON
(and) UPPER EGYPT
1. T   2. U   3. T
ANKH
1. A   2. AMEN   3. N

SPELLING:
TUTANKHA(a)MEN(n) =
image living a god (AMEN) or
living image of AMEN.

SPELLING: MU-S-S   MES-S-S
Meaning:
out of water   born of
"I drew him out of the water."

219

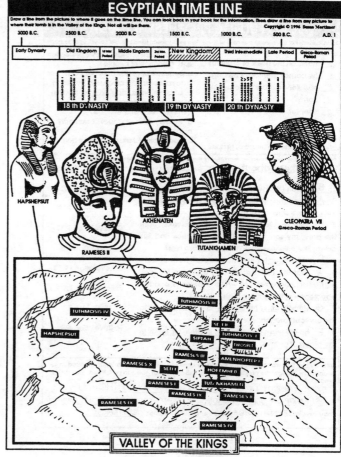

EGYPTIAN TIME LINE

Draw a line from the picture to where it goes on the time line. You can look back in your book for the information. Then draw a line from where their tomb is in the Valley of the Kings. Not all will be there. Copyright © 1996 Susan Mortimer

VALLEY OF THE KINGS

222

'SORROWS OF ISIS' HELP SHEET © 1996 Susan Mortimer

228

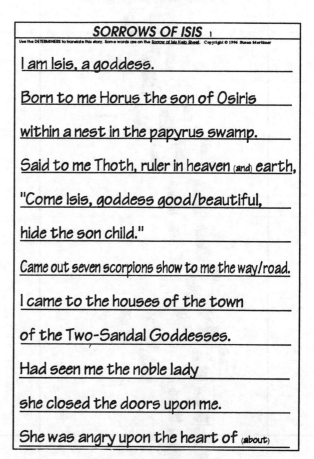

SORROWS OF ISIS

Use the DETERMINERS to translate this story. Some words are on the Sorrow of Isis Help Sheet. Copyright © 1996 Susan Mortimer

I am Isis, a goddess.

Born to me Horus the son of Osiris

within a nest in the papyrus swamp.

Said to me Thoth, ruler in heaven (and) earth,

"Come Isis, goddess good/beautiful,

hide the son child."

Came out seven scorpions show to me the way/road.

I came to the houses of the town

of the Two-Sandal Goddesses.

Had seen me the noble lady

she closed the doors upon me.

She was angry upon the heart of (about)

229

Remembering God's Awesome Acts: Answer Page

the scorpions with me.

The scorpions placed their poisons

upon the tail of a scorpion.

The scorpion came in the doors.

She (the scorpion) killed the son (of) the noble lady.

Fire came out in the house (of) the noble lady.

Not was water to extinguish (it).

not (did) heaven rain

in house (of) the noble lady.

The heart (of) the noble lady was sad.

Not was life in him.

The heart (of) Isis was sad for the child.

231

Said to her, "Come to me, my word is life."

Isis (put) her hands upon the child to revive.

Said Isis, "The poisons of the scorpions

come fall upon the ground/earth."

Live the child, die the poisons.

(The) fire was quenched.

Isis hide Horus, (the) child,

in the papyrus swamp.

Hidden not from his enemies.

The scorpion killed him.

Stung Horus, (the) child good/beautiful of gold.

Child, he is no more, his heart is still

233

with foam upon his lips.

Came Isis weeping. She embraced him

leaping about with him like a fish upon the fire.

Not was anyone to revive Horus.

Isis said to heaven,

"Come (the) boat of Ra to (the) son, Horus."

Ra came today in (the) boat

to heal Horus for his mother.

Triumphant is Horus from his enemies.

Lives the child Horus,

dies the poisons.

234

ARE ISIS AND HORUS LIKE GOD OR LIKE HUMANS?

1. BROWN

2. BROWN

3. GOLD

4. BROWN

5. BROWN

6. BROWN

7. BROWN

235

Two Stories about the Sun

Fill in the name of the correct god in each space, using the information from <u>The gods of Egypt</u> page.   © 1996 Susan Mortimer

<u>Ra</u>, the sun god, was considered by all the most powerful god. Every day the people of Egypt would give sacrifices to <u>Ra</u>, the sun god, so that he would shine down blessings on them.

Days and nights were divided into twelve hours each. Each hour was dedicated to and ruled by a different descendant of <u>Ra</u>. So each god in some way shared in being a sun god with him. Over time, however, <u>Ra</u>, the sun god, became so old and feeble that he could do was sit and slobber. His spittle dribbled down his face and fell to the earth. <u>Isis</u>, the goddess of dawn, wanted all his power. She took the spittle and created a serpent from it. The serpent gave a painful bite to <u>Ra</u>, the head god of Egypt.

Then <u>Isis</u>, the goddess of dawn, demanded that <u>Ra</u>, the sun god, tell her his secret name; for with the taking of this sacred name, she would get the powers of the sun and moon. In his agony, he finally gave in and let <u>Isis</u>, the mother of Horus, come into his head and find his name. <u>Isis</u> then became the most powerful of all the gods of Egypt.

Khepera, the scarab beetle god

Another story about the sun involved <u>Khepera</u>, the scarab beetle. Scarab beetles were considered to be able to create life out of non-living matter. The reason for this is that the scarab beetle would roll a one and a half inch ball of dung (manure), then lay an egg in it. The dung would serve as food for the larvae. In time, a scarab beetle would emerge. The Egyptians, not understanding that the egg had been laid, believed that life was created by itself in the lifeless matter. With this thinking in mind, the sun was depicted as a dung ball rolled by the self-created <u>Khepera</u>, radiant with the forces that create life.

Remembering God's Awesome Acts: Answer Page

TERRIBLY TONGUE-TIED

Match the lines of this Hebrew poem. First write how the lines relate to each other. Answer the questions below. © 1996 Susan Mortimer

Exodus 4:10-12

In the boxes, mark the relationship of each pair of letters using these symbols:

= (reword/repeat)
> (expand upon)
≠ (opposite)

A Moses said to the Lord
B "O Lord, I have never been eloquent
C neither in the past
_C_ nor since you have spoken to your servant.
_B_ I am slow of speech and tongue."

_A_ The Lord said to him,
D "Who gave man his mouth?
_D_ Who makes him deaf or mute?
E Who gives him sight
_E_ or makes him blind?
F Is it not I,
_F_ the Lord?
　　Now go;
G I will help you speak
_G_ and will teach you what to say."

A	≠	A
B	=	B
C	≠	C
D	≠	D
E	≠	E
F	=	F
G	=	G

1. Did God get rid of Moses' speech problem? __NO__ How do you know? _GOD OFFERED TO TEACH HIM & HELP HIM SPEAK, NOT CURE HIM_

2. What did Moses say after God told him that He would help him speak and teach him what to say? Exodus 4:13 _PLEASE SEND SOMEONE ELSE_

3. What was God's two-part response to Moses? Exodus 4:14-15 A. _GOD WAS ANGRY_ B. _GOD MADE PROVISION BY ALLOWING AARON TO SPEAK FOR MOSES_

4. Every person feels inadequate in some area in their lives. If God spoke to you about an area in your life in which you feel inadequate, what would it be and what would He say to you? _____

237

God's Promise to His People in Bondage

Read Exodus 6:2-8 and fill in the blanks from the word bank. Copyright © 1996 Susan Mortimer

God said,

I _am_ The Lord
　I have _heard_ the groanings
　　I have _remembered_ my covenant
　　　I will _free_ you from being slaves
　　　I will _redeem_ you
　　　　I will _take_ you as my own people
　　　　　I will _be_ your God
Then you will _know_ that I Am The Lord your God,
　who _brought_ you out from under the yoke of slavery
　I will _bring_ you to the land.

Word Bank:

brought	redeem	be	know	free
bring	am	heard	take	remembered

238

COMPARISON OF THE GODS AND GODDESSES

Fill in each column with the information below. First write in the Egyptian planets in order, starting with the moon. Then, from either its name or the planet associated with it, fill in the Roman gods. Next write in what each Roman god was said to rule over besides its planet. From these clues fill in the equivalent of the Germanic and Norse gods. Copyright © 1996 Susan Mortimer

Number assigned to each god or planet	The Egyptian Planetary order	Roman gods	What, other than a planet, were they gods of?	Germanic and Norse gods
7	Moon	Diana	the hunt	Uller
6	Mercury	Mercury	dead/messenger	Woden
5	Venus	Venus	lovers	Frigg
4	Sun	Apollo	music/poetry	Bragi
3	Mars	Mars	war	Tui
2	Jupiter	Jupiter	storms/thunder	Thor
1	Saturn	Saturn	harvest	Balder

The Egyptian's Order of the Known Planets

The Egyptians ordered the planets from what they observed from earth.

Earth You are here — 7 Moon — 6 Mercury — 5 Venus — 4 Sun — 3 Mars — 2 Jupiter — 1 Saturn

Roman gods	Germanic and Norse gods
☐ Apollo was the sun god and the god of music and poetry.	☐ Balder was the god of harvest. He died at the hand of his brother.
☐ Mars was the god of war.	☐ Thor was the god of thunder and lighting.
☐ Diana was the moon goddess and the goddess of the hunt.	☐ Woden was the god who brought messages from the dead.
☐ Venus was the goddess of lovers.	☐ Uller was the god of archery and hunting.
☐ Saturn was the god of the harvest.	☐ Tui was the god of winter, law and war.
☐ Jupiter was the god of storms and thunder.	☐ Bragi the god of music and poetry.
☐ Mercury was the god of the dead and the messenger god.	☐ Frigg the wife of Woden, was the goddess of lovers and fertility.

240

TRACING THE DAYS OF THE WEEK BACK IN TIME

According to an ancient theory, the Egyptians could have had one of the seven known planets (in reverse order) rule every hour of the day and night. Fill in each day's column with the number of the planet. Use one for each hour. Start with 1 and go to 7. When you get to the last planet (7) start over again with 1 (Saturn). Begin the next column where you left off. The first hour of the day (the top box) would give the day its name. Use the information and number assigned each planet and god from the Comparison of the Gods and Goddesses page to figure out how we may have gotten the name of each day. Copyright © 1996 Susan Mortimer

	1st day	2nd day	3rd day	4th day	5th day	6th day	7th day
Name of planet.	Saturn	Sun	Moon	Mars	Mercury	Jupiter	Venus
Name used to name day.	Saturn's day	Sun's day	Moon's day	Tui's day	Woden's day	Thor's day	Frigg's day
Name of day.	Saturday	Sunday	Monday	Tuesday	Wednesday	Thursday	Friday
1	①	④	⑦	③	⑥	②	⑤
2	2	5	1	4	7	3	6
3	3	6	2	5	1	4	7
4	4	7	3	6	2	5	1
5	5	1	4	7	3	6	2
6	6	2	5	1	4	7	3
7	7	3	6	2	5	1	4
8	1	4	7	3	6	2	5
9	2	5	1	4	7	3	6
10	3	6	2	5	1	4	7
11	4	7	3	6	2	5	1
12	5	1	4	7	3	6	2
13	6	2	5	1	4	7	3
14	7	3	6	2	5	1	4
15	1	4	7	3	6	2	5
16	2	5	1	4	7	3	6
17	3	6	2	5	1	4	7
18	4	7	3	6	2	5	1
19	5	1	4	7	3	6	2
20	6	2	5	1	4	7	3
21	7	3	6	2	5	1	4
22	1	4	7	3	6	2	5
23	2	5	1	4	7	3	6
24	3	6	2	5	1	4	7

(Number of hours Egyptians divided the day into.)

241

Remembering God's Awesome Acts: Answer Page

ANSWER KEY: ANCIENT EGYPT REVIEW

TRACING THE DAYS OF THE WEEK BACK IN TIME 2

A more likely ancient theory is that the Egyptians divided the day into four parts with one of the seven known planets ruling over each 6-hour segment of time. Fill in each day's column with the name of the planet. Start with the moon and go to Saturn. When you get to Saturn start over again with the moon. Begin the next column where you left off. The first segment of the day (the top box) would give the day its name. Use the information and planet order from the *Comparison of the Gods and Goddesses* page to figure out how we may have gotten the name of each day.

Copyright © 1996 Susan Mortimer

Name of planet	1st day moon	2nd day Mars	3rd day Mercury	4th day Jupiter	5th day Venus	6th day Saturn	7th day Sun
Name used to name day	moon's day	Tui's day	Woden's day	Thor's day	Frigg's day	Saturn's day	Sun's day
Name of day	Monday	Tuesday	Wednesday	Thursday	Friday	Saturday	Sunday

Number of hours Egyptians divided the day into.							
1 2 3 4 5 6	moon	Mars	Mercury	Jupiter	Venus	Saturn	Sun
7 8 9 10 11 12	Mercury	Jupiter	Venus	Saturn	Sun	Moon	Mars
13 14 15 16 17 18	Venus	Saturn	Sun	Moon	Mars	Mercury	Jupiter
19 20 21 22 23 24	Sun	Moon	Mars	Mercury	Jupiter	Venus	Saturn

242

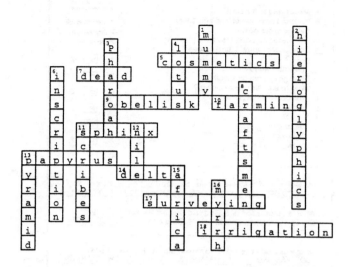

Crossword answers:
- 1 mummy
- 2 hieroglyphics
- 3 Phoenician
- 4 statuary
- 5 cosmetics
- 6 inscription
- 7 dead
- 8 craftsmen
- 9 obelisk
- 10 farming
- 11 sphinx
- 12 Nile
- 13 papyrus / pyramid
- 14 delta
- 15 afraid
- 16 monarch
- 17 surveying
- 18 irrigation
- tribes

243

Moses and Jesus Compared

The verses listed below contain many similarities found in the lives of Moses and Jesus Christ. Read these verses and write each reference in the correct box. Also answer the detail questions in the grid below.

Copyright © 1996 Susan Mortimer

Similarities	Moses	Jesus
Born when Israel was dominated by an oppressive ruler	Exodus 1:8-14	Matthew 2:1
Ruler was killing all the baby boys	Exodus 1:22	Matthew 2:16-18
Rescued by parents	Hebrews 11:23	Matthew 2:13
Spent 40 days in the wilderness	EXODUS 34:28	Matthew 4:1-2
Ministry did not start until adulthood	Exodus 3:1-2	Luke 3:23
Was sent by God	Exodus 3:13-14	John 8:18
Was not received by his own people	Exodus 2:14	John 1:10-11
Had a glorious mountaintop experience	Exodus 34:29	Matthew 17:1-3
Gave commandments	Deuteronomy 31:9	John 13:34-35
Performed signs and wonders	Exodus 7:8-10	John 20:30-31
Leaders hardened their hearts against him	Exodus 7:3	John 12:37
Said, "Man does not live on bread alone."	Deuteronomy 8:3	Matthew 4:4
Blood of the 'Passover Lamb' saved others	Hebrews 11:28	I Corinthians 5:7
Was the savior of his people	Exodus 14:30-31	1 John 4:14

I Corinthians 5:7	Matthew 2:1	Luke 3:23	Matthew 17:1-3
Exodus 1:22	Exodus 3:13-14	Exodus 2:14	Exodus 1:8-14
Matthew 4:1-2	Matthew 2:16-18	John 8:18	Matthew 2:16-18
John 1:10-11	Exodus 7:3	John 13:34-35	Deuteronomy 31:9
Hebrews 11:23	Matthew 2:13	Exodus 14:30-31	John 20:30-31
Exodus 3:1-2	Exodus 7:8-10	Matthew 4:4	Deuteronomy 8:3
Deuteronomy 8:2	1 John 4:14	Exodus 34:29	John 12:37
		Hebrews 11:28	

244

Evaluating the Egyptian Gods & Goddesses

Check one in each group of two. Give an example from the accounts of the Egyptian gods that demonstrates your choice.

© 1996 Susan Mortimer

Egyptian gods and goddesses:

- ☐ are holy.
- ■ are evil.

Example: ANY EXAMPLE FROM THE LESSONS ABOUT THE GODS AND GODDESSES OF EGYPT WHICH ILLUSTRATES THEIR CHARACTERISTICS IS CORRECT.

- ■ can become old and senile.
- ☐ are the same yesterday, today and forever.

Example: _____

- ■ can die.
- ☐ are eternal.

Example: _____

- ■ have limited power.
- ☐ are all powerful.

Example: _____

- ☐ have nothing to fear.
- ■ can be frightened.

Example: _____

- ■ turn on each other and their followers.
- ☐ are faithful and true.

Example: _____

- ■ can be outwitted.
- ☐ have the final word.

Example: _____

- ■ have a beginning.
- ☐ have no beginning.

Example: _____

- ■ have a confused concept of nature.
- ☐ explain nature by order and design.

Example: _____

Look at the choices you did not check. Do they describe the God of the Bible? Write a sentence comparing the gods of Egypt with the God of the Bible.

_____

_____

245

Remembering God's Awesome Acts: Answer Page

For each of the plague pages, the student will be doing one <u>The God of Israel Challenges the 'gods' of Egypt</u> page and then another page specific to each plague. At the bottom of the specific page is a section called: <u>What is the Challenge?</u> The challenges are numbered below and will be referred back to for each plague.

WHAT IS THE CHALLENGE?

1. Who is the source of natural and spiritual light—Ra and all the other sun gods, or He who said, "Let there be light"? (p. 265—Darkness)

2. Who can create life out of inert matter—He who formed man from dust and breathed life in him, or Khepera? (p. 253-Insects)

3. Who has conquered death and who will rule in eternity—Jesus or Osiris? (p. 263—Locust)

4. Who is the source of all creation, the sustainer of life on earth and the source of eternal life after death—Nu and Hapi, or the God of the Bible? (p. 249—Nile)

5. Who protects and insures the livelihood of the people—the gods Apis, Osiris and Hathor, or the One who cares for even the flowers and sparrows? (p. 255—Livestock)

6. Who protects from disease and infection—amulets and charms, or the One who heals all our diseases? (p. 259—Boils)

7. Who will always win the final confrontation with a fatal blow to the opponent—the 'I AM' or all the gods of Egypt? (p. 267-Firstborn)

8. Who is the resurrection and the life—Jesus or Hathor? (p. 251—Frogs)

9. Who owns, governs and is God over all nations—the 'ancient serpent' or the One who will defeat him? (p. 247—Serpent)

10. Who is in control of the forces of nature and the elements—the gods Nut and Ra, or He who can speak and calm the storm? (p. 261—Hail)

247/249/251/253/255/259/261/263/265/267

Answers may vary slightly on the plague pages, but count correct if the student can show evidence from the passage to support his choice.

Snake—Ex. 7:1-13   Challenge #9   Nile/Blood—Ex. 7:14-24   Challenge #4

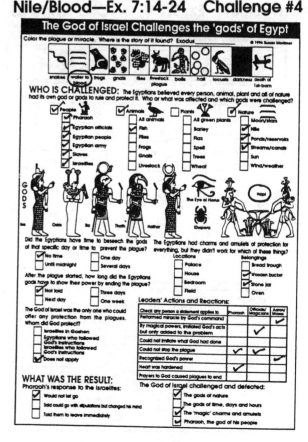

246/247   248/249

Remembering God's Awesome Acts: Answer Page

Frogs—Ex. 7:25 to 8:15   Challenge #8

250/251

Insects—Ex. 8:16-32   Challenge #2

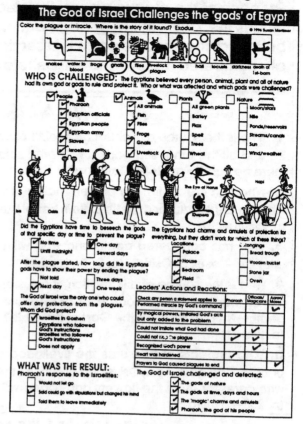

252/253

Livestock—Ex. 9:1-7   Challenge #5

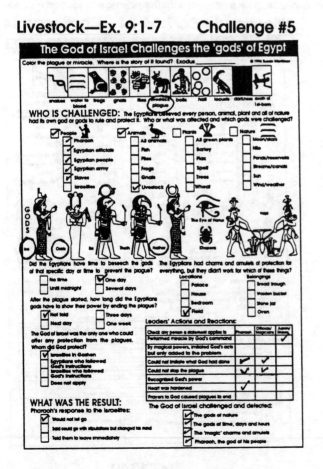

256/257

Boils—Ex. 9:8-12   Challenge #6

258/259

Remembering God's Awesome Acts: Answer Page

Hail—Ex. 9:13-35   Challenge #10

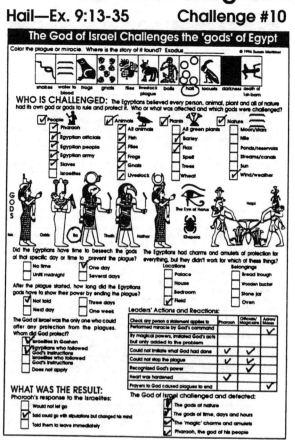

260/261

Locust—Ex. 10:1-20   Challenge #3

262/263

Darkness—Ex. 10:21-29   Challenge #1

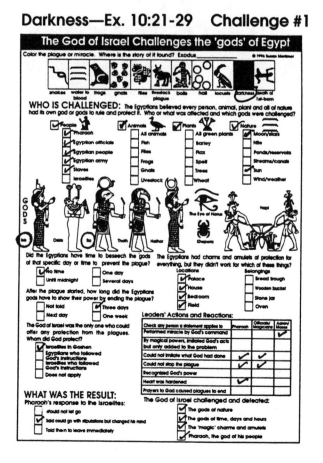

264/265

Firstborn—Ex. 11:1-12   Challenge #7

266/267

FIRSTBORN

(There may be some slight variation due to translation of the hieroglyphics, but it should closely parallel Exodus 12:12.)

on the same night I will pass through Egypt and strike down every firstborn both men and animals and I will bring judgment on all the gods of Egypt I am the Lord

267

BY FAITH

Read Hebrews 11. Then complete each statement by filling in the matching number. Try to do it without looking back. © 1996 Dawn Mortimer

By faith we understand that the universe __2__
By faith Abel __13__
By faith Enoch was taken from this life, __4__
By faith Noah, when warned about things not yet seen, __5__
By faith Abraham, when called to go to a place he would later receive as his inheritance, __3__
By faith Abraham, even though he was past age—and Sarah herself was barren— __9__
By faith Abraham, when God tested him, __15__
By faith Isaac __8__
By faith Jacob, when he was dying, __6__
By faith Joseph, when his end was near, __14__
By faith Moses' parents __7__
By faith Moses, when he had grown up, __11__
By faith he (Moses) left Egypt, __12__
By faith he (Moses) kept the Passover and the sprinkling of blood __10__
By faith the people passed through the Red Sea on dry land; __1__

1. but when the Egyptians tried to do so, they were drowned.
2. was formed by God's command.
3. obeyed and went, even though he did not know where he was going.
4. so that he did not experience death.
5. in holy fear built an ark to save his family.
6. blessed each of Joseph's sons.
7. hid him for three months after he was born...and they were not afraid of the king's edict.
8. blessed Jacob and Esau in regard to their future.
9. was enabled to become a father because he considered Him faithful who had made the promise.
10. so that the destroyer of the firstborn would not touch the firstborn of Israel.
11. refused to be known as the son of Pharaoh's daughter. He chose to be mistreated along with the people of God....
12. not fearing the king's anger; he persevered because he saw Him who is invisible.
13. offered God a better sacrifice than Cain did.
14. spoke about the exodus of the Israelites from Egypt and gave instructions about his bones.
15. offered Isaac as a sacrifice.
Taken from Hebrews 11, NIV.

What is faith?   Write out Hebrews 11:1 _____

From the examples of men of faith, where should we place our faith? (Hebrews 11:6b) _in God_
What is faith about? (Hebrews 11:1b) _things we can't see_
When will our faith be fulfilled? (Hebrews 11:16-17) _in the next life/heaven_
Why is faith important? (Hebrews 11:6a) _without faith it is impossible to please God_
How do we live our faith? (Hebrews 11:8) _in obedience, doing what God tells us to do_

Everyone has faith in something.
Faith can be big or little; it can grow or be destroyed.
It can be shared or be denied; it is given but must be used.
It can be placed rightly or wrongly; it can be encouraged or be abandoned.
It must be practiced now but is rewarded later.
What was Jesus' example to us? (Hebrews 12:1-3) _Jesus endured the cross for the future joy_

268

Jesus, the First and the Last

c   Creation

b   Serpent's defeat

j   Adam's sin

l   Abel's death

d   The ark of Noah

a   The tower of Babel

h   Abraham's covenant

i   Isaac and the ram

m   Melchizedek

f   Lot's rescue

g   Jacob's struggle

e   Joseph's grain

n   Judah's prophesy

k   Moses frees people

269

A PICTURE OF A **VULTURE** MEANS **MOTHER** In Egyptian, "vulture" and "mother" are homonyms. ①	A PICTURE OF AN **EGG** MEANS **FEMALE** OR **QUEEN** ①	A PICTURE OF **HAIR** MEANS **FLOW** OR **HAIR** ①	A PICTURE OF A **DUCK** MEANS THE **'SA'** SOUND OR ALONE MEANS **SON** ①
A PICTURE OF A **MAN** WITH **AX** MEANS **ENEMY** ①	A PICTURE OF A **MAN SITTING, HAND ON HEAD** MEANS **THINK, EAT** OR **HEAR** ①	A PICTURE OF A **CROOK** MEANS **RULER** OR **ROYALTY** ①	A PICTURE OF A **DOOR** MEANS **DOOR** OR **OPEN** ①
A PICTURE OF A **WOMAN SITTING** MEANS **FEMALE** OR **LADY'S NAME** ①	A PICTURE OF A **SITTING LADY GIVING BIRTH** MEANS **BORN** ①	A PICTURE OF THE **SUN** WITH **DOT** MEANS **SUN, SHINING, DAY** OR **SEASON** ①	A PICTURE OF A **SEPTER** MEANS **POWER** ①
A PICTURE OF A **SITTING CHILD SUCKING THUMB** MEANS **CHILD** ①	A PICTURE OF A **SUN SINKING** BETWEEN **TWO HILLS** MEANS **SUNSET** ①	A PICTURE OF A **BEARDED MAN SITTING** MEANS **MALE** OR **MAN'S NAME** ①	A PICTURE OF A **LOTUS FLOWER** MEANS **FLOWER** ①

A PICTURE OF A **FEATHER** MEANS **TRUTH** ①	A PICTURE OF A **SANDLE STRAP** MEANS **LIFE** OR **LIVING** (PRONOUNCED 'ANKH') ①	A PICTURE OF **MOUNTAINS** MEANS **LAND** OR **COUNTRY** ①	A PICTURE OF AN **ARROW** MEANS **VICTORY** ①
A PICTURE OF A **CIRCLED X** MEANS **TOWN** OR **CITY** ①	A PICTURE OF A **PAPYRUS ROLL** MEANS **WRITE** OR **BOOK** OR **ABSTRACT IDEA** ①	A PICTURE OF A **FLOOR PLAN** MEANS **HOUSE** OR **CAVE** OR **BUILDING** ①	A PICTURE OF A **BULL** MEANS **BULL** OR **CATTLE** ①
A PICTURE OF A **FISH** MEANS **FISH** ①	A PICTURE OF **SAILS** MEANS **AIR** OR **WIND** ①	A PICTURE OF A **STAR IN THE SKY** MEANS **NIGHT** ①	A PICTURE OF A **HAND HOLDING HOOK** MEANS **PERSON WHO DOES THE ACTION** ①
A PICTURE OF A **CAT** MEANS **CAT** ①	A PICTURE OF A **DOG** MEANS **DOG** ①	A PICTURE OF AN **EYE** MEANS **EYE** OR **SEE** ①	A PICTURE OF A **LAMP** MEANS **FIRE** OR **LIGHT** ①

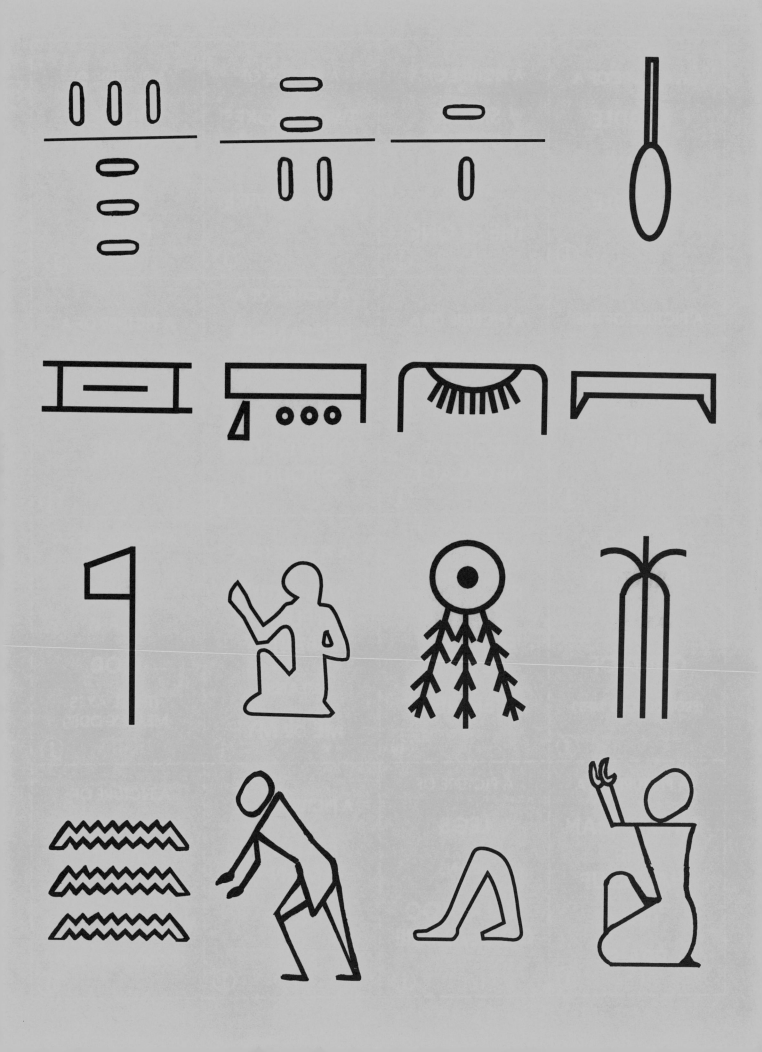

A PICTURE OF A	A PICTURE OF A	A PICTURE OF	A PICTURE OF
PADDLE	**SINGLE STROKE**	**TWO STROKES**	**THREE STROKES**
MEANS	MEANS	MEANS	MEANS
PADDLE	**THE OR ONE**	**TWO OR TWICE**	**PLURAL**
①	①	①	①

A PICTURE OF THE	A PICTURE OF A	A PICTURE OF A	A PICTURE OF A
SKY	**NECKLACE**	**RECTANGLE OVER 3 DOTS**	**WATERCOURSE**
MEANS	MEANS	MEANS	MEANS
SKY	**GOLD OR NECKLACE**	**LAND/EARTH/ GROUND**	**LAKE**
①	①	①	①

A PICTURE OF A	A PICTURE OF	A PICTURE OF A	A PICTURE OF AN
FOUNTAIN	**RAYS FROM THE SUN**	**MAN SITTING WITH ELBOWS BENT**	**AX**
MEANS	MEANS	MEANS	MEANS
CHILD OF	**SHINE**	**ME OR MY**	**GOD**
(PRONOUNCED 'MES')			(THREE AXES MEAN 'GODS')
①	①	①	①

A PICTURE OF A	A PICTURE OF	A PICTURE OF A	A PICTURE OF
SITTING MAN WITH HANDS UP	**LEGS**	**FALLING MAN**	**WAVES OF A RIVER**
MEANS	MEANS	MEANS	MEANS
PRAISE	**WALK OR GO COME/CAME**	**FALL**	**WATER OR RIVER**
			(PRONOUNCED 'MU')
①	①	①	①

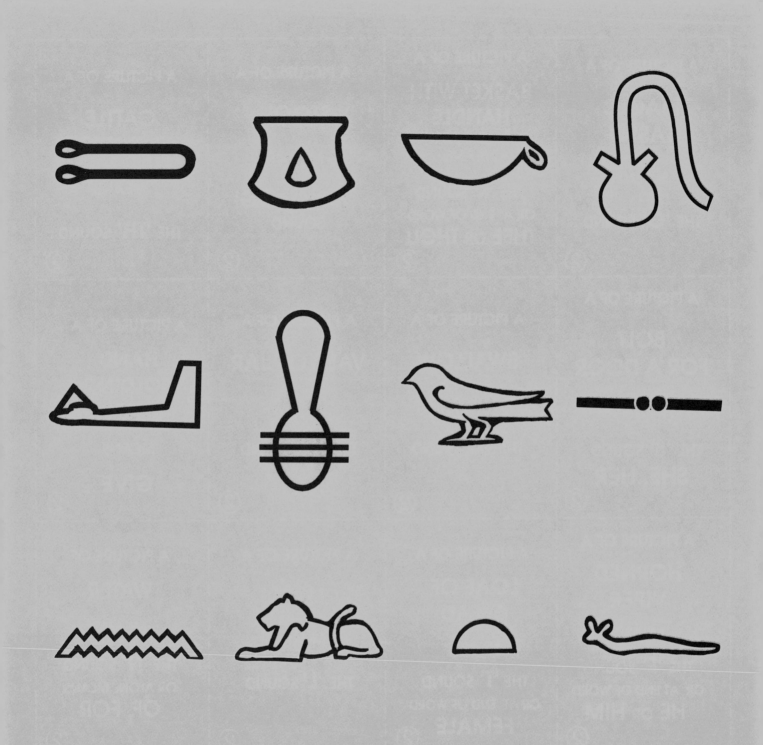

A PICTURE OF A **MAGIC LASSO** MEANS THE 'O' SOUND ②	A PICTURE OF A **BASKET WITH HANDLE** MEANS THE 'K' SOUND OR AT END OF WORD **THEE** OR **THOU** ②	A PICTURE OF A **STOOL** MEANS THE 'K' OR 'G' SOUND ②	A PICTURE OF A **CATTLE HOBBLE** MEANS THE 'TH' SOUND ②
A PICTURE OF A **BOLT FOR A DOOR** MEANS THE 'S' SOUND , **SHE, HER** ②	A PICTURE OF A **SWALLOW** MEANS THE 'U' SOUND ②	A PICTURE OF A **VASE OR JAR** MEANS THE 'M' SOUND ②	A PICTURE OF A **HAND HOLDING OBJECT** MEANS **GIVE** ②
A PICTURE OF A **HORNED VIPER** MEANS THE 'F' SOUND OR AT END OF WORD **HE** OR **HIM** ②	A PICTURE OF A **LOAF OF BREAD** MEANS THE 'T' SOUND OR AT END OF WORD **FEMALE** ②	A PICTURE OF A **LION** MEANS THE 'L' SOUND ②	A PICTURE OF **WATER** MEANS THE 'N' SOUND OR ALONE MEANS **OF, FOR** ②
A PICTURE OF AN **OWL** MEANS THE 'EM' SOUND OR ALONE MEANS **AS** ②	A PICTURE OF A **RABBIT** MEANS THE 'U' SOUND OR **BEAUTY, WAS** OR **IS** ②	A PICTURE OF A **MOUTH** MEANS THE 'R' SOUND OR **MOUTH, TO** OR **FROM** ②	A PICTURE OF AN **EGYPTIAN EAGLE** MEANS THE SHORT 'A' SOUND ②

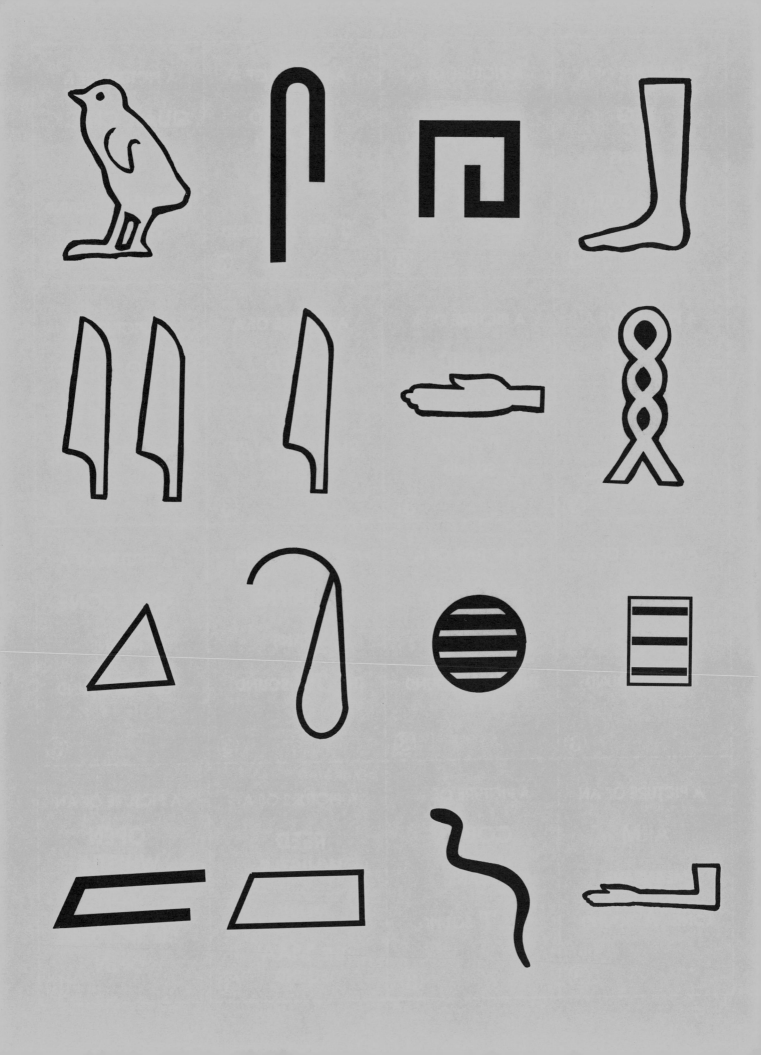

A PICTURE OF A **LEG** MEANS THE 'B' SOUND ③	A PICTURE OF A **REED SHELTER** MEANS THE 'H' SOUND ③	A PICTURE OF A **FOLDED CLOTH** MEANS THE 'S' OR 'Z' SOUND ③	A PICTURE OF A **QUAIL CHICK** MEANS 'U'/'W'/'V' SOUND ③
A PICTURE OF A **TWISTED FLAX** MEANS THE 'H' SOUND ③	A PICTURE OF A **HAND** MEANS THE 'T' OR 'D' SOUND ③	A PICTURE OF A **REED** MEANS THE SHORT 'A'/'E' SOUND ③	A PICTURE OF **TWO REEDS** MEANS THE 'I'/'Y' SOUND ③
A PICTURE OF A **DOOR** MEANS THE 'P' SOUND ③	A PICTURE OF A **PLACENTA** MEANS THE 'CH' SOUND ③	A PICTURE OF AN **EARRING** MEANS THE 'TH' SOUND ③	A PICTURE OF A **KNEE BONE** MEANS THE 'Q' SOUND ③
A PICTURE OF AN **ARM** MEANS THE LONG 'A' SOUND ③	A PICTURE OF A **COBRA** MEANS THE 'T' SOUND ③	A PICTURE OF A **REED WHISTLE** MEANS THE 'MAA' SOUND ③	A PICTURE OF AN **OPEN WHISTLE** MEANS THE 'M' SOUND OR IN ③

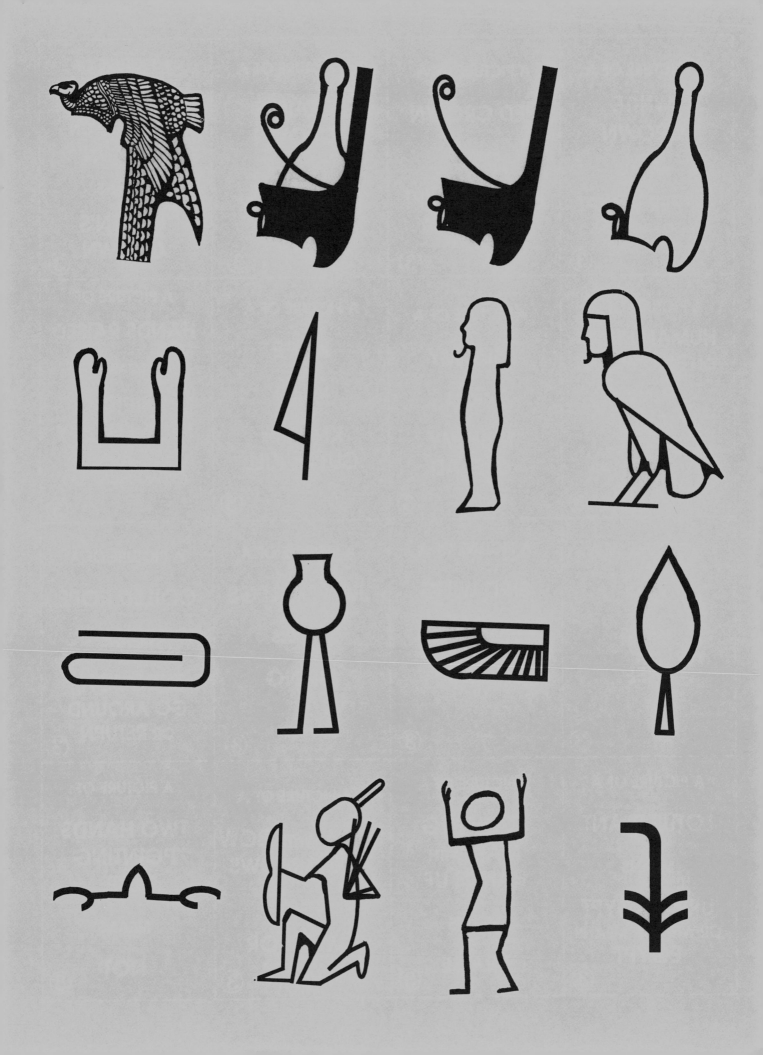

A PICTURE OF A	A PICTURE OF A	A PICTURE OF A	A PICTURE OF
WHITE CROWN	**RED CROWN**	**DOUBLE CROWN**	**FEATHERS** AND **SUN** ON **CROWN**
MEANS	MEANS	MEANS	MEANS
UPPER EGYPT ALSO KNOWN AS WHITE LAND	**LOWER EGYPT** ALSO KNOWN AS RED LAND	**UNITED EGYPT**	**QUEEN'S CROWN**
③	③	③	③

A PICTURE OF A	A PICTURE OF A	A PICTURE OF A	A PICTURE OF
HUMAN HEAD ON **BIRD BODY**	**MUMMY**	**KNIFE**	**HANDS RAISED**
MEANS	MEANS	MEANS	MEANS
SOUL (PRONOUNCED 'BA') PART OF DUAL SOUL 'BA' AND 'KA'	**MUMMY** OR **DEAD**	**KNIFE** OR **CUT** OR **KILL**	**SPIRIT** OR **VITAL ENERGY OF MAN** (PRONOUNCED 'KA')
③	③	③	③

A PICTURE OF A	A PICTURE OF A	A PICTURE OF A	A PICTURE OF A
TREE	**BIRD WING**	**JUG ON LEGS**	**COILED ROPE**
MEANS	MEANS	MEANS	MEANS
TREE	**FLY**	**BRING**	**THROUGH/ GO AROUND** OR **RETURN**
③	③	③	③

A PICTURE OF A	A PICTURE OF A	A PICTURE OF A	A PICTURE OF
LOTUS PLANT	**STANDING MAN** WITH **HANDS UP**	**MAN** WITH **BOW** AND **ARROWS**	**TWO HANDS POINTING OUT**
MEANS	MEANS	MEANS	MEANS
UPPER EGYPT OR WITH BEE MEANS **EGYPT**	**PRAISE**	**WARRIOR**	**NOT**
③	③	③	③

A PICTURE OF A **BASKET** MEANS **ALL/EVERY/ LORD/BASKET** ③	A PICTURE OF AN **UPRIGHT MAN** WITH **STAFF** MEANS **CHIEF** ③	A PICTURE OF A **PERSON** IN AN **ENCLOSURE** MEANS **HIDE** ③	A PICTURE OF A **FORKED TWIG** MEANS **WITH** ③
A PICTURE OF A **DUCK** AND **FEMALE SIGN** MEANS **DAUGHTER** ③	A PICTURE OF A **PERSON SITTING** AND **POINTING DOWN** MEANS **SIT** ③	A PICTURE OF A **FEEBLE MAN** WITH **STAFF** MEANS **OLD** ③	A PICTURE OF A **MOON** MEANS **MOON** OR **SEASON** ③
A PICTURE OF A **SCOURGE** MEANS **GOD, KING** OR **DOMINION** ③	A PICTURE OF A **ROAD** WITH **PLANTS** MEANS **ROAD** OR **WAY** ③	A PICTURE OF **WATER** AND **A WOMAN SITTING** MEANS **TO ME** ③	A PICTURE OF **WATER, A LOOP,** AND **ONE STROKE** MEANS **ME, I** ③
A PICTURE OF AN **EYE, THRONE** AND **SITTING MAN** MEANS **OSIRIS** ③	A PICTURE OF A **FALCON** MEANS **THE GOD HORUS** ③	A PICTURE OF A **THRONE, FEMALE SIGN, EGG** AND **COBRA** MEANS **ISIS** ③	A PICTURE OF A **SUN, ONE STROKE,** AND **MAN SITTING** MEANS **RA** ③

A PICTURE OF A **ROW BOAT** MEANS **GOING/BOAT** ③	A PICTURE OF AN **OVAL FRAME** **(CARTOUCHE)** ENCIRCLES A **ROYAL NAME** ③	A PICTURE OF A **BOAT** WITH SIGNS FOR **TRUTH + GOD** MEANS **AFTERLIFE** OR **NETHERLANDS** ③	A PICTURE OF A **SCRIBE'S** **TOOLS** MEANS **SCRIBE** OR **WRITE** ③
A PICTURE OF A **BOARD GAME** IS PRONOUNCED **'AMEN'** AND MEANS **ETERNITY** ③	A PICTURE OF A **SCARAB** **BEETLE** MEANS **CREATE** ③	A PICTURE OF A **SPEAR** MEANS **GREAT** ③	A PICTURE OF A **BASKET** AND **FEMALE SIGN** MEANS **QUEEN** ③
A PICTURE OF A **MUSICAL** **INSTRUMENT** MEANS **GOOD** OR **BEAUTIFUL** OR **HAPPINESS** ③	A PICTURE OF THE **TREE TRUNK** ENCASING OSIRUS MEANS **STABILITY** OR **ETERNITY** (PRONOUNCED 'TET') ③	A PICTURE OF **HORUS' EYE** (WITH FALCON MARKINGS) MEANS **HEALING** ③	A PICTURE OF A **THRONE** MEANS **RULE** ③
A PICTURE OF A **HEART** MEANS **HEART** ③	A PICTURE OF A **BEE** MEANS **BEE, HONEY,** **LOWER EGYPT** ③	A PICTURE OF A **PREGNANT** **LADY SITTING** MEANS **CONCEIVE** ③	A PICTURE OF **SCALES** MEANS **JUDGEMENT** **SCALES** ③